CAVALRY TRUMPETER, KHAKI UNIFORM, 1900.

FROM YORKTOWN TO SANTIAGO

WITH THE SIXTH U. S. CAVALRY

BY

LIEUTENANT-COLONEL W. H. CARTER

AUTHOR OF "HORSES, SADDLES, AND BRIDLES."

Introduction by John M. Carroll

STATE HOUSE PRESS
Austin, Texas
1989

Library of Congress Cataloging-in-Publication Data

Carter, William H. (William Harding), 1851-1925.
From Yorktown to Santiago with the Sixth U.S. Cavalry / by W. H. Carter ; new introduction by John M. Carroll ; illustrated by Frederic Remington . . . (et al.).
p. cm.
Reprint. Originally published: Baltimore : Lord Baltimore Press, 1900.
Includes bibliographical references.
ISBN 0-938349-42-2 : $24.95. — ISBN 0-938349-43-0 (deluxe lim. ed.) : $50.00
1. United States. Army. Cavalry, 6th—History. 2. United States—History—Civil War, 1861-1865—Regimental histories. 3. United States—History—War of 1898—Regimental histories. 4. Indians of North America—Wars—1866-1895—Regimental histories. 5. United States—History, Military—To 1900. I. Title.
UA31.6thC37 1989
357'.183'0973—dc20

89-19734
CIP

Manufactured in the United States of America

State House Press
P.O. Box 15247
Austin, Texas 78761

INTRODUCTION

One of the rarest of the major histories of any U. S. Cavalry regiment has long been W. H. Carter's *From Yorktown to Santiago with the Sixth U. S. Cavalry,* published in 1900. The book covers the first thirty-seven years of the 6th's history, most of which Carter experienced as a member of the unit. Although Carter had previously written military articles for professional journals, this was his first book and something that he could certainly be proud of with its illustrations by Remington and Zogbaum, gilded top edge and handsome printing by the Lord Baltimore Press in Baltimore, Maryland. However his pride was to be short-lived. Soon after the book's publication most copies were destroyed in a warehouse fire and Carter did not have additional copies printed. Because of the rarity of the original edition, this reprint edition is virtually a new book in the military library. The publishers have also improved the book for research use by adding an index of people, places and events.

The history of the 6th U. S. Cavalry through the Spanish-American War is well covered by Carter in narrative form. However, some capsule information of that period and activities of the 6th Cavalry to date is desirable and is therefore added in this introduction.

The 6th U. S. Cavalry's identification has long been "The Fighting Sixth," much like the 7th U. S. Cavalry's "Garryowen."

Coat of Arms: 1. Shield - Azure, with a unicorn rampant. 2. Crest - On a wreath of the colors an imperial Chinese dragon rampant, grasping in its dexter claw four arrows sable, armed and feathered gules.

Motto: Ducit Amor Patriae (Led by Love of Country).

In the official army lineage, the symbolism is stated thusly: "The regiment took part in the eastern campaigns of the Civil War, its outstanding feats being at Williamsburg, Virginia, 1862, when it assaulted entrenched works, and at Fairfield, Pennsylvania, 1863. At Fairfield the unit engaged two enemy brigades of cavalry, completely neutralizing them and saving the supply trains of the Army, but in the process was literally cut to pieces. This is symbolized by the unicorn, held to represent the knightly virtues and, in the rampant position, a symbol of fighting aggressiveness, combined with speed and activity. The shield is blue, the color of the Federal uniform in the Civil War. The Chinese dragon represents the regiment's entrance into the Forbidden City in Peking in 1900. The arrows symbolize service in the Indian Wars."

It was on 5 May 1861, when the regiment was constituted in the Regular army as the 3rd Cavalry, and it was organized on 18 June 1861, at Pittsburgh, Pennsylvania. Six weeks later, 3 August 1861, it was redesignated as the 6th Cavalry. It was assigned to the 3rd Cavalry Division from 15 August 1927 to 1 December 1939. On 21 July 1942, it was reorganized and redesignated as the 6th U. S. Cavalry, Mechanized.

The regiment was broken up on 1 January 1944, and elements were reorganized and redesignated as Headquarters and Headquarters Troop, 6th U. S. Cavalry Group, Mechanized, and 6th and 28th Cavalry Reconnaissance Squadrons, Mechanized. These units were converted and redesignated as Headquarters and Headquarters Troop, 6th U. S. Constabulary Regiment, and 6th and 28th Constabulary Squadrons, respectively. This was on 1 May 1946. These units were in turn converted and redesignated 20 December 1948 as elements of the 6th Armored Cavalry.

On 24 October 1963, the unit was inactivated at Fort Knox, Kentucky, and activated once again on 23 March 1967, at Fort Meade, Maryland. Currently the unit has been reorganized into the 6th U. S. Cavalry Aviation, and organized under O&E into five battalions.

The 6th Cavalry's long and honorable service includes campaign participation credit in the Civil war for the Peninsula, Antietam, Fredericksburg, Chancellorsville, Gettysburg, Wilderness, Spotsylvania, Cold Harbor, Petersburg, Shenandoah, Appomattox, Virginia from 1862 to 1865, and finally, Maryland in 1863. The Indian Wars credit includes the Comanches, Apaches, Pine Ridge, Texas in 1867 & 1874, Oklahoma in 1874, Arizona in 1876, 1877, 1881 and 1882, New Mexico in 1882, and Colorado in 1884. In the War with Spain they were in the Battle of Santiago and subsequently received participation credit for the China Relief Expedition, the Philippine Insurrection, the Punitive Expedition Against Mexico, and World War I. In World War II they received participation credit in the following campaigns: Normandy, Northern France, Rhineland, Ardennes-Alsace and Central Europe.

William Giles Harding Carter was seventh in descent from a family first identified in Henrico County, Virginia. His father, Samuel, was living in Nashville, Tennessee, when William was born in 1851, and where he was living at the time of the Civil War.

The family was not in sympathy with the secession movement, and did not join in the general flight of the residents on the appearance of the Federal army. At the age of twelve, William became employed in the Quartermaster's Department of the Federal Army, as a mounted messenger.

At the close of the war, the Carter family moved to New York. President Andrew Johnson granted young Carter an "At Large" appointment to the United States Military Academy when he was but sixteen years of age. He entered in 1869 and graduated in 1873, standing 35 in a class of 41. The loss of educational facilities during the Civil War was a disadvantage to almost all the Cadets from the South at the time, which made West Point more difficult than it would have been had they received all the advantages of public school in their earlier years.

After graduation the newly commissioned 2d Lt. Carter served briefly with the 8th U. S. Infantry in Montana and Wyoming. In November, 1874, he went to the Arizona Territory to become a member of the 6th U.

S. Cavalry. At Cibucu, Arizona on August 30, 1881 Lt. Carter rescued the wounded while under heavy fire by hostile Indians. For his bravery he was awarded the Medal of Honor. He remained in Arizona for ten years before returning to the East for recruiting duty. He was next assigned to duty for several years in the Adjutant General's Department in Washington, D. C.

During Carter's tour of duty in Washington, he was promoted to Lieutenant Colonel and Colonel in the Adjutant General's Department, and Brigadier General of the line. During this period he had become recognized as an expert in Army organization. In January, 1904, General Carter was reassigned to the Philippines where he commanded a Department until the latter part of 1905, when he returned to the United States to command the Department of the Lakes for several years and then Department of Missouri in 1908. The year 1909 once again found him in the Philippines with the rank of Major General. At the request of Secretary of War Dickinson, he was assigned to duty in Washington, D. C. once more, as Assistant Chief of Staff. He then held successive command and staff positions in the United States and Hawaii until his retirement from active service by operation of law in November, 1915.

General Carter was called to duty from the retired list for five months in 1916. His duty was with the Senate Military Committee in preparing the National Defense Act. He was once again called to duty and placed in command of the Central Department at the onset of World War I. On June 3, 1918, after 50 years of service, General Carter was finally retired from active service.

Before his death on May 24, 1925 at age 73, in Washington, D. C., General Carter was awarded the Distinguished Servce Medal for especially meritorious and conspicuous service as Department Commander, Central Department, August 26, 1917 to March 13, 1918.

Carter was a prolific writer throughout his long career, much of his published writings being articles on military affairs which appeared in various historical and professional publications. Besides *From Yorktown to Santiago,* Carter also wrote *Horses, Saddles and Bridles,* 1902; *Old Army Sketches,* 1906; *Giles Carter of Virginia,* 1909; *The American Army,* 1915 and *Life of Lt. Gen. Chaffee,* 1917.

JOHN M. CARROLL
Bryan, Texas
March, 1989

William H. Carter
Courtesy West Point Library.

PREFACE.

The title given this volume was selected to indicate the first and last battles in which the Sixth Cavalry participated. To-day the news was flashed from the Golden Gate of the Pacific that the regiment had passed out on the transport "Grant," bound for China. To conserve the truth of history it may soon be necessary to amend the title to read "From Yorktown to Pekin."

Histories of military organizations are usually found in two classes: one being a biographical record of the members, usually accompanied by photographs; the other a general history of the campaigns in which the organization served. The author has endeavored to avoid both schools, and the reader must decide as to the degree of success which has attended the effort.

The historical scheme of the chapters devoted to the period of the Civil War follows the successive campaigns; those devoted to the subsequent period are localized by the tours of service on various frontier stations and by the Santiago campaign.

The regiment will always hold in high esteem the artists—Remington, de Thulstrup, Zogbaum, Gaul, Klepper and Christy—who have generously aided in making this volume a worthy memento of long years of service under the flag of the Republic.

The author desires to express his personal appreciation of the kindly assistance rendered by these gentlemen and to make due acknowledgment to Colonel C. W. Larned, C. H. Ourand, F. L. Mast and St. G. R. Raby, Jr. for drawings which have served both an artistic and historical purpose.

Two of Remington's sketches made in the Sixth Cavalry camp during the Pine Ridge campaign are reproduced through the courtesy of Harper and Brothers.

July 3, 1900.

CONTENTS.

CHAPTER IX.

CHAPTER X.

CHAPTER XI.

CHAPTER XII.

LIST OF ILLUSTRATIONS.

INTRODUCTORY.

WAR forms the grim background while nations play unceasingly at diplomacy. Sometimes the drifting clouds of human passion are dispelled, but the possibilities of the background are always in evidence. The character of war varies directly with the motives which actuate an appeal to the arbitrament of arms, and soldiers are but average exponents of the good and evil of their own communities, their conduct by flood and field representing what may be again expected under like conditions. Volumes have been written upon the fortunes of individual soldiers, and hero-worship has ever been more or less blind in the adulation bestowed upon successful commanders.

No great nation has yet been able to establish a permanent form of government without an armed power to sustain it, and the crucial periods of national life have all been marked more or less by war or armed intervention. The history of wars, showing their causes and resulting effects upon civilization, has enlisted the services of the wisest students of the civilized world. The history of armies deals more or less with political and strategical considerations; the history of a regiment naturally hinges somewhat on its reputation, as established by its officers and men.

The history of war is not always the story of success, but American manhood has ofttimes been exalted by defeat as well as by victory. Hypocrisy and cant may revel in academic discussion of the rights of mongrel nations, but as long as there remain upon the pages of history the stories of Valley Forge, of Yorktown, of Mexico, of Chickamauga, of Gettysburg, of Manila and of Santiago, so long will children lisp with proud mien the stories of their fathers' swords. There is no pride akin to that which comes of a knowledge that one's ancestors have rendered the State some service.

It should be remembered that the stories of a few eye-witnesses to battle, by no means constitute true history. To arrive at a correct understanding of military operations, the general plans of campaign must be studied and the statements of all the commanders, whose duty it is to make reports, must be carefully weighed. By making due allowance for varying temperaments, powers of expression and the essential element of time, the calm historian is enabled to make a fair estimate of events as they actually occur in war. If this system be not followed and the story of a single participant is accepted, the real truth will be swamped under the errors of the personal equation which exists more or less in all men.

It is the fate of nations to witness the rise and fall of popular military idols. So with organizations, for sometimes it happens in war that, through specious pleas and friendly correspondents, the public gaze becomes, for the moment, riveted upon individual regiments to the detriment of others equally, if not more, deserving.

Truthful history disposes of ephemeral reputations, for no regiment has ever been organized, in this or any other country, which has maintained on many consecutive battlefields, its claim to superiority. Some individuals have more personal courage and calmness in the hour of danger than others, but cowardice is not an attribute of men who voluntarily enter the ranks in defense of their country's honor, and average regiments are but assemblages of average men.

During the period of the Revolution, the marvelous leader, Tarleton, made a fiery path with his light-horsemen, only to go down with the wreck at Yorktown. The Mexican Lancers, whose self-appointed duty was to sink the rising star of Texas, trailed their fluttering pennons in retreat when gallant May sent them scurrying through the gates of the Mexican capital. The "Louisiana Tigers" and the "Black Horse Cavalry," of Confederate renown, exercised an uncanny influence only until the hour of battle arrived, when it was discovered, as of old, that no one organization has an exclusive title to courage.

In the lines of battle around Santiago there were thousands of highly trained and gallant soldiers, sustaining the honor of renowned American regiments on whose battle-flags were emblazoned scores of blood-bought titles. Being regulars, they were all but forgotten by the Press become hysterical over the newly-risen "Rough Riders."

Recently, the war in South Africa has given to the world an unexpected picture in the sight of the "Gordon Highlanders," the "Black Watch" and Britain's pride, "The Guards," recoiling before the unerring aim of the rustic Boers. "Up Guards, and at them!" will live as long as boys read the story of Waterloo, notwithstanding Wellington protested, in the name of truth, that no such words were ever uttered.

In the preparation of much of the history it has been practicable only to "blaze the trail" of the regiment by its itinerary of marches and battles, without entering more than is absolutely necessary into plans of campaign or movements of other organizations. In following a cavalry regiment for nearly forty years, by means of its records, the trail is often found dim and sometimes completely obliterated. To illustrate the difficulties of the situation the naive remark is quoted from one of the morning reports: "The company was not paid to-day because the company-clerk was captured yesterday with the muster-roll in his pocket."

It has been the constant endeavor, in the preparation of the story, to present an honest and unpretentious representation of service as substantiated by the records, avoiding alike the tempting realms of speculation and tradition. The search for facts has developed a perfect mine of interesting incidents and regimental tales, but the author has felt constrained not to enter this field.

All these years of regimental life have constantly added to the list of heroes who have distinguished themselves while following the guidons. Sometimes it is the lonely dispatch courier, threading his dangerous course through hostile Indians; sometimes a gallant soul risking, perhaps sacrificing, a life to save that of a comrade; and sometimes it is in that awful moment of battle when fortune seems to hang in the balance and something beyond mere courage is needed to carry forward exhausted lines, as at Sailor's creek, when the cavalry corps was pressing hard upon Lee's army to force a surrender; here the sadly depleted ranks of the Sixth wavered under the fearful fire from some log huts, when Lieutenant McLellan cried out, "Men, let us die like soldiers!" and led them at a run through a shower of bullets and drove the enemy from his cover.

The regiment has ever been celebrated for modest and successful performance of duty rather than vainglorious efforts to enhance its reputation by specious claims. Simple language and plain statements of facts are required to fitly honor the deeds of men whose veteran association had the courage to adopt for a motto, "Fairfield," the name of the one battle in which all was lost save honor and the regimental standard.

This volume contains but a fraction of the incidents essential to a complete history, but it should be remembered that during the Civil War there were periods when skirmishes, which would now be designated battles, were of daily occurrence, and yet were considered so unimportant that, in many instances, they can only be traced by the casualty columns of the muster-rolls. The frontier period, covering thirty years of regimental life, is inadequately presented for the reason that the regiment was generally much scattered, and although the service was of a kind to try men's souls, the officers, nearly all of whom had participated in the Civil War, did not consider it important enough to perpetuate in detailed reports.

The nation has seldom taken to heart the services of the regular army on the frontier; in fact, it was not until Remington and his confrères pictured the life in all its character-making incidents and rough manhood that general interest was awakened.

While the country was supposed to be in a state of profound peace, the little frontier garrisons, which made the settlement of half a continent possible, unostentatiously went about their work of carving the path of an empire without expectation of other reward than a consciousness of duty right nobly performed. It was the self-reliance which this frontier training brought about that enabled the generals at Santiago to feel confident that each subordinate would lead his little band of followers through the chaparral straight for the "red house on the hill."

The regiment had the honor, as the advance guard, to lead the Army of the Potomac, under McClellan, from Yorktown up the Peninsula, to the battlefields around Richmond; and at Santiago, when the flag of freedom slowly rose to the mast-head on the palace, replacing the Spanish emblem, which for more than three centuries had floated over the city, it was the Sixth Cavalry band which saluted it with "Hail, Columbia."

The search for and tying together of historical facts have been a labor of love with the author, who, for nearly a quarter of a century, rode in the ranks of the distinguished regiment, the services of which he has endeavored to chronicle. It has only been possible to give the subject brief moments, snatched from an active career; but the results are presented to his old comrades with a feeling of assurance that, recognizing the difficulties under which he has labored, they will welcome the rescue of these fragments from oblivion.

No attempt has been made to picture the social life of the old frontier, a life so apart from that "in the States," that no one could share it without becoming partisan. To a few it was indescribably lonely, but to the large majority there was a strange fascination about it all that comes back to memory like a fond dream. All the hardships are forgotten and the dangers are mellowed by the lapse of years. Over their cigars old sabreurs discuss their scouting days with quickened pulse and heightened color, while their goodly spouses speak with tearful eyes of the days of Auld Lang Syne, when all was blessed comradeship in the old regiment.

CHAPTER I.

The Organization of the Regiment.

Conditions in 1861—President Lincoln issues Proclamation increasing Regular Army—Regiment organized as Third Cavalry and Headquarters established at Pittsburg—Designation changed to Sixth—Camp at Bladensburg—Camp east of Capitol, Washington—Equipment and Training of Regiment.

HE breaking point of the long continued strain between the sections was reached on the day when the election of Abraham Lincoln was made known, and yet the North was slow to believe that the South would hazard the fate of the republic because of political disappointment.

Events followed each other in evil combination, until at last the veil was lifted from the eyes of the amazed men of the North. The stupendous war, which was to follow with all its attending horrors, was beyond the conception of the wisest thinkers of the age. He who dared to intimate that enormous armies would be called into being before the rebellion could be crushed, was scorned as of unbalanced mind.

No one could base a calculation upon the past, for there was grave misunderstanding between the sections as to their relative strength; the southerners strangely vain of their individual prowess, the northerners more phlegmatic, slow to move, but once aroused neither defeat nor disaster could swerve them from their purpose. This awful strife was soon to afford opportunity for the world to witness real war as waged by the progeny of American pioneers, who carved a republic in the face of almost insurmountable obstacles and placed a new and a great name on the roll of nations.

When the old flag was lowered at Sumter, the gauge of battle was thrown down and there was naught to do but prepare for the coming struggle. The few regiments of the little regular army were scattered over an immense domain and could not be readily concentrated, even for the defense of the nation's capital. The early calls for volunteers did not indicate, in the light of subsequent events, any very decided or comprehensive plan beyond immediate defense.

It soon became apparent to the Administration that the war was to be much more than a brief insurrection, and on the 3d day of May, 1861, the President issued a proclamation which directed the addition to the regular establishment of one regiment of cavalry, one of artillery, and eight of infantry. Within four years it was found necessary to put in service two hundred and seventy-two regiments of cavalry, two hundred and thirty-two batteries of artillery, and one thousand and ninety-six regiments of infantry, numbering more than two million men.

On May 4th, General Order No. 16, Adjutant General's Office, was published, and prescribed the plan of organization for the new regiments. This order provided that the new cavalry regiment should be composed of three battalions, each battalion of two squadrons, and each squadron of two companies. The order also provided that two-thirds of the company officers should be appointed in the same manner as officers of like rank in the then existing army, and the remaining one-third should be taken from among the sergeants, on the recommendation of the colonel of the regiment, approved by the general commanding the brigade. This plan assured to the regiment the presence of a number of subalterns, thoroughly trained in all the minute details of company administration and drill, things which, while second nature to old soldiers, appear like the uncut pages of a new book to recruits, no matter how patriotic and enthusiastic they may be.

The organization of the Third Regiment of Cavalry was announced in General Order No. 33,

Adjutant's General Office, June 18th, 1861, with the following assignment of officers:

NAMES AND RANK.	BREVETS AND FORMER COMMISSIONS.
Colonel.	
David Hunter	Paymaster.
Lieutenant-Colonel.	
William H. Emory	Lieutenant-Colonel, 1st Cavalry.
Majors.	
Daniel H. Rucker	Captain, A. Q. M., Brevet Major.
Edward H. Wright	
Captains.	
Isaiah N. Moore	Captain, 1st Dragoons.
August V. Kautz	1st Lieutenant, 4th Infantry.
Andrew W. Evans	1st Lieutenant, 7th Infantry.
William S. Abert	1st Lieutenant, 4th Artillery.
David McM. Gregg	1st Lieutenant, 1st Dragoons.
Joseph H. Taylor	1st Lieutenant, 1st Cavalry.
Irvin Gregg	
John Savage	
George C. Cram	
Charles R. Lowell	
1st Lieutenants.	
John K. Mizner	1st Lieutenant, 2d Dragoons.
William W. Averell	2d Lieutenant, Mounted Rifles.
Herbert M. Enos	2d Lieutenant, Mounted Rifles.
Ira W. Claflin	2d Lieutenant, Mounted Rifles.
Sewall H. Brown	
Benjamin T. Hutchins	
Hancock T. McLean	
Tattnall Paulding	
Frederick Dodge	
John B. Johnson	
James F. Wade	
Mark F. Leavenworth	
2d Lieutenants.	
John W. Spangler	1st Sergeant, Co. H, 2d Cavalry.
Peter McGrath	1st Sergeant, Co. I, Mounted Rifles.
Hugh McQuade	1st Sergeant, Co. F, Mounted Rifles.
Curwen B. McLellan	Sergeant, Co. H, 2d Cavalry.

CAVALRY TRUMPETER, CIVIL WAR PERIOD, FULL DRESS.

This order also directed that the colonel should assign the officers to battalions and companies, and that recruiting should be commenced at once and conducted under the superintendence of the colonel or lieutenant-colonel. The headquarters was directed to be established at Pittsburg, Pa.

Prior to this time the mounted force of the army was organized as dragoons, mounted riflemen and cavalry. In order to simplify matters for the large volunteer army then being organized, Congress enacted, on August 3d, 1861, that all mounted regiments should be known as cavalry, and General Order No. 55, Adjutant General's Office, August 10th, 1861, prescribed that "The six mounted regiments of the army are consolidated in one corps, and will hereafter be known as follows:

The 1st Dragoons	as the 1st Cavalry.
The 2d Dragoons	as the 2d Cavalry.
The Mounted Riflemen	as the 3d Cavalry.
The 1st Cavalry	as the 4th Cavalry.
The 2d Cavalry	as the 5th Cavalry.
The 3d Cavalry	as the 6th Cavalry."

It was not, however, until July 17th, 1862, that the old regiments were provided by law with the same organization as the Sixth, that is, twelve companies and a full complement of field officers.

The assignment of companies to squadrons, and

of officers to companies, was announced in Regimental Orders No. 1, August 15th, 1861, and recruiting was immediately begun in Pennsylvania, Ohio, and western New York. The enthusiasm for the war was at its height, and no difficulty was experienced in securing a splendid body of men.

The regiment was recruited just as volunteer regiments were raised, except that there was no election of officers. It was only necessary for the officers who had already been appointed to direct the energy and courage of this fine body of patriots to make the regiment what it soon became,—one of the best in the Army of the Potomac, on the returns of of which were borne many celebrated organizations.

Colonel Hunter never joined for duty with the regiment, and of those appointed to original vacancies, Major Rucker, Captain Moore and Lieutenant Mizner declined. Major J. H. Carleton and Major L. A. Williams were appointed to date from September 7th; the former vice Major Rucker and the latter to an original vacancy. Captain Moore's vacancy was filled by the promotion of that gallant soldier William P. Sanders, of the old Second Dragoons. October 25th, 2d Lieutenants I. M. Ward, Albert Coats, Joseph Kerin and Christian Balder were appointed, and on November 1st, other vacancies were filled by the appointment of Andrew Stoll, Samuel M. Whitside and Daniel Madden.

There were a number of officers and sergeants selected from the old army who were familiar with the drill, traditions and customs of the mounted service on the western frontier. The value of this experience is best attested by the long list of distinguished commanders during the Civil War whose early training was acquired in operations against the Indians who then roamed over half a continent. To the enthusiasm and hard labor of these officers the regiment owed its early instruction in the details of cavalry work, which enabled it to serve without embarrassment in that celebrated organization, the First Brigade, Cavalry Reserve, Army of the Potomac.

On September 12th the regiment mustered six hundred and seven men, and was moved on that date to Bladensburg, Maryland, where it was mounted during the following month.

Even in an old troop of cavalry the annual arrival of the remounts is attended with much interest and more or less speculation as to the relative merits of the various horses. The scenes and incidents attendant upon mounting the new regiments of volunteer cavalry at the beginning of the Civil War were almost indescribable, and the regimental historians usually draw the broad mantle of charity over that period. The organization and mounting of the Sixth was not entirely devoid of similar experiences, but the presence of regular officers and many ex-regular soldiers, who had enlisted with a view to securing commissions, saved the regiment from much of the difficulty and delay encountered by volunteer organizations.

It was, of course, impossible to supply trained officers to the hosts of volunteers of 1861, but a modified plan on similar lines was adopted recently (1899) in the organization of thirty-five thousand volunteers for service in the Philippine Islands. The remarkable success attendant upon the recruitment, organization and equipment of these regiments under regular officers is something for the nation to be proud of, and were it not for the supposed antagonism of such a scheme to the interests of the national guard organizations, there can be little doubt that the plan, through its own virtues, would force itself upon the attention of the people when the services of volunteers are again required.

The regiment remained in camp at Bladensburg until October 12th, 1861, when it was marched to the camp of instruction, east of the Capitol, Washington, D. C., companies B, D, E, F, G, H, I and K having been organized. On October 15th Lieutenant Dodge arrived with sufficient recruits for "A" company, which was organized on that date.

On November 1st, the band was organized and a sufficient number of recruits had arrived to complete the organization of company M. Company C was not organized until December 23d, owing to the absence of all the officers. Company L was subsequently organized at the old camp in Washington, but did not join until July 13th, 1862, when the regiment was camped at "Westover," near Harrison's Landing, Virginia, after the Seven Days' Battles.

As soon as the regiment was established in the new camp east of the Capitol instruction was undertaken in earnest, and before the end of October the companies were ordered to appear in full marching order at drills, which were by squadron in the afternoon and regimental in the morning. At this period a squadron consisted of two companies instead of four, as at present. During the autumn, quarters and stables were commenced, and by the end of December men and horses were comfortably housed. Throughout the winter the drills and other routine work of camp were kept up regardless of weather. Drills by brigade and regiment frequently took place in the rain, and the mud about the barracks and stables was often half knee deep to a horse; but the regiment was preparing for grim war and this preparation enabled it to acquit itself well on its first field of battle.

The regiment, except one squadron, was equipped as light cavalry with pistols and sabres only. Owing to the large number of volunteers being organized, it was impossible to secure carbines at this time, and in fact much difficulty was encountered in obtaining ordinary supplies, as may be illustrated by the following appeal to the Quartermaster-General for necessary garments for soldiers about to take the field:

"Headquarters 6th Cavalry,
Camp east of Capitol, November 27th, 1861.

SIR:—I send Lieutenant Spangler, Regimental Quartermaster, to represent to you that he has failed to obtain pantaloons for this regiment, and I am satisfied he used the proper exertion to get them. The men are suffering for these garments very much, and it has occurred to me, after the conversation which took place on the field yesterday, that there is a misapprehension in some quarter on this subject.

I am, very respectfully,
Your obedient servant,
W. H. EMORY,
Lieutenant-Colonel Commanding."

It was to be expected, as a matter of course, in a country which kept so small a force scattered over a wide expanse of territory, that the staff corps and departments would not be able to at once set in motion the trained machinery so essential to the administration of large armies. The enthusiasm and patriotism of the American soldier can always be relied upon in any just cause, but guns, munitions of war, tents, transportation and, above all, training, do not materialize at the mere movement of the magician's wand. This has been the teaching of history from time immemorial, and the higher the civilization and the more advanced nations become in mechanical arts, the more necessary it is to provide and maintain a reasonable store of things essential to successful war. Any other course results just as the condition of affairs in 1861 resulted,—long delay and enormously expensive preparation because of higher prices demanded under war conditions.

At this early period of the war, before the bounty system had demoralized patriotism, recruits were still easily obtained, but the absence of officers soon became a fruitful source of complaint which continued throughout the war. Much of this resulted from the temporary promotion of regular officers to higher commands in the volunteers; many were detached as aides-de-camp and for other duties which did not advance them professionally, yet deprived a fine regiment of the influence and example which trained officers exert over young men eager to learn. Lieutenant-Colonel Emory, to whom, for his painstaking care and intelligent direction in its early existence, the regiment owes a debt of gratitude, commented on this subject in a letter dated January 17th, 1862, as follows:

"The unremitted instruction given this regiment is all in vain without the presence of officers to retain and enforce the instruction. A few tours of detached service or inclement weather interfering with the exercises effaces the labors of a month.

The best old cavalry requires more officers in proportion to the men than are with this, a regiment of a few months' standing. Without proper officers, no effort can make good cavalry, and all military authorities agree that bad cavalry is worse than useless.

It is not only the positive inconvenience resulting from the absence of these officers, but it is the discontent fastened in the minds of those left behind, who are equally desirous of obtaining high commands in the volunteer forces."

The regiment continued in the camp at Washington until March 10th, 1862, furnishing its share of details for provost-guard duty in the city. Instruction was pushed unremittingly to bring the thousand men then in the ranks, up to the "old army" standard. As late as February, 1862, Lieutenant-Colonel Emory was still struggling for needful supplies, amongst other deficiencies being carbines, pistol cartridges and saddle blankets. It was only a few days before the regiment took the field that carbines were secured for the flank squadron, as it was then called, composed of companies B and H. Inspections of horses and equipments were carefully made and everything done to put the squadron in light but perfect marching order.

The regiment was now about to enter the field where it remained for more than three years, participating in all the campaigns of the Army of the

Potomac, and returning to Washington only in time for the Grand Review at the close of the war. It will be shown from the simple story of the records that General Emory, and those who so loyally aided him in organizing and preparing this fine body of men for the service of their country, may justly be proud of the results of their patriotic and thorough work.

CHAPTER II.

THE PENINSULA CAMPAIGN.

REGIMENT TAKES THE FIELD—CENTERVILLE AND MANASSAS—EMBARK AT ALEXANDRIA ON TRANSPORTS—YORKTOWN—WILLIAMSBURG—ADVANCE UP PENINSULA—SLATERSVILLE—NEW KENT COURT HOUSE—HAWES' SHOP—ARREST OF MAJOR WILLIAMS—HIS BROTHER'S CAREER—NEW BRIDGE—MECHANICSVILLE—WINSTON'S FARM—HANOVER COURT HOUSE—BURNING BRIDGES—SOUTH ANNA—PICKETING—STUART'S RAID—MOVEMENT TO JAMES RIVER—BLACK RIVER—WESTOVER—RECONNOISSANCE, MALVERN HILL—EVACUATION, HARRISON'S LANDING—REAR GUARD.

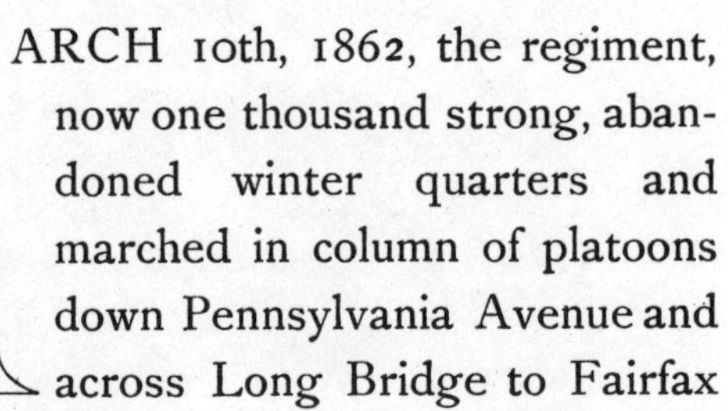

MARCH 10th, 1862, the regiment, now one thousand strong, abandoned winter quarters and marched in column of platoons down Pennsylvania Avenue and across Long Bridge to Fairfax Court House. Here it was assigned to General P. St. George Cooke's command, and camped for the first time in the open field.

On the following day a reconnoissance was made to Centerville and Manassas Junction, driving in the Confederate pickets near the latter place, the regiment returning to and camping at Centerville until the 13th, when the reconnoissance was pushed as far as Catlett's station and Cedar Run, where the regiment stood to horse in a meadow all night, during a heavy rain.

During the next day the regiment formed line of battle three times, the men removing their overcoats so that they could use the sabre to advantage. The night was a repetition of the previous one, so far as comfort was concerned, the command bivouacking in deep mud without fires.

On the 15th the regiment returned and occupied the abandoned Confederate huts at Manassas, and next day built a bridge at Blackburn's Ford on Bull Run, crossed and marched back to Fairfax Court House. During this movement the men had an opportunity to examine the "Quaker" guns, mounted the previous winter by the Confederates, and which exerted a strong moral influence, notwithstanding they were of home manufacture from native trees, without even the bark removed.

On March 18th, the regiment marched to Alexandria and encamped near the Seminary until the 27th, when it was embarked on transports for Fort Monroe under Major L. A. Williams, the former commander, Lieutenant-Colonel Emory, having been promoted to Brigadier-General of Volunteers and assigned to command of the First Brigade, Cavalry Reserve, to which the Sixth belonged. The companies disembarked, as the various vessels arrived, at Fort Monroe, and on the 30th went into camp near Hampton, where the regiment remained until April 5th, when it moved to Big Bethel, and on the following day to within six miles of Yorktown.

The regiment had been in service nearly a year and had been put through its paces by some of the best drill-masters of the old army; it had not yet been in action, however, and some of the old dragoons in the brigade were inclined to chaff the men as volunteers. Upon one occasion this led to some embarrassment when a Sixth Cavalry sergeant allowed his resentment to lead him into difficulty with the camp guard of the First Cavalry. The result of the investigation is shown in the following extract from a letter to Captain Magruder, commanding the First Cavalry near Yorktown:

"The Major Commanding directs me to say, relative to Sergeant Palmer, that he has investigated the case and finds from an ex parte statement of the Sergeant, who is a very quiet and reliable man, that the Sergeant of the guard of your camp used very abusive language towards him, calling him a 'damn recruit and volunteer,' drawing his sabre upon him and threatening to cut him down; this without his having refused to obey any order. It is difficult to arrive at the truth of these matters except before a court. If you desire it, the Major Commanding directs me to say, that on the presentation of the charges against him, Sergeant Palmer shall be brought to trial."

There was no more trouble after the enemy was once sighted, for no men ever proved their right to the knightly title of "soldier" more gallantly than those of the Sixth.

At this time the heavy rains had put the ground in very bad condition, and, transportation being limited, the regiment was compelled to pack its forage on the horses from Ship Point until April 11th, when camp was pitched on the York river. On April 21st Camp Winfield Scott was established about three miles from Ship Point, and two weeks were spent in perfecting the instruction of the regiment in the details of field service.

On May 1st, 1862, the Confederates abandoned their lines at Yorktown, and General Stoneman was sent forward early in the morning with four batteries of horse artillery and all available cavalry in pursuit, by the Yorktown and Williamsburg road, with orders to harass the enemy's rear and cut off such of his forces as had taken the Lee's Mill and Williamsburg roads. When the head of the column reached the road near the breastworks at Yorktown, several horses were killed by the explosion of torpedoes, sunk in the ground, and set off by contact with the horses' shoes. About two miles from Williamsburg, General Cooke's advance guard and flankers encountered the rear guard of the enemy. Captain Savage's squadron, Sixth Cavalry, was ordered to advance and charge, but the enemy retreated, leaving two wagons, in flames, and a spiked howitzer.

When the head of the column reached a strip of swampy woods, the central battlefield of the next day, Captain Savage's right flank platoon reported field works in front and to the right. General Cooke, having learned that there was a forest road which turned the enemy's left flank, ordered Major Williams with four large squadrons of the Sixth against the enemy's left, while Gibson's battery was brought into action, as rapidly as the deep mud would permit, to reply to the fire which had opened on the head of the column from Fort Magruder. While the regiment was making its way to attack the enemy's left, Magruder's squadron of the First and Savage's squadron of the Sixth Cavalry, charged the enemy close up to the works, and later charged again to save some of the guns, when their capture appeared imminent. Lieutenant Joseph Kerin, Sixth Cavalry, who was with Savage's flankers, captured a Confederate captain at this time.

Subsequently some trifling controversy took place as to exactly what message Major Lawrence Williams received from Lieutenant Frank Beach, General Cooke's Aide-de-Camp, who carried the order for attack. What actually took place may be best shown by quoting Major Williams' report:

"I was ordered to make a detour through the woods and take a battery on the enemy's extreme left flank. I accordingly proceeded with the Sixth Cavalry through the woods indicated, and after going about half a mile at a trot, debouched upon an open but undulating ground in front of the enemy's line of fortifications. The ground was very heavy, and between the woods and the fieldworks there was a deep ravine only passable by file. The ravine was about equidistant from the woods and the works. It was passed and the regiment formed about one hundred yards from the fortifications. Lieutenant Madden with a platoon was sent to reconnoitre the gorge. This was during the time its occupants were engaged with Gibson's battery in front. Lieutenant Madden reported that the ditch and rampart would have to be surmounted before we could effect an entrance, and also that infantry was approaching on the near side of a wood which skirted the back of the fort. I saw three regiments advancing in line; our position was critical, equally exposed to the guns of the fort and the advancing infantry. I determined to retire. Four of the squadrons and a portion of the fifth had already passed the ravine (*it was belly deep to the horses in mud*), when two squadrons of rebel cavalry rushed from the barracks in rear of the fort, and endeavored to cut off Captain Sanders' company. Captain Sanders wheeled his company about, charged and repelled the enemy with great gallantry. I cannot speak too highly of the officers and men on this occasion. Though every one felt that few would survive if the guns of the fort were turned upon us, not one showed the slightest concern. Captain Sanders showed great prudence and bravery in the timely manner in which he met the enemy, though taken at a disadvantage by superior numbers. I regret to report that Lieutenant McLellan was wounded in the leg by a shell while engaged."

When Lieutenant Madden led his platoon at a trot towards Fort Magruder, the occupants were engaged in firing on the army in their front. There were several rows of huts near by and outside the works, which concealed the platoon until the men arrived at the outer edge of the ditch, along which they were trotting in search of a crossing, when some of the Confederates looking over the crest called out "They are Yankees!" It was apparent that a cavalry regiment could accomplish nothing here, and, besides, Lieutenant Madden discovered the enemy's cavalry coming out of the woods in force. He put his platoon at a gallop and by winding in and out of the rows of huts concealed his men from the fire of the fort, but came out facing a brigade of Confederate infantry, and so close that he clearly recognized the General in command, his former Captain in the old army who had resigned and gone south to cast his fortunes with the Confederacy. Lieutenant Madden realized that his platoon had been saved by being mistaken for Confederates, and he lost no time in galloping hastily down the slope, followed by the Confederate cavalry supports which had discovered the column, and warned the regiment to withdraw from its critical position.

When the regiment retired from the position near Fort Magruder, Captain Sanders' squadron composed of Companies A and M was in the rear. In order to cross the long, narrow ravine, it was necessary to march by twos or file. Just before reaching the ravine the enemy's artillery began dropping shells into the column with considerable accuracy. While

Captain Sanders was endeavoring to cross, and in the worst part of the ravine, the enemy's cavalry appeared on the edge and opened a severe fire. The squadron pushed across and formed column of platoons on the hillside. The enemy followed up the hill, when Sanders quickly wheeled about by platoons and charged, driving them into and across the ravine with considerable loss.

Captain Sanders had sent Lieutenant Madden to report to the regimental commander the condition of things in the rear. A part of Captain J. Irvin Gregg's squadron, under Lieutenants Paulding and Ward, wheeled about and joined in the charge. Captain Lowell's and the remainder of Captain Gregg's squadron wheeled about and formed to support Captain Sanders and remained until he had driven back the enemy.

Some of the men were unhorsed in the deep mud of the ravine, by the plunging and falling of wounded horses, and were captured and taken to the rear before the counter-charge drove the enemy back. These were the first losses of the regiment by capture. The prisoners were marched to an old tobacco warehouse in Richmond and subsequently sent to Salisbury, North Carolina, for confinement. After a brief imprisonment, however, they were paroled, sent to Washington, North Carolina, and thence delivered to the Union fleet. They embarked on the "Virginia," and after inspection by General Burnside, at Newbern, they sailed for New York, and subsequently rejoined the regiment.

Captain Sanders specially mentioned Captain Hays, Lieutenant McLellan, First Sergeants Joseph Bould and Michael Cooney, and Sergeant Durboran for their gallant conduct in this affair, and Captain Gregg commended Sergeants Andrew F. Swan, of G company, and Emil Swartz (wounded), of F company.

On May 7th the regiment left Williamsburg in pursuit of the enemy, and after a march of about five miles, overtook the rear guard, with which the carbine squadron, composed of B and H companies, became engaged. After a brief but lively skirmish the enemy withdrew. Nine men were wounded in this affair and were left to be cared for in houses in the vicinity.

The pursuit was continued and on the 9th the advance reached Slatersville about 3 p. m. It was reported to the regimental commander that a detachment of about twenty Confederate cavalrymen were near by, and he sent a part of Captain Lowell's squadron, consisting of fifty-five men, and Captain Sanders' company of thirty-two men, to make a detour of the town and cut them off. Soon after the column started a vedette was discovered in the edge of the woods on the right of the village. He signaled to the company of cavalry to which he belonged and it wheeled about. Captain Lowell, who was in advance, immediately took up the gallop, and on reaching the opening he led his squadron to the charge in person. The enemy retreated before the advancing troopers in the direction of some buildings, from which a heavy fire was poured into Captain Lowell's men as soon as the enemy had uncovered them.

At this moment, and before Captain Sanders' company had completely emerged from the wood, a squadron of Confederate cavalry, heretofore concealed, suddenly approached on the left. Captain Sanders' company was immediately diverted from the road through a gap in the fence, and boldly charged down upon the squadron, which greatly exceeded in strength his own force. The sudden attack by Captain Sanders threw the advancing squadron into confusion and caused it to retreat. At this juncture some consternation was produced by the appearance of still another squadron of the enemy advancing rapidly. Captain Sanders showed his signal ability as a cavalryman by rallying his small company, which he had well in hand, wheeling about, charging the Confederate squadron which had last come upon the field, throwing it into confusion and compelling a retreat.

It was apparent that the small force was greatly outnumbered and the recall was sounded. Captain Sanders quickly rallied his men and withdrew. Captain Lowell, in the meantime, had pursued through the town beyond the sound of recall, but by prompt action he managed to withdraw before the enemy had recovered sufficiently to recognize the smallness of the force opposed to them. Lieutenants Hutchins, Whitside and Coats were engaged in this affair and were commended for their good conduct. The loss in this action was four killed, eight wounded and three missing.

The regiment was very proud of this little fight, for the companies engaged were greatly outnumbered at every turn, and it was only by the exhibition of perfect confidence and unhesitating courage that the command was enabled to withdraw, after it was discovered that the supposed small detachment of the enemy had suddenly grown to several squadrons, backed up by infantry.

The Confederates continued their retreat and the regiment remained in close proximity to the rear guard through the 10th and 11th; on the latter date a sharp engagement, lasting nearly two hours, took place at New Kent Court House, when the enemy withdrew and the regiment pushed on to Cumberland Landing, on the Pamunkey river. During the pursuit, near New Kent Court House, the enemy's rear guard was constantly driven back, and Lieutenants Balder and Kerin behaved with such fearlessness and gallantry as to call forth a special report to the brigade commander.

On May 12th the regiment reached White House Landing, a place which subsequently became quite familiar to the Army of the Potomac. On the 14th the movement was continued to Dr. Macon's house, from which place B and H companies were sent, on the 15th, to scout in the direction of Hanover Court House. The advance guard captured at Hawes' Shop seventy-five mules and three six-mule teams from Winder's Confederate brigade. The companies rejoined the regiment the same night.

It was at this camp and on this date that some of the pickets reported Major Williams for alleged communication with the enemy, and he was promptly arrested. Two days later he addressed the following letter asking an investigation:

"Headquarters 6th Cavalry, May 17th, 1862.
Assistant Adjutant-General,
Advance Guard, Army of Potomac.

SIR:—On the evening of the 15th instant, I was placed in arrest as a prisoner of State, a guard of four of my own men put over me, and with orders to shoot me if I attempted to leave the tent. A procedure so extraordinary in itself, independent of the humiliation and disgrace which it must impose upon a soldier of spirit and a gentleman of pride, could only have been resorted to from reasons of the greatest importance. The General Commanding the advance guard believed the information which subjected me to this mortifying restraint sufficient to justify his order no doubt, but, as the fact of my arrest is known to the men of my regiment and the army generally, and as the arrest itself casts an imputation upon my fidelity as an officer, I respectfully request that a

Board of Examination be appointed by the General Commanding to investigate the circumstances.

I am sir, very respectfully,

Your obedient servant,

L. A. WILLIAMS,

Major, 6th Cavalry."

On the same day, May 17th, he was released by an order from Headquarters of the Army of the Potomac and resumed command of the regiment, which he continued to exercise until June 26th, when he was disabled and remained absent sick until September 3d, 1862. He was then placed on duty in New York City, where he continued until dismissed by order, March 11th, 1863.

In the calm deliberation which should be given such a subject, after the lapse of years, it must be frankly acknowledged that the services of this officer in battle with his regiment should have precluded suspicion as to his loyalty. A year previous, when resignations were matters of daily occurrence, there was much uncertainty as to how officers stood on the burning questions of the day, but this should have been obliterated in the cases of all who had actually participated in battle.

Major Lawrence Williams was an officer of the old army and was promoted by selection from captain, Tenth Infantry, to be major of the Sixth Cavalry. At the time of the advance from Yorktown, up the Peninsula, Mrs. Robert E. Lee and her daughter, were at the White House, and Major Williams was a kinsman of the Lees. When arrested on the picket line by Lieutenant Madden and men of his own regiment, the matter was not reported, but Major Williams was warned back inside the lines. He was subsequently arrested outside the lines in front of the First Cavalry, and when brought in was ordered confined to his tent, under guard, for attempting to communicate with the enemy. There can be no reasonable doubt but that Major Williams, having learned of Mrs. Lee's presence at the White House, contemplated a friendly visit, without any criminal motive whatever. The last thing to expect of the Lees, if they received him at all, would be for them to allow a kinsman to imperil his honor by secret and disloyal communication. Two centuries of family pride would have forbidden the thought of such a transaction. General Fitzhugh Lee, when asked for any information he could give concerning Major Williams and this charge against him, replied:

"I saw him on the Peninsula as McClellan's army was advancing on Richmond. At the time I was commanding two regiments of cavalry, drawn up in line of battle on an open field, just in rear of a slight elevation upon which a road ran. Lawrence Williams charged down this road at the head of what looked like a squadron of cavalry, but turned off immediately upon seeing the line of battle, just as he was in front of me and not very far off. I recognized him and shot at him with my pistol. He and his men quickly disappeared behind a portion of McClellan's advance. I did not know that he had been arrested between the lines on the Peninsula. During these movements, I remember that Mrs. General Robert E. Lee and one of her daughters were down at the White House. It is possible that Williams attempted to communicate with them in some way for social purposes. I am quite satisfied that he was not a traitor to the Union cause."

While still absent from the regiment, reported sick, Major Williams was placed on duty in New York by General Scott, who had been a friend and admirer of the Lees, in the old army.

His younger brother, William Orton Williams, who had cast his fortunes with the Confederacy, had a strange career, which ended in a tragic manner. He was appointed a 2d lieutenant, Second U. S. Cavalry, in March, 1861, and promoted in April to 1st lieutenant. The records at the War Department contain these instructions: "To join his company which arrived in this city. His services will be required for a few hours daily at the Headquarters of the Army; not to interfere, however, with his company duties." He was placed in arrest on May 7th, 1861, and ordered to report to the commanding officer at Fort Columbus, New York Harbor, where he arrived May 10th, 1861. He resigned from the service June 10th, 1861.

He first came into public notice in the Confederate service as a captain of artillery, under General Leonidas Polk at Columbus, Kentucky. He was tall, had a fine figure, a military air and was considerable of a martinet. The horses of his battery were stabled at this camp. One day, while attending the morning stables of his battery, and having completed his inspection, he was passing out when he stopped in front of a young soldier and asked him why he did not salute him, and received the reply "I saluted you, sir, as you passed down and I did not think I had to salute afterwards, every time you might pass by me in going about the stable." The soldier was then ordered to salute him, but failed to do so. Williams drew his sabre and thrust it into the man's body, killing him. The matter was investigated and Williams called upon for a report of the affair, which he submitted in writing, and which concluded as follows: "For his ignorance, I pitied him; for his insolence, I forgave him; for his insubordination, I slew him."

About this time General Polk was ordered to evacuate Columbus, and move in the direction of Corinth, Mississippi. The confusion arising from the movement caused the matter to be dropped; but Williams was transferred to duty elsewhere, and did not reappear for a year or more. He was assigned to various places on unimportant duty.

He was next heard of in the Western army, returning from Richmond with a commission as colonel of cavalry, with orders to report to General

Bragg, at Shelbyville, Tennessee, in 1863. At this time, General Van Dorn had a large body of cavalry, including Forrest's command, at Columbia, Tennessee. Colonel Williams was ordered to report to Van Dorn, for assignment to a Tennessee regiment, made up of two independent battalions, one of which was under the command of Major Dick McCann. General Van Dorn issued the order and Colonel Williams went to assume command. The entire regiment, officers and men, promptly refused to accept him as their colonel, and notified him that they would not serve under him. General Van Dorn did not attempt to force or persuade them. This assignment was not at all in accordance with the practice of the Confederate troops in the appointment of their officers, and it was recognized that the attempt to foist him on this regiment could not succeed. Colonel Williams remained around Columbia for a while. He had Lieutenant Peter, who had been assigned to duty with him by the War Department, as an adjutant, and he appears to have commanded the second brigade of Martin's Cavalry Division, in April, 1863.

Apparently without any authority whatever, or mentioning the object of his expedition to any one, he took Lieutenant Peter and visited the Federal post at Franklin, where they were arrested. Both of them were hung as spies, because they were in the uniform of the Federal army and within the lines. The official history of this is shown briefly in these dispatches from the Rebellion Records:

"Franklin, June 8th, 1863. 11.30 p.m.

Brigadier-General GARFIELD:

Two men came in camp about dark, dressed in our uniform, with horses and equipments to correspond, saying that they were Colonel Orton, Inspector-General, and Major Dunlap, Assistant, having an order from Adjutant-General Townsend and your order to inspect all posts, but their conduct was so singular that we have arrested them, and they insisted that it was important to go to Nashville to-night. The one representing himself as Colonel Orton [W. Orton Williams] is probably a regular officer of the old army, but Colonel Watkins, commanding cavalry here, in whom I have the utmost confidence, is of the opinion that they are spies, who have either forged or captured their orders. They can give no consistent account of their conduct.

J. P. BAIRD,
Colonel, Commanding Post."

* * * * * * * * * * * * * * *

"Headquarters Department of the Cumberland,
Murfreesborough, June 8th [1863]. 12 p.m.

Colonel J. P. BAIRD, Franklin:

The two men are no doubt spies. Call a drum-head court-martial to-night, and if they are found to be spies, hang them before morning without fail. No such men have been accredited from these headquarters.

J. A. GARFIELD,
Brigadier-General and Chief of Staff."

* * * * * * * * * * * * * * *

"Franklin, June 9th, 1863.

General GARFIELD, Chief of Staff:

The men have been tried, found guilty and executed, in compliance with your order.

J. P. BAIRD,
Colonel, Commanding Post."

* * * * * * * * * * * * * * *

This affair has never been understood by Confederate officers. In fact, Williams' whole career seems to have been incomprehensible from beginning to end. The value of any information he could have gotten about Franklin, as to the works or forces there, would have been of no especial importance to General Van Dorn, whose troops were quartered in a part of the State where forage was abundant, and who had a sufficient number of men to have defeated any attempt of that portion of the army around Franklin to assail him.

It should be observed that Colonel Williams had, in the meantime, changed his name from W. Orton Williams to Colonel Lawrence W. Orton.

Lieutenant Peter was a kinsman of the Williams brothers and all were connected with well-known families. G. W. P. Custis, of "Arlington," Virginia, and Mrs. Peter, of "Tudor Place," Georgetown, were brother and sister. The former was the father of Mrs. R. E. Lee, and the latter the mother of Mrs. Williams. It seems strange that such untimely fate should have overtaken these officers, when their kinsmen, the three Lees, emerged from the four years of fratricidal strife with the high regard of the entire country, notwithstanding they had all previously held commissions in the regular army.

It was a matter of great regret on the part of all, that young Lieutenant Peter should have forfeited his life through Williams' folly. Many Confederate officers believed that Williams, finding his usefulness within the Confederate lines entirely destroyed, intended going within the Federal lines with a view to either reaching Canada, or quietly remaining north. His whole career was certainly an eventful one and any good within him seems to have been stultified by the entire want of stability in his character.

On May 18th the regiment moved to Cold Harbor and on the 20th A and M companies were sent on a reconnoissance to New Bridge on the Chickahominy, where an engagement took place, in which A company lost a corporal, killed, and two men wounded. On May 21st the regiment marched to Gaines' Mill, and on the 24th to Mechanicsville, where it was engaged with the enemy for about three hours, and at the close of the action was sent on picket at Shady Grove and Bethesda Church.

On May 25th the regiment moved at 7 a. m., in the direction of Hanover Court House, and at noon came in contact with the enemy at Winston's Farm.

During the engagement which ensued, the regiment acted as support for Benson's Battery and lost one man and two horses wounded. The enemy soon retreated in the direction of Hanover Court House, which was promptly occupied by a squadron under Captains Sanders and Hays. While pursuing the retreating enemy beyond Hanover Court House, the brigade was recalled to resist an attack from the rear, which, having been accomplished, the regiment camped for the night on the battlefield.

On the morning of the 28th the regiment was ordered to burn the railroad bridge over the South Anna river. Four squadrons proceeded to Wickham's Farm, with materials for firing the bridge. Colonel Wickham was laid up with a sabre wound received in the action with Captain Sanders, and was captured and paroled. The nature of the ground was not favorable for action of any considerable body of cavalry, so that Lieutenant Kerin was detached with a platoon, and he accomplished the entire destruction of the bridge, although it required about three hours, the regiment being held on the road to support the detachment. At midnight of the same day, Lieutenants Kerin and Coats left camp with twenty men and successfully destroyed the county bridge, about two hundred yards above the railroad bridge previously burned. Another bridge was destroyed by Captain Cram. It had been fired on the 27th by Rush's Lancers, who were prematurely withdrawn.

On the night of May 28th orders were received to destroy still another bridge over the South Anna, which belonged to the Virginia Central Railroad. The enemy was supposed to be in force near this bridge, and a section of artillery and two companies of infantry were sent with the Sixth Cavalry. Captain Abert was sent with his squadron in advance and destroyed the bridge. Captain Kautz with his squadron supported Captain Abert while engaged in this work. On its return to camp, the regiment was ordered at once to Cold Harbor, where it arrived shortly after midnight, and continued to occupy the camp at that point for some time, performing picket and scouting duty.

To illustrate these duties, on June 2d Captain Kautz proceeded with his squadron and two squadrons of lancers on an expedition to Wormley's Ferry, on the Pamunkey, and destroyed a sloop and a number of smaller boats concealed there. Sergeant George Platt swam across the river and secured a canoe in which Lieutenant Balder and six men crossed the turbid stream and arrested Doctor Wormley, at whose place the boats had been hidden by towing them into a creek and felling trees to cover the entrance with foliage. As usual, in such cases, the slaves carried information of the location.

In closing his report of these operations, General Emory says:

"The first squadron of the Sixth U. S. Cavalry, composed of Companies B and H, commanded by Captains Kautz and Savage, led the advance, which they have done most of the way from Yorktown, in the most gallant style."

The regiment had now been undergoing such constant marching and fighting, all the way from Yorktown, that the horses were rapidly becoming unserviceable, not only from exhaustion, but because of the condition of their feet. There was a scarcity of horseshoes and nails, little or no coal, and although the companies had three forges, there was only one anvil amongst them. The regimental return of February 28th shows that twenty-eight officers and nine hundred and fifty-three men were present for duty, and the return for May, made at camp, eight miles from Richmond, Virginia, shows twenty-four officers and six hundred and seventy men. The difference represents the loss,—killed, wounded, captured, etc.,—incident to the incessant labors of the cavalry in advance of the Army of the Potomac, which was confronted at all times by active and alert foemen, commanded by capable and courageous generals.

While the regiment had its camp at Cold Harbor, during the period the army was before Richmond, it was charged with picketing at Atlee station, and a part of the time on the extreme right, near Old

Church, and made frequent reconnoissances to Ashland and Hanover Court House.

On June 13th, when General J. E. B. Stuart made his celebrated raid to the rear of the Army of the Potomac, the regiment participated actively in the futile attempts made to capture and destroy his command. This raid made Stuart so famous and created such a feeling of insecurity concerning trains and supplies, that it will not be amiss to briefly sketch its history.

General Lee gave written instructions to General Stuart to select twelve hundred cavalrymen and a section of artillery and penetrate to the rear of the Army of the Potomac. The instructions and the destination of the command were kept profoundly secret. The personnel included Fitzhugh Lee, W. H. F. Lee, Mosby and other daring and accomplished cavalrymen.

The force was quietly concentrated near the Chickahominy, and camped after the first day's march opposite Hanover Court House, twenty-two miles from Richmond. Without sound of trumpets or display of flags, the march was resumed early the following morning and directed on Hanover Court House, through which Gregg's squadron of the Sixth was just passing toward Mechanicsville, ignorant of Stuart's column being in the vicinity. Fitzhugh Lee reached the intersection of the road just after the squadron passed and in time to capture a straggling sergeant.

The march was then directed on Hawes' Shop, and the column was discovered by a company of the Fifth Cavalry, under Lieutenant E. H. Leib, which was scouting from Old Church in the direction of Hanover Court House. The approach of the Confederates was reported at once to Captain Royall, who commanded the outpost at Old Church. Lieutenant Leib was being steadily driven back, and Captain Royall hastily relieved the pickets, joined him with such force as he could collect, and attacked Stuart's advance, driving it back in a sabre charge. Royall was immediately attacked by a largely superior force, but in order to gain time for his messengers to warn the troops in rear, he twice wheeled about and charged the enemy. The sabre charges were made in columns of fours by both combatants, and Captain Royall was credited with killing Captain Latane, who led the Confederate squadron, which advanced in the second charge. Captain Royall was wounded several times and compelled, through weakness, to turn over the command.

Captain Royall had previously sent Lieutenant Watkins, of his regiment, to report to General Cooke, commanding the Cavalry Division. Orders were quickly given for Major Williams to take the

Fifth and Sixth Cavalry to Royall's assistance. The Sixth started at once, and by taking a short cut, came into the road ahead of Whiting's command—the Fifth—and assuming command of both regiments, Major Williams hastened to the cross-roads where the enemy had fought Captain Royall's squadron, and encountered Stuart's pickets there about 3.30 p. m.; the main body had passed half an hour before, and the pickets now withdrew to follow them. Lieutenant Watkins had been sent back to notify Captain Royall of the coming of relief, but returned reporting the camp burned, and that the enemy had passed on in the direction of the White House. Lieutenant Balder was sent with a platoon of the Sixth to follow and locate the enemy, which he accomplished without difficulty, by following rapidly along the road taken by the vedettes, who had just withdrawn, and who led his platoon directly to Stuart's rear guard.

Just at the moment when Lieutenant Balder reported the whereabouts of and direction taken by Stuart's column, Major Williams received an order from General Cooke to hold his position, scour the roads and collect information. This was done, while Stuart went almost unmolested on his rapid march, creating so much confusion that twenty-five non-commissioned officers and privates of the Fifth Cavalry caught up with his rear guard, under a flag of truce, and surrendered, with horses and arms, under the impression that they were surrounded.

Lieutenant Spangler, Regimental Quartermaster, was near Garlick's Landing with the wagon train, and discovered Stuart's column about an hour after the regiment had halted at the scene of the Royall fight. This discovery was reported, but seems not to have been received by General Warren, who had been hurried forward with infantry, until about midnight. General Warren's infantry marched back and forth, over forty miles, between 5 p. m. on the 13th and 7 a. m. on the 15th, but the enemy proved so elusive that they only traced them by rumor.

Stuart left a squadron at Garlick's Landing long enough to destroy a couple of transports and some stores, but continued the march of his column towards Tunstall's station, where he captured a wagon train en route, but failed to capture a railroad train which, at high speed, brushed away the obstructions which had been placed on the track. There was no time for Stuart to tarry, for he had reason to know that he had aroused the whole Federal army. He continued his rapid march during the bright moonlight night, with which he was favored, and recrossed the Chickahominy at Forge Bridge about daylight. Stuart summarized the results of his raid as 165 prisoners, 260 horses and mules, and the creation of such a panic in the Federal army, that he estimated that not less than ten thousand men would be detached from the fighting line to guard against similar expeditions.

General Emory in his report, said:

> "The damage done by the enemy is not commensurate with the bold spirit with which the raid was dictated. He left faster than he came, and the attempt to break up the railroad communication was an entire failure, resulting in cutting telegraph wires, tearing up a single rail, and burning one carload of corn. The whole business, however, is suggestive, and shows on the part of the enemy great knowledge of localities within our pickets, even that of the sutler establishment."

There was no doubt that all those remaining at home in the region occupied were in sympathy and communication with the enemy. Major Williams arrested and sent to the rear a number of supposed citizens, one of whom the negroes reported as an officer of the Hanover Legion, and whom they accused of offering a bribe to one of their number to conduct the Confederate column by a circuitous route to Captain Royall's camp, so as to surprise and capture his entire command.

Stuart's raid did more damage through its effect on the public mind than it really accomplished against the army, but it taught him what he could expect from his followers, and he was not slow to profit by the knowledge.

The cavalry of the Army of the Potomac had not yet, however, been equipped and trained for the independent action for which it subsequently became so justly celebrated. General Cooke (father-in-law of J. E. B. Stuart, his opponent) was a thorough cavalryman, as were many of the distinguished officers under him, a number of whom subsequently rose to important commands. But the American cavalry idea was, day by day, crystallizing, and all the regiments were begging and struggling for carbines and the equipment which enabled them later on to be comparatively independent of infantry supports. On June 21st, 1862, just after Stuart's raid, and a year after the regiment had been organized, there were only one hundred and forty men present, armed with carbines, whereas the Confederate cavalry was quite generally equipped with firearms, including carbines, shotguns and rifles.

During the operations around Richmond, June 25th to July 2d, 1862, known as the Seven Days' battles, the Sixth Cavalry was detached from the Reserve Brigade to duty with General Stoneman, and Gregg's squadron was on the extreme right when the action opened. General P. St. George Cooke personally commanded the cavalry which formed the extreme rear guard, and really saved Fitz John Porter's batteries, which had been left without support at Gaines' Mill. General Cooke, in his report, specially commended two men, one of whom was Private D. F. King, Troop B, Sixth Cavalry, "for serving above that position with intelligence, bravery and promptness."

June 25th the regiment moved from Cold Harbor to Hanover Court House, and the next day to Tunstall's station. The movement of the army from the Chickahominy to the James having commenced, the cavalry retired by way of York river. There was a large quantity of stores at White House Landing to be moved, and the pursuit of the retiring column by the enemy's cavalry was so energetic that it became necessary to take some steps to check it. The Sixth Cavalry, with a section of artillery, was placed at the crossing of Black river, which was not fordable for some distance above and below this crossing. The enemy attacked and endeavored several times to force a passage, but every attempt was defeated; the position was defended until after dark, when the torch was applied to such stores as could not be moved. The regiment then withdrew and, acting as rear guard, marched all night, arriving at Williamsburg about 8 a. m. of the 27th, and on the following day continued the march back to Yorktown.

On July 2d camp was moved to a point near Hampton, where the regiment remained until it embarked on the 7th, at Fort Monroe, for Harrison's Landing on the James, in the vicinity of which place the Army of the Potomac had concentrated after the Seven Days' battles. The regiment was camped at "Westover," one of the most famous of the old Virginia estates, where it remained until August 4th, employed in picketing the extreme left towards Haxall's.

While the regiment lay at "Westover," news was received of the death of Lieutenant McQuade in prison at Richmond of wounds received at Bull Run the preceding summer, at which time he was captured. The death of Lieutenant Peter McGrath was also reported at this time from New Mexico, where he had continued on duty after his appointment in the Sixth. He died of wounds received in action at Apache Canon with the Confederate column, which came up from Texas and invaded New Mexico. A number of officers were detailed from the regiment while in this camp as aides for Generals McClellan, Sumner, Pleasanton, and others, and it was not long before their loss was keenly felt.

On August 4th the regiment formed a part of General Pleasanton's brigade of General Hooker's command, and it had, as usual, the advance of the reconnoissance in force to Malvern Hill, where it participated in the action of August 5th, losing four men killed and a number of wounded and prisoners.

The regiment acted as rear guard returning to Haxall's Landing and remained outside the works, forming part of the grand guard, under General Pleasanton, and picketing towards Malvern Hill and Richmond. On August 14th the evacuation by the Army of the Potomac had proceeded so far that General Pleasanton was directed to withdraw all troops except the First and Sixth Cavalry, and Robertson's and Benson's horse batteries; this brigade was forced to occupy a line of about fifteen miles, with pickets and scouts covering all the roads leading into Harrison's Landing. About midnight of the 16th the pickets were withdrawn from Haxall's; the enemy followed, and the next afternoon charged the pickets to the west of Harrison's Landing, wounding one man.

Amongst the few specially recommended by General Pleasanton for favorable notice were Captains Sanders and Gregg, and Lieutenants Ward and Spangler, Sixth Cavalry.

The evacuation of Harrison's Landing having been completed on August 18th, the regiment marched as the rear guard of the army through Charles City Court House, and on the following day crossed the Chickahominy, reaching Yorktown on the evening of the 20th, and remained there until the last day of the month, when it was embarked on transports for Alexandria, Virginia. In closing his report of the operation of covering the withdrawal and the performance of very arduous duties as rear guard, General Pleasanton said:

"I respectfully request of the General commanding that an appreciation of the gallant bearing of the men of this command may be evinced by permitting the following named regiments and batteries to inscribe on their colors "Malvern Hill, August 5th, 1862": the Sixth Regular Cavalry, the Eighth Pennsylvania Cavalry, the Eighth Illinois Cavalry, Robertson's battery of horse artillery and Benson's battery of horse artillery. These were the only troops that were actually engaged with the enemy on that day; the only troops that followed in pursuit, and that were the last to leave the field when the army was withdrawn. They victoriously closed the fighting of the Army of the Potomac on the Peninsula."

The regiment, in its first brief but arduous campaign, had won the right to now emblazon upon its standard the names of ten engagements in which it had participated with honor. The gallantry and ability of its officers had marked many of them for higher commands, which unfortunately, in too many instances, was to sever forever their connection with the regiment. Losses had begun to thin the ranks, but the experience already gained by those remaining made them no unimportant factors in the solution of the difficult problems which faced the Army of the Potomac during the next three years:

At the outbreak of the war, the Confederate cavalry was composed of the flower of the Southern youth. Each trooper was required to provide his mount at his own expense, and the ranks were filled from those accustomed to an outdoor life in the saddle; until the long-continued struggle had completely ruined their country and made it impossible to secure proper remounts, these lusty young followers of Stuart gave their opponents blow for blow and enhanced the power of their infantry many fold. Called upon constantly to test its powers against these brave and active horsemen, the regiment added to its reputation at each and every encounter.

CHAPTER III.

Maryland Campaign.

Back to Alexandria—Falls Church—Sugar Loaf Mountain—Petersville—With Franklin's Corps—Stuart's Maryland Raid—Carbines received at Sharpsburg—Charlestown—Hillsboro—Expedition to Leesburg—With General Hancock—Arduous Cavalry Service.

THE preceding chapter left the regiment on transports returning from the scenes of the Peninsula Campaign, the army having been summoned for the defense of the capital, which was menaced by the presence of a victorious enemy marching into Maryland, thereby threatening both Washington and Baltimore, as well as Pennsylvania. Alexandria was reached September 1st, and as soon as the weary men and horses could be disembarked, they were placed in camp near Fort Albany where the precious hours were spent in the preparation for the coming conflict with Stuart's cavalry, which had already advanced to Fairfax Court House.

A part of the regiment was detached to Dranesville, under General Sigel, and the remainder advanced to Falls Church, where the enemy's cavalry outposts were encountered. In the short engagement which ensued the regiment lost one man killed and three wounded.

Lee's troops were now actively threatening Washington and the cavalry was pushed rapidly to the front to retain contact with and determine the strength of the invading army. During the night of the 5th the regiment crossed the Aqueduct bridge and proceeded to Tennallytown, which was reached the next day. The day following the march was resumed via Darnestown and Dawsonville, where the regiment halted for a rest. September 8th, the regiment reached Barnesville, and sent scouting parties towards Frederick City and Point of Rocks. Picketing roads and scouting were actively continued until the 10th, when the enemy was encountered at Sugar Loaf Mountain, where Captain Sanders with the regiment, reinforced by two guns, endeavored to dislodge them, but was unsuccessful. The regiment lost one man killed and four wounded in this action.

On the 12th the regiment marched through Greenfield Mills and Licksville and arrived at Middletown at 2 a. m. From this place companies were sent to guard the fords of the Potomac from the mouth of the Monocacy to Knoxville. Companies I and L, while scouting near Petersville, became engaged in a skirmish with the enemy and drove them from that place. The regiment operated a part of the time with Franklin's Corps. The Battle of South Mountain took place on the 14th, and Antietam on the 16th and 17th.

It will be remembered that on September 10th Stuart had crossed the Potomac at McCoy's Ferry, on his raid into Maryland and Pennsylvania, making it necessary to use all the available cavalry against him. General Pleasanton was ordered to cut off his retreat, should he make for any of the fords below the position of the main army. He arrived at Mechanicstown about an hour after Stuart passed on his retreat to the river, and pushed him so close that he prevented his crossing at the mouth of the Monocacy and drove him to White's Ford, which had been ordered occupied by a regiment. The regiment had not reached its appointed station, however, and Stuart crossed back into Virginia under fire of Pleasanton's guns, on September 19th, after passing around the entire army. The exhaustive service endured by the cavalry broke down a large percentage of the horses. To illustrate the vigorous manner in which the pursuit was conducted, it need only be stated that General Pleasanton marched his command seventy-eight miles in twenty-four hours.

After much hard scouting and reconnoissance duty the regiment arrived at Sharpsburg on the evening of the 21st, where carbines, which had been repeatedly asked for during the preceding year, were at last obtained. Up to this time the regiment, excepting one squadron, had been equipped with pistols and sabres upon the European model of light cavalry.

The regiment marched by way of Knoxville to Harper's Ferry, and arrived at Bolivar Heights September 23d. After a brief respite, the regiment, together with the Fifth Cavalry and Robertson's Battery of horse artillery, made a reconnoissance to Charlestown, Virginia, on the 25th, and on the 27th one squadron was sent across Loudoun Heights to Hillsboro. It will be remembered that Lee's army had recently captured the garrison at Harper's Ferry, consisting of about 10,000 men, in fact, all but the cavalry under the gallant Colonel Davis, who not only made his way out, but captured an important ammunition train and forced the drivers to take the wagons along at a rapid gait until he delivered them within the Federal lines.

On the 28th the regiment was sent on a second reconnoissance to Charlestown, where five prisoners were captured, and on the following day went to Hillsboro and captured three more prisoners. On October 1st, the regiment left Bolivar Heights and, crossing the Shenandoah to Loudoun Heights, joined the expedition under General Kimball to Leesburg, Virginia.

The expedition left the Potomac about five miles from Harper's Ferry, and, passing through the gorge of Dutchman's Creek, entered the Catoctin valley, which was being devastated by Confederate cavalry. On approaching Waterford, Captain Sanders, who commanded the regiment, charged with the advance platoon, which was under Lieutenant Nolan, and captured six of the enemy's pickets. The summit of Catoctin Mountain was reached at night, and at daylight of the 25th, the advance guard entered Leesburg and captured a number of sick and convalescent patients left by the enemy, who were reported at Aldie and Snicker's Gap. Returning to Bolivar Heights, the command moved into the valley between the Blue Ridge and Short Hills, and encountered the enemy's pickets all along the route, but they constantly withdrew into the side valleys. The regiment arrived at Bolivar Heights before daylight of the 3d, and changed camp on the 4th to Knoxville, Maryland.

In closing his report, General Kimball said:

> "I desire to express to you my admiration of the soldierly conduct of both officers and men of the Sixth U. S. Cavalry, under the command of Captain Sanders, as well as that of Major Robertson of the horse artillery."

October 8th, the regiment with the Fifth Cavalry and Robertson's horse battery accompanied General Hancock to Charlestown, Virginia, and occupied the town, with the loss of one man wounded. The regiment subsequently returned to the camp at Knoxville.

While at this camp, C company, which had been on the eve of organization several times, when the recruits were taken for other companies, was finally organized on October 25th; this completed the organization, but the next day the regiment was again on the march and as C company had not received equipments or horses, it was left behind with other dismounted men, over three hundred in all.

Upon leaving Knoxville, the command crossed the Potomac on the pontoon bridge at Berlin, and proceeded to Lovettsville, where H company was detached for duty at General Pleasanton's headquarters. While here, on October 27th, four companies, A, E, K and M, were detached for picket duty at Hillsboro. As the advance guard entered the town, it was charged by a squad of Confederate cavalry, and a corporal of E company was captured through his horse falling in the street. The enemy was promptly driven from the town, which was then occupied by the two squadrons until the 31st, when they joined the regiment at Purcellville to which place it had advanced.

The brief time which had elapsed since disembarking at Alexandria had been taken up with hard marching, screening, scouting and picket duty,—purely cavalry work, but involving much hardship, constant activity, courage and quick judgment.

While the regiment had no conspicuous part in the main battle of Antietam, it was constantly striking the enemy's outposts during the entire campaign and driving them in with loss to itself as well as the enemy. General Pleasanton, in making his report of the operations resulting in driving Lee's army back into Virginia, said:

"The services of this division (cavalry) from the 4th of September up to the 19th were of the most constant and arduous character. For fifteen successive days we were in contact with the enemy, and each day conflicts of some kind were maintained, in which we gradually but steadily advanced. The officers and men have exerted themselves to insure the success of every expedition and these efforts have been fortunate. The officers entitled to mention for gallant services are .... Captains W. P. Sanders, George C. Cram and Henry B. Hays, and Lieutenant Albert Coats, Adjutant."

Lieutenant Isaac M. Ward, A. D. C., and J. W. Spangler, Division Quartermaster, belonging to the Sixth were also commended for valuable services.

At the muster of October 31st, there were present nineteen officers and five hundred and ten men. It will be recalled that the regiment embarked for the Peninsula Campaign the previous April, one thousand strong.

CHAPTER IV.

On to Fredericksburg.

Pursuit of Lee—Philamont—Uniontown—Upperville—Barbee's Cross Roads—Amissville—General Pleasanton's Report—Sulphur Springs—Picketing the Rappahannock—Fredericksburg—Squadron crosses to develop Enemy's Line—Camp at Falmouth—Some Difficulties of Service—Stoneman's Raid—Buford's Raid to Gordonsville—Absence of Cavalry from Chancellorsville—Captured by Guerrillas—Dahlgren's proposed Raid—Cavalry Battle Beverly Ford—Incidents.

LEE'S army having withdrawn from the vicinity of the battlefield of Antietam, the pursuit was taken up by a portion of the Army of the Potomac. There was considerable controversy at this period between General McClellan and the authorities in Washington, because the army did not immediately move forward and crush the Confederates. General McClellan reported that the army, which had been hurried back from the Peninsula and marched at once to meet Lee's army and relieve Harper's Ferry, was now in no state to follow up the victory of Antietam, but needed supplies of all kinds, and that the cavalry must be remounted. Supplies and animals were forwarded with all haste possible, but many of the horses were in no condition for active work against such horsemen as composed Stuart's command. It developed that in one instance a lot of horses for remounts, had been kept on the cars fifty hours without water or forage, before delivery to the cavalry.

The Cavalry Division moved forward, and the regiment marched by way of Philamont, Uniontown and Upperville, participating in the cavalry action at the first named place, on November 1st. On the second, the regiment was dismounted and supported a battery during the engagement at Uniontown, and on the 3d, participated in a running fight all the way from Uniontown to Upperville. Next day the pursuit was continued to the Manassas Gap railroad, and on the 5th to Barbee's Cross Roads, where the regiment came under a heavy fire of artillery and dismounted cavalry. The command was dismounted to fight on foot and drove the enemy from the field.

On the 6th, the command reached Orleans, and on the 7th again came up with the Confederates at Amissville and drove them out of that place. On the 8th the regiment marched to Little Washington and engaged in a skirmish, capturing a wagon, a dozen horses, an officer and one man, and then returned to Amissville. While here, on November

10th, the Confederate cavalry attacked and drove in the pickets. The command moved out at once, repulsed the enemy and re-established the line. The Confederates indulged in considerable artillery firing with but little result. The following extract from a detailed report of General Pleasanton, in which the efficient services of the Sixth Cavalry are frequently mentioned, is of interest to cavalrymen generally:

"Headquarters Cavalry Division,
Camp near Warrenton, Virginia, November 17th, 1862.

General:—I have the honor to submit the following report of the operations of this command from the crossing of the Potomac, at Berlin, to the arrival of the Army of the Potomac in the vicinity of Warrenton, Virginia, and the relinquishment of the command of the army by Major-General McClellan:

* * * * * * * * * * * * * *

In closing this report, it is but justice to the troops I have had the honor to command that I should mention the results of their laborious exertions and the chivalrous gallantry, constantly exhibited under many adverse circumstances. From the time the army left Washington to the end of the campaign at Warrenton, the cavalry of my command had taken from the enemy six pieces of artillery, four stands of colors, and 1000 prisoners of war, without losing a single gun or color. These facts show that the officers and men of our cavalry have the energy, the intelligence, the courage and enterprise to make them superior to any cavalry they have to contend with, and yet no one is more painfully conscious than myself that the opinion is entertained that our cavalry has been deficient in its duty in the present rebellion. I will, therefore, mention a few facts to show that, wherever there exists a foundation for such an opinion, the fault does not rest with the cavalry. The rebels have always had more cavalry in the field than we, and whenever we have fought them, their numbers were two to three to one of ours. Such a difference is always an encouragement to brave soldiers, for they never stop to inquire their number; but such a difference tells fearfully upon the hard service the horses have to perform. Good horses are broken down by it; inferior ones are literally thrown away in such service.

The rebel cavalry are mounted on the best horses in the south, while our cavalry are furnished a very inferior animal, bought by contract, which is totally unfit for efficient service. The best horses in my command are the horses my men have captured from the rebel cavalry in their different engagements with them. As an instance, one of my companies has twenty-two rebel horses out of fifty-three, and these horses are the best in the company. Out of eighteen horses furnished this same company by the quartermaster's department at Knoxville, only two are left in the company, and these are very inferior. Does not this show that the officers and men who thus wrest the elements of success from the hands of the enemy are superior to the circumstances surrounding them, and are not responsible for those failures which are used as illustrations against them?

A. PLEASANTON,
Brigadier-General, Commanding Division.

Brigadier-General R. B. MARCY,
Chief of Staff, Army of the Potomac."

The regiment marched by way of Waterloo, Liverpool and Warrenton, and arrived at Sulphur Springs, November 17th, and picketed the ford of the Rappahannock river, near that village. November 18th, when General Pleasanton's division was withdrawing from Sulphur Springs, the enemy opened with a battery on the rear guard, composed of the Sixth, and a section of Pennington's battery.

WADE'S SQUADRON RETURNING FROM RECONNOISSANCE CONFEDERATE LINE OF BATTLE, FREDERICKSBURG.

The section replied and the Confederates crossed two squadrons, which were driven off, and the march of the rear guard resumed.

The regiment arrived at Falmouth on the 20th; B and E companies were immediately detached for escort duty with General Sumner. Belle Plain was reached on the 24th, when the regiment was assigned to the duty of picketing the fords on the Rappahannock, which was continued until December 12th, when, at daylight, the regiment marched to the Philips House, near Fredericksburg, to participate in the battle about to begin on that historic field.

The army had already begun crossing below Fredericksburg and a pontoon bridge was under construction immediately opposite the city. This bridge was completed about noon of the 12th, and at 3 p. m., Lieutenant J. F. Wade's squadron, composed of D and K companies, was ordered to cross and make a reconnoissance of the enemy's works.

The squadron marched through the town and thence out into the open country at the foot of Marye's Heights and the adjoining ridges. The advance guard, well to the front, was allowed to approach the Confederate position from which the main infantry strength of the magnificent Army of the Potomac was soon to recoil in defeat.

When the squadron had proceeded as near as the

Confederates deemed it wise to permit it to approach the artillery opened. The advance guard turned to the right and, moving rapidly along the lines, developed the infantry fire. It was evident that no further reconnoissance of this position was possible with this single squadron, which, although in rapid motion, suffered within a few minutes a loss of two men and eight horses wounded.

The squadron retired in good order, under fire, and recrossed the bridge. The result of the reconnoissance was communicated to General Burnside. The infantry skirmish lines were soon pushed out beyond the town while the army was being massed on the Fredericksburg side of the river.

The battle which followed was an infantry and artillery fight of great magnitude, and, although unsuccessful, the Army of the Potomac could not well afford to efface from history the record of its defeat, for the valorous charges on Marye's Heights could have been repulsed only by soldiers of the highest type. It is a matter of honest pride for the opposing armies that, when positions were reversed at Gettysburg, Pickett's gallant column went down to defeat, but left behind a record for future history, beside which the story of "The Charge of the Six Hundred" pales almost into insignificance.

During the fierce engagement the regiment was posted on the opposite side of the river, above and to the rear of Falmouth, in support of the batteries guarding that flank. During the evening of the 13th of December it was withdrawn and went into camp about two miles from Falmouth, where it remained throughout the winter and until April 13th, 1863.

During these four months the cavalry performed picket duty along the Rappahannock, the Sixth having the posts at United States, Richard's and Banks' fords above, and at Corbin's Neck, below Fredericksburg.

On November 27th, 1862, General Wade Hampton, with selected detachments from his command, crossed the Rappahannock at Kelly's Mill, and entered the Federal lines and captured various pickets, to within eight miles of Falmouth, returning safely to the Confederate lines after a most successful expedition. He says in his report:

> "A part of my plan was to have cut off the force at Richard's Ferry, but though I got completely in their rear, I found my number so reduced that I was forced reluctantly to abandon my design. The Sixth Regiment Regulars was on post there, and I had to leave them for another time."

The distance from camp was so great that these tours of picket duty were regulated so that each detail remained out a week at a time. The duty was not only very trying and disagreeable for the men, but was ruinous to the horses. In fact, the continuous hard service had brought the regiment to a point where its commanding officer recognized that it must be built up and encouraged.

The regiment had been serving with great credit under General Pleasanton as shown by its record of numberless advance and rear guard actions. Captain Sanders finally concluded, on the march from Maryland, that the regiment was not being accorded fair treatment, and addressed to the Adjutant General, Army of the Potomac, the following letter:

"Headquarters 6th Cavalry,
Camp at Upperville, Virginia, November 4th, 1862.

GENERAL:—I have the honor to request that, in justice to my regiment, the 6th U. S. Cavalry be relieved from duty with General Pleasanton's brigade.

General Pleasanton now has three officers from my regiment on his staff, one company and its officers as provost marshal, and almost every detail of men is made from this regiment. I am willing to go on any duty where the regiment will be justly treated. I have also the honor to request that some of the officers and men on duty at brigade headquarters be relieved.

Very respectfully,
Your obedient servant,
W. P. SANDERS,
Captain, 6th U. S. Cavalry, Commanding."

No reply having been received, the regimental commander requested information as to whether the brigade commander had forwarded the communication. In this letter, dated November 24th, 1862, Camp near Belle Plain, Virginia, appears the following:

"Previous to making a similar request to that of Captain Sanders, I would state that, in my opinion and that of every officer in the regiment, more than a fair portion of duty is assigned it. I have also to inform you that in direct violation of the published order of march, this regiment was placed in rear and made to do rear guard duty for two consecutive days, thereby compelling the regiment to encamp after night in a country destitute of forage, and for forty-eight hours the horses were without feed. I am now compelled to send my companies sixteen miles on picket and relieve them myself. On account of the numerous heavy details ordered by your office from the 6th Cavalry, it is impossible for me, with the limited number of men left, to do the full duty of a regiment. The 6th Cavalry has served faithfully and deserves well of the country, and I consider it no part of my duty to see injustice done it. Enclosed you will find a report of the condition of the regiment, consolidated from this morning's report of company commanders. I desire that you will communicate these grievances to the General without delay, in order that justice may be done this command."

Matters did not mend rapidly, for the following letters were sent during January, at a time when the strength of the cavalry should have been husbanded with great care for the spring campaign:

"Headquarters 6th U. S. Cavalry,
January 16th, 1863.

SIR:—I have the honor to report for the information of Brigade Headquarters, that the three squadrons of my regiment now on picket duty have a strength of 505 enlisted men. The three companies now in camp awaiting will turn out to-morrow 121 enlisted men. Present, absolute available strength mounted of the six troops and the three in camp, of which my command consists, 426.

There are three troops on detached service at General Sumner's and General Pleasanton's headquarters. Of ineffectives I shall leave in camp, mostly dismounted, 292. From the above it will be perceived that I can march with one hundred and seventy-one men as the strength of my three disposable companies. I succeeded in getting thirty-six carbines and sabres from Pennington's battery to-day. To-morrow I shall be obliged to send out two days' forage and three days' rations to my six companies on picket; this is essential to provide for their subsistence and forage. It requires six wagons to enable them to return during the day (they must be lightly loaded), which will cripple my transportation seriously, should I have to use it for general purposes to-morrow.

Very respectfully, Your obedient servant,

(Signed) G. C. CRAM,

Captain, 6th U. S. Cavalry, Commanding.

To Lieutenant MAHNKEN,
Acting Assistant Adjutant-General,
2d Cavalry Brigade."

"Headquarters 6th U. S. Cavalry,
January 21st, 1863.

SIR:—I have the honor to request to be informed whether I am at liberty to run out forage to the six companies of my regiment, now on picket; their forage is out this morning; also whether I can start my train to depot for forage. I have a scant two days' in camp ahead for the whole command, and forage must be sent this morning to the detail on picket.

My entire command is rationed for three days, from this morning, in their haversacks. Am I to construe the circular received this morning as a standing order to run out the necessary transportation daily, to my detail on picket, with one day's rations, without further orders, as it is only by that, that I can keep them three days ahead?

Very respectfully, Your obedient servant,

G. C. CRAM,

Captain, 6th U. S. Cavalry.

To Lieutenant H. MAHNKEN,
Acting Assistant Adjutant-General,
2d Cavalry Brigade."

"Headquarters 6th U. S. Cavalry,
Camp near Falmouth, Virginia, January 29th, 1863.

SIR:—I have the honor to transmit herewith approved requisitions for six wagons and requisitions for tools rendered absolutely necessary under orders from Headquarters 2d Cavalry Brigade, Cavalry Division, January 28th, 1863, requiring me to employ the troops under my command to construct and keep in repair the bridges on the road between General Hooker's headquarters and 'Stoneman's switch.' I have the honor to officially state my belief that, unless I am furnished with the means called for in such requisitions, it will be impossible for me to perform the duty assigned to me under the above-noted order, as my regimental resources are already insufficient for the purpose of foraging and rationing my command. I have also the honor to very respectfully request to be informed if it is intended to retain this regiment on the roster for picket while discharging this duty of road and bridge construction and police, and if, while assigned to such fatigue duty, it will also be required to do its usual outpost duty. The requisitions are based upon a careful survey and examination made to-day of the roads and line of country assigned me.

* * * * * * * * * * * * * * *

I am, sir, very respectfully,
Your obedient servant,
(Signed) G. C. CRAM,
Captain, 6th U. S. Cavalry, Commanding.

To Lieutenant H. MAHNKEN,
Acting Assistant Adjutant-General,
2d Cavalry Brigade."

From a number of letters written about this time the following has been selected to illustrate picket duty on the Rappahannock from the trooper's point of view:

"Banks of the Rappahannock, Virginia,
Sunday morning.

DEAR MOTHER:—Being very hard off for paper and ink and something to write on, I take one-half of the sheet of paper you sent me and sit down to answer your welcome letter which I received this morning.

At present I am on picket duty, only a short distance across the river from the Rebel pickets. We are in sight of each other. I am writing this on the butt of my carbine. There is another man on post with me; he is a Scotchman. He keeps me in good humor all the time telling stories. He is talking to the Secesh all the time. They asked him to what regiment he belonged. He told them it was the 1st Dublin. We don't fire at one another unless someone attempts to cross the river. The weather is very pleasant at present, but the nights are cold. We get along very well. We have a fire to warm ourselves. I like to stand picket in good weather; but it is very nasty work in bad weather. We are going to have a good dinner. One of the boys has killed a hog, so we will have pork steaks to-day. We get plenty of corn cakes from the farmers. We have to stop out here eight days. We are out six now.

There are a great many stories afloat. Sometimes we hear that the army is going to the west, and at other times we hear that we are going to the Peninsula again. We do not know where we are going. Time will tell. I wish the war was at an end. As soon as the war is over I shall quit the service for good and settle down.

* * * * * * * * * * * * * * *

Your affectionate son,
JAMES,
Company M, 6th U. S. Cavalry."

The true uses of cavalry and its capabilities when properly handled were apparently not understood up to this time by any one powerful enough to rectify abuses and stop the enormous waste of horses. In the early part of the war subordinate generals were constantly seen with so-called "body guards" of cavalry, and the strength of fine organizations was frittered away with unnecessary details.

The extracts given from the regimental records show how useless it was for junior commanders, who understood the use of cavalry, to seek justice for their organizations. Think of such a born cavalryman as Sanders witnessing his regiment keeping roads in repair and picketing camps for infantry corps! Yet this is what went on from month to month, to the great distress of many able and clever officers who, under more advantageous conditions, would have wrested victory from Stuart without waiting for the advent of General Sheridan.

The cavalry exhibited magnificent fighting qualities on various fields, but it remained later for Sheridan with his determination and strong will to force the cavalry corps into its true position, relative to the remainder of the Army of the Potomac.

Every effort was made to drill and equip the regiment while in the camp at Falmouth; the drilling was necessarily confined to those not on outpost duty, and the exposure and hard work prevented the horses from improving very fast. Nevertheless, when "boots and saddles" sounded on April 13th, 1863, owing to the diligent and intelligent efforts of officers and men, the regiment turned out six hundred and sixty-one men mounted and equipped for the expedition, which started on that date and known as "Stoneman's Raid."

On the 14th the regiment reached Kelly's Ford, and on the 15th Rappahannock station, where it remained in a heavy rainstorm until 10 p. m., when it returned to Deep Run. The rain had raised the stream so that it could not be forded. At daylight a raft was constructed and, the property having been conveyed across, the regiment swam the horses and pack-mules over and proceeded to Morrisville to guard the train.

On the 22d the regiment marched to Bealeton station; on the 23d to Warrenton Junction, and on the 29th back to Kelly's Ford, which was crossed and pickets thrown out towards Brandy station. The fighting on this date was confined to driving in the enemy's pickets on the roads to Brandy station and to Stevensburg, the latter being performed by the Sixth. On the 30th the regiment crossed the Rapidan at Raccoon Ford.

On May 1st the march was continued through Louisa Court House, where the railroad and telegraph lines were destroyed, and thence to the North Anna river. The next day the South Anna was crossed and the command marched to Thompson's Cross Roads, and on the day following a squadron was detached to scout towards the Virginia Central Railroad.

On May 4th details of selected men were sent, under Lieutenants Wade and Carpenter, with General John Buford's command on his raid to Gordonsville, where the column arrived at daybreak. As the place was occupied in force, no attack was made beyond some firing by skirmishers. This column returned and, on the morning of the 6th, overtook the main command, which had marched all night in the mud and rain near the North Anna river. Raccoon Ford was reached on the 7th; after swimming the command across, the march was continued to Rappahannock station. Although the march was resumed on the 11th, this practically ended the Stoneman raid, which had been conducted under conditions involving unusual hardship.

Starting from Falmouth, each trooper packed thirty pounds of grain on his horse, besides rations. The average load carried by the pack-mules, of which there were six to each company, two for the hospital and two for the band, was two hundred pounds. Owing to improper packing and the necessity for keeping the packs on for long periods in very bad weather, the mules were quickly disabled by sore backs.

From May 2d until the 8th the command was out

of supplies, except such as could be obtained by foraging in a despoiled country, and while on a rapid march. While on a foraging expedition, with a detachment of ten men, Lieutenant T. C. Tupper, Sixth Cavalry, captured General Stuart's chief quartermaster, in sight of one of their squadrons. Ninety-three horses gave out, fifty-one were killed and seven lost to the enemy through capture. The regiment captured twenty-nine horses and thirteen mules, not enough to make an appreciable showing as compared with the loss. Years afterwards this raid was pronounced, by those who participated in it, as being unrivaled in the annals of war for discomfort and hardship, taking into consideration the time consumed.

There is a view of this raid which has received much consideration at the hands of those military students who deal in theories as to "what might have been." It will be remembered that the battle of Chancellorsville was fought by the army during the absence of Stoneman with the cavalry, and that Stuart's presence with Lee's army had a marked effect on the grand flank movement which brought the Army of the Potomac to the verge of ruin. What might have happened if Hooker had kept his cavalry in hand must remain locked in the realms of speculation.

The success which attended the passage of the artillery and infantry across the river could hardly have been improved upon had the cavalry been present. What would have resulted from the cavalry being thrown against Jackson in his march across the front, and to Hooker's right flank, can only be surmised. This might have changed the whole tide of battle. One thing, however, from the cavalryman's point of view is quite certain, that is, no good results attended this raid commensurate with the efforts and labor involved; the loss of efficiency was keenly felt and impossible to repair in the brief time which elapsed before Lee started on his march to Gettysburg.

When Stuart was massing his magnificent cavalry corps in the vicinity of Beverly Ford early in June, General Hooker reported that he intended to attack and break up the raid in its incipiency, but added: "As many of my cavalry are still unserviceable from the effects of Stoneman's raid, I am too weak to cope with the numbers of the enemy, if as large as represented."

On May 11th the march was resumed to Hartwood Church, which was reached on the 13th, and where the regiment camped until the 18th, picketing Richard's and United States Fords.

While at this camp, Captain G. C. Cram, the regimental commander, accompanied by Assistant Surgeon W. H. Forwood and two orderlies, rode to General Buford's headquarters, about a mile and a half distant. Towards evening they started back to camp, and while passing along a country road, were suddenly surrounded and compelled to surrender by about thirty of Mosby's men, under Lieutenant Fairchild.

The guerrillas had ridden close to the camps, under cover of the dense forest, and, secreting their horses in the underbrush, had posted themselves on both sides of the road and captured several troopers passing back and forth between the camps.

The officers were not armed, and both were entirely unsuspicious of any danger until confronted with a demand for surrender, backed up by cocked carbines. It was a daring ambush, laid in the midst of the cavalry corps, on a piece of road supposed to be covered by patrols and pickets, yet resistance would have been foolhardy.

The captors mounted and conducted their prisoners through the forest to a house, which appeared to be their headquarters. Here Captain Cram and the enlisted men were released on parole, after being deprived of horses and equipments, and started to camp.

Assistant Surgeon Forwood declined to sign the parole and insisted upon his right, as a medical officer, to be released. This was refused, and he was turned over to a guard to be taken to some interior point as a prisoner of war. The guard started after midnight, the prisoner being placed

CAPTURED BY MOSBY'S GUERRILLAS.

on foot between mounted detachments in front and rear. While passing through a dense growth of young pines, the gallant surgeon made a dash for liberty and escaped without injury from the carbine and pistol shots, which resounded through the forest.

The escaping prisoner floundered along over fallen timber and through swamps until nearly daylight, when he succeeded in reaching the main road, where Captain Cram and his party had already arrived, and at a point not far from General Buford's headquarters. Surgeon Forwood rejoined the regiment and continued to share its fortunes, by flood and field, with the same daring spirit which dictated his dash into the dark forest amidst the flying bullets of the guerrillas.

Considerable controversy arose over this capture, and the result was a general order forbidding the acceptance of parole under such circumstances. The order referred to, dated July 3d, 1863, contains the following language:

> "It is understood that captured officers and men have been paroled and released in the field by others than commanders of opposing armies. * * *
>
> Any officer or soldier who gives such parole will be returned to duty without exchange, and, moreover, will be punished for disobedience of orders. It is the duty of the captor to guard his prisoners, and if, through necessity or choice, he fail to do this, it is the duty of the prisoner to return to the service of his Government."

On May 18th the regiment marched to Brooks' station. Captain Cram having been exchanged, reported and resumed command June 2d.

It was while at Brooks' station that Colonel Dahlgren, then an aide-de-camp, contemplated his celebrated expedition to Richmond, and actually proposed to the commanding general to undertake it with the Sixth Cavalry alone.

"Camp near Falmouth, Virginia,
May 23d, 1863.

Major-General HOOKER,
Commanding Army of the Potomac.

GENERAL:—I respectfully submit the following plan for a cavalry expedition, and ask, if it should meet with your approval, permission to prepare and attempt it. The rebel cavalry are again feeling along our lines, probably to find a weak point to enter at, as is their custom. If they should attempt a raid, this would offer a fine chance for a small body of our cavalry to penetrate their country, and I would respectfully ask, in such case, permission to have the Sixth U. S. Cavalry and take the following course: Cross above on the Rappahannock and at Raccoon Ford, on the Rapidan River, or at points which appear best just before starting; thence somewhere near Louisa Court House; thence somewhere between Columbia and Goochland; thence over the James River to the arsenal at Bellona, which we would destroy; thence either burn the bridges in rear of Richmond over James River, and dash through the city and on to the White House, or any safe place near there, or, after burning the bridges, move to Petersburg, and thence to our forces near Suffolk. The greatest obstacle would be passing their picket line on the Rappahannock, which, if accomplished without being discovered, would leave the roads open before us; but I know several men in the provost-marshal's service who feel confident of guiding such an expedition, and have offered to do so. I think it would be impossible to accomplish anything unless the rebel cavalry are off on a raid, which would give us four or five days start of them and no cavalry to oppose.

The object of the expedition would be to destroy everything along the route, and especially on the south side of the James River, and attempt to enter Richmond and Petersburg. If the general proposition should meet with your approval, I will submit more minute details.

I have the honor to be, General, with great respect,

Your obedient servant,

ULRIC DAHLGREN,

Captain and Aide-de-Camp."

The proposition was not accepted, but some months later Colonel Dahlgren was authorized to proceed on his errand with selected men, and General Kilpatrick was dispatched to the opposite side of Richmond to aid him as far as possible.

The Sixth was not detailed, but Colonel Dahlgren was allowed to select a small detachment, under Sergeant James R. Wood, for duty as scouts. The regiment had been on all the cavalry raids of the Army of the Potomac, and the men, generally, were familiar with the country. The scouts led a detachment across the Rapidan, and in a very clever manner captured the pickets and reserve at Ely's Ford without creating any unusual alarm. The detachment rendered excellent service until the outer works of Richmond were reached and Kilpatrick's guns could be heard far away on the opposite side of the city.

After a conference, Colonel Dahlgren sent Sergeant Wood and another scout to open communication with General Kilpatrick. Sergeant Wood was captured and his companion killed by a party of Confederate cavalrymen on the Brook turnpike. The sergeant was sent to Libby Prison, where he was soon joined by others, captured when Colonel Dahlgren was killed. Wood cleverly effected his escape, succeeded in passing through the Confederate lines, and rejoined the army. Some of the others were held as prisoners until the close of the war.

The continued accessions to Stuart's cavalry camp created much uneasiness, and General Hooker decided to add some infantry to his available cavalry and make an attack. The Sixth moved with the cavalry corps to near Beverly Ford on the 8th, and on June 9th crossed the Rappahannock and took a gallant part in the great cavalry battle of that day.

The regiment, five squadrons strong, crossed the Rappahannock shortly after daylight in brigade column and formed as a support to Elder's Horse Artillery, in which capacity it acted for about one hour after crossing. The first squadron was, by order of the brigade commander, detached to observe the enemy on the left flank, remaining on that duty till the close of the day, when withdrawn by General Buford, after most of the brigade had recrossed the river.

The remaining four squadrons were moved to

close-supporting distance and on the left of the Sixth Pennsylvania Cavalry, and advanced through the woods in front under a heavy fire of shell till the open ground was reached, when it promptly charged the enemy who had just successfully resisted the Sixth Pennsylvania Cavalry. Owing to the overpowering numbers opposed to it, and being exposed to a heavy artillery fire at close range on its left, the regiment was compelled to retire through the woods, instantly reforming on its edge to re-advance. The timber on the left was so dense that, but for the coolness of the officers and men, the formation of squadrons would have been an impossibility. It was in this advance that 2d Lieutenant Madden was seriously wounded by a shell. The regiment, besides losing severely in horses and men disabled, met with a serious loss in having the regimental adjutant, Lieutenant Kerin, taken prisoner at the side of the commanding officer, while gallantly assisting him to reform the command after the charge.

The regiment was then again used as support for Elder's Horse Artillery, remaining several hours, a portion of the time under a heavy fire, until ordered to the extreme right with the Second U. S. Cavalry. At that time—in the afternoon—the fifth squadron reported, under Captain Brisbin, who, with his command, had been detached since the day before. During the morning he had, with six companies dismounted, including four of volunteer cavalry, engaged in obstinately disputing with the enemy the possession of a fence and stone wall on the right and near the river.

After again supporting the artillery in its new position on the right, and sending a squadron to dislodge the enemy from a point of woods on the extreme right flank, the regiment moved into the timber, deploying two squadrons as skirmishers to the front, connecting with the Second Cavalry line, and drove the enemy from its edge to an eminence in a plowed field beyond. The enemy attempted to flank the line of skirmishers, which was supported with the two remaining squadrons, Ward's and Balder's, which twice charged the enemy, and each time drove them with severe loss from their position to a hill beyond, and finally held them in check against heavy odds till withdrawn by the brigade commander. In this last charge fell the gallant Ward, at the head of his squadron, within grasping distance of the enemy's battle-flag, for which he had been struggling.

On being withdrawn from this hotly contested position, the regiment, for a short time, acted as a reserve for the Second U. S. Cavalry and the Sixth Pennsylvania, then engaged with the enemy in the woods, and later relieved those two regiments with four squadrons—Captain Brisbin having been again detached—which were deployed as skirmishers and drove the enemy back into the timber. Lieutenant Stoll, another squadron commander, fell mortally wounded at this time while gallantly animating his command. The enemy continued firing, and shot the bearers who were fruitlessly attempting to remove him.

In compliance with orders from the brigade commander, at the close of the engagement, the squadrons were withdrawn from the woods, retiring slowly as skirmishers, keeping the enemy in check and acting as the rear guard of the brigade which was rejoined at sunset, after crossing the Rappahannock.

The regiment had been engaged all day and had lost four officers out of twelve that went into action, viz.: Lieutenant Ward, killed; Lieutenant Stoll, missing and supposed to be dead; Lieutenant Madden, severely wounded; and Lieutenant Kerin, taken prisoner. Out of two hundred and fifty-four enlisted men actually engaged, seven were killed outright, twenty-five severely wounded, and thirty-one disabled and missing, making an aggregate loss of sixty-seven officers and men.

The report of the regimental commander, Captain Cram, commends in the highest terms the officers and men who participated in this hotly contested battle, which raged for about thirteen hours in the forests and clearings, bordering on the Rappahannock. Lieutenants Ward and Stoll fell in the front of battle after giving a splendid example of dash and courage to their comrades. At the critical moment of Lieutenant Ward's death, Lieutenant Balder rendered invaluable service by rallying the men and with desperate courage resisting successfully the onslaught of the enemy, Lieutenant Tupper was commended not only for his conduct in the battle, but for "the skillful and deliberate manner in which, at the close of the engagement, he withdrew his skirmishers, his squadron being the extreme rear guard of the brigade, checking the enemy at every step as he retired and suffering more than any other squadron." Lieutenant Wade was warmly praised not only for his impetuous gallantry in the first charge in the morning, when his horse was shot under him, but for his conduct throughout the day.

At the critical moment when the adjutant was captured, Lieutenant Coats replaced him and discharged the hazardous duties with energy and courage under a galling fire. Lieutenants Carpenter and McQuiston rendered good service, and, in fact, the conduct of all on this occasion was most creditable to the regiment. The men showed not only an unflinching readiness to follow their officers in every charge, but when, through losses of battle, three companies were left without officers, the sergeants gallantly led them in the fray, which, throughout, was a giant test of strength between the cavalry corps of the two armies.

Until this battle took place, Stuart's cavalry divisions had held those of the Army of the Potomac in great contempt so far as mounted fighting was concerned. The Federal cavalry had boldly crossed the river, captured Stuart's headquarters, developed Lee's intended march to the north, and had fearlessly engaged the enemy, fighting mounted or dismounted as the immediate occasion demanded. The corps was withdrawn only upon the approach of Lee's heavy columns of infantry and after the object of the crossing had been effected.

For many months Lieutenant Ward was supposed to be a prisoner in the hands of the enemy. He was seen by a sergeant to fall, shot through the breast, but still alive. The day after the battle the enemy gave notice that an officer of the Sixth Cavalry had been killed in the charge. He was carried on the rolls as a prisoner, notwithstanding the officers of the regiment, held in Libby Prison, had sent word that he had never been with them. During January, 1864, when the cavalry was again encamped at the scene of the battle on June 9th, 1863, a citizen living near by, recognized the insignia of the regiment and reported that an officer had been buried in the vicinity. General Pleasanton's headquarters were then camped on the hill over which the regiment had charged. There was no difficulty in finding the spot where Lieutenant Ward was seen to fall, and, with the assistance of the farmer, the grave was readily located and the body disinterred.

In this connection it may be remarked that the adjutant, Lieutenant Kerin, was confined in Libby Prison and was one of those who got out by means of the celebrated tunnel, through which so many officers escaped from captivity. It is said that just after Lieutenant Kerin had gotten down the shaft and before he could move into the tunnel, the next one to follow, fell, landing on Kerin with such force as to cause him to groan in despair, and for a moment all seemed lost. He recovered himself, however, and made his exit without alarming the guard.

CHAPTER V.

THE GETTYSBURG CAMPAIGN.

INVASION OF PENNSYLVANIA—BENTON'S MILLS—MIDDLEBURG—UPPERVILLE—FAIRFIELD—WILLIAMSPORT—FUNKSTOWN—BOONSBORO—HEAVY LOSSES OF CAMPAIGN—BRANDY STATION—CATLETT'S STATION—WINTER QUARTERS—CONDITION OF HORSES—SENTENCE OF DEATH—DRY TORTUGAS.

MAJOR STARR, who had been promoted from the Second Cavalry, vice Wright, resigned, reported on June 10th and assumed command, no field officer having been present for duty since Major Williams left the regiment a year prior to this time. The regiment moved to Catlett's station, and next day to Thoroughfare Gap, where Lieutenant Wade's squadron, composed of D and K companies, was detached as provost guard at headquarters of the cavalry corps. The remainder of the regiment went on picket until the 15th when it marched to Manassas Junction, and on the following day to Bull Run bridge.

When Hooker effected the passage of his army across the Rappahannock the previous month, Lee had good cause to worry for the safety of his army and capital. With Jackson's wonderful flank attack, where success was achieved, but at a cost to the Confederacy of his valuable life, Lee was not only relieved of anxiety, but at once made his plans to carry the war to the north.

General Hooker proposed to the President that Lee be met by such other troops as could be marshalled to confront him, while he moved on Richmond with the Army of the Potomac. President Lincoln, who developed into one of the greatest strategists of the Civil War, promptly announced: "I think Lee's army, and not Richmond, is your sure objective point. If he comes toward the upper Potomac, follow on his flank and on his inside track, shortening your lines while he lengthens his. Fight him, too, when opportunity offers. If he stays where he is, fret him and fret him."

The race for the north began, the Army of the Potomac moving between Lee's army and Washington. The cavalry corps was kept constantly in contact with the enemy, and the Sixth participated in many fights during the campaign, the first of which occurring at Benton's Mills, June 17th, while on the march from Aldie, on the road leading to Middleburg. The regiment encamped near the scene of the fight until the 21st, when it joined General Gregg's command and had a running fight in which nearly all the cavalry of both armies engaged throughout the day between Middleburg and Upperville. Captain Cram's report of this affair is very interesting and given with more detail than is usual in such cases:

"Camp near Aldie, Virginia, June 23d, 1863.

SIR:—I have the honor to transmit the following report of the part taken by the Sixth U. S. Cavalry in the operations of June 21st: The regiment marched before breakfast from its position on picket near Aldie, in the brigade column, and, crossing Goose Creek, was employed at different portions of the day with the rest of the brigade as a supporting reserve until reaching the slopes on the hither side of Upperville, when, forming squadron and advancing for some time at a trot, it was suddenly called on to defeat an effort of the enemy on our left flank, the volunteer cavalry at this time being engaged with the enemy in front of us. Instantly breaking from its formation in column of squadrons, and passing through a narrow gap in a stone wall, and reforming on the other side, as well as the time allowed it, and the circumstances and ground would permit, moved immediately forward, and on the command being given, charged up to the enemy, under an harassing artillery fire and over a long stretch of heavy and marshy ground, intersected by a most difficult ditch and terminating in a hill of plowed ground, beyond which, on the firm ground in the edge of the woods, the enemy in large force awaited it. The charge was unsuccessful, the most of the horses being so blown that it was impossible to bring or keep them for such a distance at a charging pace.

On the regiment rallying and reforming on the nucleus of the second squadron, commanded by Captain Claflin, on more favorable ground, the enemy being within easy reach and everything favorable for a successful charge, for which it was then preparing, the regiment was then ordered to dismount and fight on foot, and was used dismounted, under the cover of stone walls, to protect our left flank, the enemy retiring at the same time into the woods on our front.

On being relieved from this position, and the engagement having terminated, it moved in column of squadrons, with the rest of the brigade, through the woods and toward the entrance of Ashby's Gap, till it succeeded in attracting the fire of the enemy's artillery, when it was withdrawn, and went into bivouac on the hither side of the town of Upperville. The regiment marched out twelve commissioned officers and two hundred and forty-two enlisted men strong.

Its casualties were Second Lieutenant Henry McQuiston, severely wounded; Privates John Might, of troop E, slightly wounded; C. F. H. Roemer, troop A, mortally; Jacob Couts, troop G, slightly; (Michael) Slattery, troop F, slightly; (Michael) Kurnan, troop A, slightly. Privates (Joshua W.) Dubois, troop E; Thomas McKeffrey, troop F, and Nelson H. Turner, troop B, missing.

In closing this report, out of justice to my regiment, I would respectfully call attention of my superiors to the dispiriting circumstances attending the unsuccessful charge, before described. The men were exhausted and worn out by the recent imposition of incessant picket duty in their position near Middleburg. They were taken from behind stone walls, which they had been guarding all night and the day before, mounted on horses as famished as themselves, and immediately marched with the column, and at the end of a fatiguing day were required to charge over ground almost impracticable in its nature and 750 paces in extent, as proved by the measurement of experienced officers on the morning of the 22d.

I am, sir, very respectfully,

Your obedient servant,

G. C. Cram,

Captain, 6th U. S. Cavalry, Commanding Regiment.

Lieutenant James F. McQueston,
Acting Assistant Adjutant-General,
Regular Cavalry Reserve Brigade."

The regiment returned to Aldie on the 22d, and on the 26th marched to Leesburg, and thence across the Potomac at Edwards' Ferry and the Monocacy, close to its mouth, and went into camp, on the 27th, near Point of Rocks, Maryland. On the 29th Middletown was reached, and here General Merritt assumed command of the brigade, relieving Major Starr, who resumed command of the regiment. The march was continued to Frederick and Mechanicstown, where the regiment remained until July 2d, when it was marched to Emmitsburg.

In the meantime Buford, with his cavalry division, had halted the head of Lee's invading column, near Gettysburg, and gallant Reynolds and other eminent commanders had hastened to the sound of the guns, bringing on that historic conflict which had been raging July 1st and 2d, while Merritt's brigade lay off on the flank.

But the red-letter day in the history of the regiment had now arrived; after leaving the bivouac it was detached from the main column and went down to defeat against overwhelming odds, but without dishonor.

General Merritt ordered the regiment to Fairfield, Pennsylvania, on the road leading to Gettysburg from the northwest, to capture a wagon train, the rest of the brigade moving toward Gettysburg by way of Farmington. Fairfield was reached at noon, where two troops were detached to proceed along the base of the mountain, the regiment keeping the road to Gettysburg. About a mile from Fairfield the enemy's pickets were encountered and driven back to their supports, when another squadron was added to the line, and the enemy—the Seventh Virginia—was driven back to the forks of the road from which their main body could be seen, consisting of about four regiments of cavalry. Clue's Virginia battery opened on the regiment as soon as the wreck of the Seventh Virginia cleared the way. The regiment was close enough to hear the command, "Draw sabres!" of the enemy, as they were formed for the charge.

The two advance squadrons were in between post and rail fences, and could not form line or join those in the fields before they were charged by the Sixth Virginia Cavalry, supported by the Confederate brigades under Generals Robertson and Jones. Caught in such a trap the men remained firm, firing and inflicting severe loss on the advancing column, until literally ridden down. Some escaped to the fields and made for the town, but the Confederates reached there first. Lieutenant Balder, who was ordered to surrender, called on the few men near him to follow, and had nearly cut his way out, when he fell mortally wounded. The squadron which was on the road near the mountain was also overpowered and hurled back.

Of this part of the action Lieutenant Nicholas Nolan says:

"When about two miles from the regiment, I saw the enemy's cavalry charge in the direction of Millerstown (Fairfield). I immediately notified the squadron commander of the fact. He then moved the squadron on the enemy's right and charged them, when he (Captain Cram) was captured. I, being the only officer then left with the squadron, took command. I found I was entirely cut off from the regiment, and had the enemy on both flanks and rear of me. After the regiment was repulsed from Millerstown (Fairfield), I immediately commenced retreating, disputing every inch of ground with the enemy. Finding the enemy in force, I gradually fell back in the direction of Mechanicstown, where I found the regiment, and also ascertained that the commanding officer was wounded and in the hands of the enemy. I, being the senior officer, assumed command of the regiment, which I found in command of Lieutenant L. Henry Carpenter. I then received orders to join the brigade. On my arrival at the brigade, I turned over the command of the regiment to Captain Claflin."

The regiment lost Lieutenant Balder, killed; Major Starr and Lieutenants Tucker, Wood and Chaffee, wounded; Captain Cram, Lieutenants Bould and Paulding, and Surgeons Forwood and Notson, captured. The loss of men was 232 killed, wounded and captured, out of a total less than 400. Lieutenant Bould escaped and Captain Cram was paroled.

At the moment when the charging column of the enemy encountered the head of the regiment, the standard-bearer was shot. As the Confederates were about to seize the standard some of the Sixth Cavalrymen charged into the melee. Sergeant George C. Platt rescued the standard and, sticking close to the fence, put spurs to his horse, dashed past the enemy and escaped. The slashed and torn emblem, for which men had fought and died, remained in the hands of the gallant little remnant who had followed it on many hotly contested fields. Sergeant Platt was awarded a medal of honor for his distinguished bravery.

The fight made at Fairfield by this small regiment against two of the crack brigades of Stuart's cavalry, which were endeavoring to get around the flank of our army to attack the trains, was one of the most gallant in its history and was really a part of the battle of Gettysburg. The efforts of these brigades were frustrated and their entire strength neutralized for the day, by the fierce onslaught of the small squadrons. The regiment was cut to pieces, but it fought so well that the squadrons were regarded as the advance of a large body of troops. The senior officer of these brigades was adversely criticised for allowing his command to be delayed by such an inferior force. Had the regiment not made the desperate stand, the two brigades of Virginians might have accomplished incalculable injury in the Federal rear, before sufficient force could have been gathered in their front.

The small portion of the regiment which escaped retreated to Emmitsburg, joined the brigade the next day near Gettysburg, and proceeded to Frederick City, Maryland, July 5th, and to South Mountain and Williamsport, July 6th, participating in the engagement at the latter place with the loss of one sergeant killed.

While making a reconnoissance to Funkstown, July 7th, the remnant of the regiment became heavily engaged with superior numbers, and lost Captain Claflin severely wounded, and 85 men killed, wounded and missing.

Lieutenant Nolan again found himself in command and says of this action:

"On the 7th instant, the regiment was ordered to make a reconnoissance in the direction of Funkstown, under command of Captain Claflin. On arriving in the vicinity of the town, we drove in the enemy's pickets; immediately afterward made disposition of the regiment to resist the enemy, who was in force. The captain commanding proceeded to the front to reconnoitre, and when about 150 yards in front of the regiment (and with the advance guard) was wounded in the shoulder by one of the enemy's sharpshooters. I, being the senior officer with the regiment, again assumed command. I immediately proceeded to the front, where my advance guard was posted, when I saw the enemy's cavalry preparing to charge my command. I then made preparations to meet them, but, being overpowered by superior numbers, was forced to fall back, inflicting, however, great damage to the enemy in a running fight of four and one-half miles, my command losing 59 men killed, wounded and missing; ten of the above were brought in dead by the 1st U. S. Cavalry the same afternoon. In closing my report, I would respectfully call attention of the General commanding to the following named officers of the regiment: 2d Lieutenant T. C. Tupper and Lieutenant L. Henry Carpenter, for their gallantry in rallying the regiment, and for their general bravery throughout the whole affair. I have also to call the attention of the General commanding to the following non-commissioned officers and privates of the regiment: Chief Bugler Jacob K. Schuck, who fought his way through the enemy's lines and rendered great assistance during the engagements of the 3d and 7th instants;

Sergeant John McCaffery, troop A, who, during the fight at Funkstown, shot the enemy's standard-bearer, made a gallant effort to capture the flag, but, being overpowered, was unable to accomplish the act; Sergeant Martin Schwenk, troop B, who cut his way through the enemy's lines at Millerstown, Pennsylvania, when sent by me to communicate with the regiment, but was unable to accomplish his mission; I also saw him extricate an officer from the hands of the enemy; Sergeant Michael C. Gorman, troop I, who extricated an officer from the hands of the enemy, and during the whole of the engagement acted with the most reckless gallantry; and Private Patrick Kelly, of troop H; this man, at Fairfield, made a desperate effort to capture one of the enemy's standards, at which place he was near losing his life and rendered great service throughout both engagements.

The above non-commissioned officers and one private formed the rear guard of the regiment during the fight of the 7th instant, and maintained the honor of the regiment."

The regiment remained in contact with the enemy and was engaged, July 8th and 9th, near Boonsboro, and again engaged near Funkstown, July 10th. General Merritt, in his report, says of this phase of the campaign:

"On the 7th and 8th the brigade again met the enemy near Boonsboro, and fought him with advantage several hours each day. On the 9th he was again engaged and driven several miles, when, on the 10th, we fought him near Funkstown, and with the best success all the way through. During these combats, which were mostly on foot (the enemy's infantry being engaged), there were some dashing, telling charges made, mounted. I mention, particularly, one made by the Sixth U. S. Cavalry, followed up by the First U. S. Cavalry, on the Boonsboro and Hagerstown road. In both of these the enemy was severely punished, and captures were made in hand-to-hand conflicts."

The period between the action at Beverly Ford and the last affair at Funkstown was one of incessant marching and fighting, and although nearly decimated by the casualties of action, the brave little band hung on to Lee's army with a courageous tenacity, which remains to-day as one of the most cherished historical incidents of the regiment's existence.

General W. E. Jones, Confederate, in his report of the Gettysburg campaign, says:

"An order from General Lee required a force of cavalry to be sent at once to the vicinity of Fairfield, to form a line to the right and rear of our line of battle. In the absence of General Robertson, I determined to move my command at once into position, which met with the approbation of the General, who returned to the camp before I was in motion.

About two miles from Fairfield we encountered the Sixth U. S. Regular Cavalry en route to capture our cavalry division train, which must have fallen an easy prey but for our timely arrival. Many wagons in quest of forage were already within a few hundred yards of the enemy.

We met in a lane, both sides of which were of post and rail fences, too strong to be broken without an axe. The country is open, the fields small, and all the fences of the same character as along the lane. No estimate could be made of the opposing force; but knowing that a vigorous assault must put even a small force on a perfect equality with a large one until a wider field could be prepared, I at once ordered the Seventh Regiment, which was in front, to charge. Before the enemy could be reached, he succeeded in throwing carbineers through gates right and left, who poured into our flanks a galling fire. The leading men hesitated; the regiment halted and retreated, losing more men than a glorious victory would have cost had the onset been made with vigor and boldness.

A failure to rally promptly and renew the fight is a blemish in the bright history of this regiment. Many officers and men formed noble exceptions.

In their efforts to renew the fight fell the noble brothers Captain John C. and Lieutenant Jacob G. Shoup, the former desperately wounded and the latter instantly killed. * * * *

Fortunately, the Seventh had a chance in a day or so, and cleared its reputation.

The Sixth Virginia Cavalry (Major C. E. Flournoy commanding) was next ordered to charge, and did its work nobly. Adjutant John Allan and others fell at its head, but, nothing daunted, it passed the skirmishers, assailing and completely routing one of the best United States regiments, just flushed with victory.

The fruits were many killed and wounded—among the latter, Major Starr, commanding—and 184 prisoners taken.

* * * * * * * * * * * * * * *

The evening of the 7th, the Sixth U. S. Regular Cavalry, making a reconnoissance near Funkstown, fell in with the Seventh Virginia Cavalry, which availed itself of the opportunity of settling old scores. Sabres were freely used. The day at Fairfield is nobly and fully avenged. The Sixth U. S. Regular Cavalry numbers among the things that were."

The regiment had now lost all but a few officers and men and was ordered, July 11th, to report for duty at the headquarters of the cavalry corps. The march was resumed over the familiar ground to Berlin, and again into Virginia, where the regiment was destined to remain until the colors of Lee's brave Army of Northern Virginia were lowered forever.

Leaving Berlin on the 17th, the route led back through Lovettsville, Waterford, Union and Warrenton Junction to near Germantown, where the regiment remained in camp for more than two weeks. At the end of August many men had rejoined and eight officers and four hundred and sixty men were again ready to take the saddle against their old foemen—General Stuart's cavalry.

The regiment remained in camp near Germantown until September 12th, when it marched to Rappahannock station; crossed the Rappahannock on the following day, joining in the attack on the Confederate cavalry at Brandy station and driving the enemy beyond Culpeper; on the 14th, followed up the success of the previous day, driving the Confederates across the Rapidan, when it returned to camp at Culpeper, where it remained until the 11th of October.

The advance of the Confederates upon the position occupied by the army at Culpeper, resulted in the withdrawal of the latter across the Rappahannock to Manassas. On the 11th the regiment withdrew toward Brandy station, and took position on the right of the road, and some little distance from it, fronting toward Culpeper. The skirmish line in front was held by the Harris Light Cavalry, which withdrew and passed to the rear, leaving the regiment exposed to attack from flank, and rear, its position being at the extremity of a field surrounded on the sides with dense undergrowth.

The commanding officer, Major Morris, finding himself thus isolated was in the act of withdrawing from the position when a column of Confederate cavalry made its appearance on the other side of the field. It was of the greatest importance to gain the road and go round the point of undergrowth before the Confederates could cross the field and gain that point, as this was the only means of escape. A rapid gait was therefore taken, and as the point of undergrowth was turned a severe skirmish fire was poured into the head of the column from the Harris Light Cavalry, which was posted behind the timber. The company leading the column received the worst effects of the fire, Sergeant Ellsworth being killed, Lieutenant Chaffee, commanding the leading company, Surgeon Forwood and one private wounded. Privates Joseph and Shortel, being mounted on poor horses, were at the rear of the column, and the Confederates charging about the time of the fire from the skirmish line, succeeded in capturing them.

That night the regiment withdrew across the Rappahannock, and on the following day marched to Catlett's station, from which place it moved towards Warrenton and became engaged in a picket skirmish, resulting, however, in no loss,—thence, on the 14th, to Centerville; 23d to Gainesville; 24th to Warrenton; 26th to Catlett's station, and 30th to Warrenton.

On November 3d the regiment took up its old line of march back towards Brandy station, where it arrived on the 8th and remained until the 26th, when it marched across Germania Ford to Robertson's Tavern, on the road between Fredericksburg and Orange Court House.

December 1st the regiment left Robertson's tavern, recrossed Germania Ford and went into camp, about two miles south of Brandy station, where the men were at once put to work building huts and stables for the winter. At the end of December there were thirteen officers and six hundred and fifteen men present.

The regiment remained in this cantonment for five months, performing its share of the duty falling upon the cavalry corps. One squadron was on duty as provost guard at corps headquarters; the others were drilled and kept in as good condition as possible under the circumstances for the spring campaign. Opportunity was offered for officers and men to go home for a few days each, a privilege gladly availed of after such a long period of continuous field service. The equipment was completed, and it should be remarked that the regiment was now armed with Sharp's carbines, caliber 52, Colt's army revolvers, caliber 44, and light cavalry sabres. The animals suffered greatly during the winter from a shortage of hay, and the trouble was increased by extra issues of grain, which over-stimulated the horses in the absence of long forage.

While here sentence of death was pronounced upon a trooper for desertion. The following letters, taken from the records, will show the disposition of the case:

"Headquarters 6th U. S. Cavalry,
January 29th, 1864.

Assistant Adjutant-General,
Headquarters, Army of the Potomac.

GENERAL:—I would respectfully call attention to the case of Private Jacob Knowl, of Company G, 6th U. S. Cavalry, who was sentenced to be shot to death for desertion, in G. O. No. 103, of November 20th, 1863, Headquarters, Army of Potomac. This sentence, which was to have taken effect upon December 4th, was suspended until further orders, and the prisoner is now in irons in the guard-house of this camp. I earnestly request that this sentence may be remitted, or rather commuted to such imprisonment as may be deemed suitable.

Very respectfully,
Your obedient servant,
A. W. EVANS,
Captain, 6th U. S. Cavalry, Commanding."

"Headquarters 6th U. S. Cavalry,
March 15th, 1864.

Provost Marshal, Cavalry Corps.

SIR:—I have the honor to forward prisoner Jacob Knowl, of the 6th U. S. Cavalry, whose sentence is mitigated to imprisonment during the war at the Dry Tortugas, Florida, per General Order No. 76, War Department, A. G. O., Washington, D. C., February 26th, 1864.

Very respectfully,
Your obedient servant,
R. M. MORRIS,
Major, 6th U. S. Cavalry, Commanding Regiment."

The little island of Dry Tortugas, off the coast of Florida, contained Fort Jefferson, a magnificent example of the art of fortification, mounting over four hundred guns and costing, in the aggregate, about $15,000,000. This fort was selected as a prison, and both civil and military prisoners were confined there during the Civil War and for a short time after. The name, Dry Tortugas, is synonymous with all that is dreary and lonesome. The huge fort of brick and masonry, with all its magnificent barracks and quarters, has for many years been tenanted by an ordnance sergeant, whose sole occupation is to exist and represent the sovereignty of the United States. The frequent outbreaks of yellow fever have long since condemned the site as unsuitable, even as a prison for desperate cases.

CHAPTER VI.

With Sheridan to the End.

Sheridan in Command—Raid to Richmond—Todd's Tavern—Yellow Tavern—Meadow Bridge—Regiment detached to Fort Monroe for Supplies—Rejoins Cavalry Corps—Hawes' Shop—Cold Harbor—Trevilian Station—James River—Ream's Station—Deep Bottom—Regiment accompanies General Sheridan to the Shenandoah Valley—Joins Corps Headquarters—Berryville—Winchester—Fisher's Hill—Laying waste Shenandoah Valley—Cedar Creek—Arrival of Sheridan—Raid in Loudoun Valley—Gordonsville Raid—Army Potomac rejoined near Petersburg—Dinwiddie Court House—Five Forks—Sailor's Creek—Clover Hill—Surrender—Services of Cavalry Corps—Ordered to join Sherman—Back to Bladensburg—Grand Review—Losses—Actions in which Regiment participated.

GENERAL SHERIDAN assumed command of the Cavalry Corps of the Army of the Potomac, April 6th, 1864, and immediately set about having the cavalry relieved from much of the arduous and harassing picket duty, which had been continually forced upon that arm by General Meade and previous commanders. This afforded an opportunity to give a brief rest to the horses and fit out the various commands for the active operations about to commence, and which had for their object the breaking of Lee's communications and the defeat of Stuart's cavalry.

There had been a lamentable loss of power in the Army of the Potomac from the very beginning of the war, because the great value of concerted cavalry action was not understood or appreciated. Notwithstanding the glorious account which that arm gave of itself on every field, it was immediately returned to picket duty, much of which should have been performed by infantry and the horses saved from the consequent semi-starvation; picketing the banks of streams for miles simply made it impossible to supply proper forage to the animals.

The regiment left winter quarters for the Wilderness, May 4th, 1864, and reconnoitered Germania Ford, Mine Run and United States Ford, returning to Chancellorsville in time to go with General Sheridan to Todd's Tavern, where, on May 7th, the cavalry corps was heavily engaged with both cavalry and infantry. After a hotly contested fight, Fitzhugh Lee's and Hampton's divisions were driven toward Spottsylvania Court House.

On May 8th, General Sheridan at last received the coveted orders from General Meade to go out and engage the Confederate cavalry, instead of guarding trains and picketing around the infantry camps. The command had only one-half day's forage on hand, so General Sheridan determined to pass around Lee's flank and get to the North Anna, and if possible, the South Anna, where forage could be obtained, before engaging Stuart's cavalry seriously.

The day was spent in preparations for the raid towards Richmond, which commenced May 9th, 1864. The regiment marched on the Fredericksburg and Richmond pike, crossing the North Anna after dark. The clouds of dust having attracted the attention of the enemy, they arrived during the night and opened on the corps headquarters at daylight with a battery, the regiment being near-by and receiving a few shells without casualties. The march was resumed, the Confederates continuing in pursuit and frequently attacking the rear guard. Reaching Beaver Dam station, a train containing prisoners captured at the Wilderness was seized about nine o'clock on the morning of the 10th, and destroyed, with a large amount of muskets and small arms.

Stuart realized the danger and hastened his troops at a killing pace, so as to pass around and put his command between Sheridan and Richmond. The march was resumed, and at 11 o'clock a. m., May 11th, the enemy was encountered at Yellow Tavern, six miles from Richmond, and a severe engagement took place, resulting in the defeat of the Confederates and the death of their gallant and famous leader, J. E. B. Stuart. This was a disastrous battle to the Confederate cavalry, which was never again the same important factor which it had been in the past. In fact, Stuart's corps ceased to exist, and the cavalry divisions were assigned to duty under General Lee's personal direction.

The march was continued during the night of the 11th, after the battle at Yellow Tavern, and was very tedious because of the darkness and rain. At daylight the head of the column reached the bluffs overlooking the Mechanicsville pike, and Sheridan massed his command here, between the first and second lines of works around Richmond. Shells had been buried in the road and one of them exploded as the regiment passed, killing a horse.

The enemy's works and batteries were encountered and it became evident that the column could not pass between the works and the Chickahominy. General Custer's brigade was detailed to repair Meadow Bridge and force a crossing, which was attempted under a persistent and heavy fire from the enemy posted on the opposite side. It was necessary to repair this bridge while it was swept by the fire of a battery. General Merritt's division was sent in to do what had become too much for a brigade to accomplish. The bridge was finally floored with rails and planks and a column pushed across. The defeat of the Confederates entrenched opposite this bridge, and the repulse of the two brigades which came out from Richmond, ended their hopes of doing anything to seriously impede Sheridan's cavalry corps, which crossed and continued its march.

The regiment remained with the column until it arrived at Bottoms bridge, when, on the 14th, it was detached and ordered to Fort Monroe to hurry forward supplies. The regiment marched to Williamsburg the first day,—a distance of fifty miles,—and with little or no rest continued the march to Fort Monroe, arriving the next day and delivering General Sheridan's dispatches.

The regiment remained here until noon of May 21st, when the return march was begun and the cavalry corps was met on the 22d at the White House. The cavalry, having received the much needed supplies, rejoined the army on the 24th near Chesterfield station, on the Richmond and Fredericksburg Railroad.

The regiment participated in the general advance of the Army of the Potomac on the Pamunkey, crossing the stream on the pontoon bridge at Old Hanovertown, and proceeded to the vicinity of Hawes' Shop, where a severe cavalry fight took place on May 28th. Old Church was next occupied and the cavalry pushed out toward Cold Harbor, and on the 31st that important point was captured after a hard fight against both cavalry and infantry.

During the general engagement at Cold Harbor, June 1st, between the two armies, the regiment was on the left and did not participate actively in the fighting, and moved next day down the Chickahominy to near Bottoms Bridge, the Confederates being on the opposite side. The regiment returned to White House landing June 4th, and on the 5th started to New Castle Ferry, where the trains were to meet the corps.

On June 7th, the regiment, provided with three days' rations to last for five days, and two days' grain on the saddles, started with General Sheridan on the Trevilian raid to cut the Virginia Central Railroad near Charlottesville. The advance continually skirmished with the enemy until Trevilian station was reached on the 11th, when a severe battle took place with Hampton's and Fitzhugh Lee's cavalry divisions, resulting in their defeat. One of the objects of the raid was to effect a junction with General Hunter. This was not accomplished, and Sheridan's command returned, hampered to some extent by about five hundred wounded and a like number of prisoners. The regiment lost a few men wounded and a few prisoners.

The return march to the White House was begun on the 12th, and it was not until the North Anna had been crossed on the morning of the 13th that the horses were unsaddled and allowed to graze. They were nearly famished, having been without food for two days.

On the 15th, the corps crossed the Mattapony on the pontoon bridge, the Sixth remaining there to await the arrival of detachments left behind. After all had crossed, the bridge was taken up on the 18th, and the regiment rejoined the corps the next day. On June 21st the regiment crossed on the railroad bridge and marched to New Baltimore and thence to the James river, arriving at Wilcox's Landing on the 26th; crossed the river in boats on the 28th, and engaged the enemy at Dabney's Mills next day. The regiment returned on the 30th of June to near City Point, Virginia. The cavalry had now been marching and fighting for fifty-six consecutive days, and was placed in camp near Light House Point to rest and refit.

The regiment went with General Sheridan in his rapid march from Reams station to relieve General Wilson's division, which had been attacked by both cavalry and infantry and forced to withdraw by a circuitous route. The regiment returned to near Light House Point and encamped, remaining until General Sheridan was ordered to report with his command for temporary duty to General Hancock. July 26th the regiment crossed to the north side of the James, at Turkey Bend, on a pontoon bridge, and went with the corps to Deep Bottom, and par-

PONTOON BRIDGE AT DEEP BOTTOM.

(FROM WAR TIME PHOTOGRAPH.)

ticipated in the fight there. The river was recrossed on July 30th, and the regiment went into camp at Prince George Court House.

The movement to the north side of the James had been made to cause the enemy to weaken his strength about Petersburg, at which point the famous mine was about to be exploded. The movement back and forth over the bridge was attended with grave danger of successful attack by the enemy at the bridge head, and the sleepless anxiety told heavily on the entire command.

General Sheridan was relieved from duty with the Army of the Potomac August 1st, 1864, and assigned to the command of the Middle Military Division and the Department of the Shenandoah Valley. Company L was detached and accompanied the general as his escort.

On August 12th the remaining companies of the regiment embarked on transports at Light House Point, and were disembarked on the following day at Geisboro Point, the great depot for cavalry horses, opposite Washington, and encamped near the Navy Yard bridge. On the 15th the regiment left the latter place and marched via Rockville, Frederick and Knoxville, Maryland, to Harper's Ferry, where it encamped on Bolivar Heights on August 19th. On the following day the regiment proceeded to Berryville and joined the corps headquarters near that place, two divisions of the cavalry corps having preceded this movement to the Shenandoah Valley. The regiment remained near Berryville until the 19th of September.

About 3 a. m. on the morning of September 19th, the regiment started from the Opequon, and proceeding across the fields to the left and front of Winchester, got into position about 10 a. m. Then followed the battle of Winchester, which, with varying successes to either side, had nearly consumed the day without either gaining materially over the other, when orders were given to charge the Confederate left with the cavalry. Two divisions, 1st and 3d of the corps, were thrown with all the force possible upon the enemy's left flank, and forced it back on Winchester; the infantry at the same time attacking the front, they withdrew through Winchester in haste. Night came on and put a stop to the pursuit. During this battle the officers of the regiment which was escorting General Sheridan acted as his aides.

On the 20th the march was resumed along the main road leading south through the valley, and over which the Confederates had retreated. Near noon on the 22d the Confederates were in position at Fisher's Hill, an eminence which commands the valley from side to side, and quite a defensive place naturally. No attempt was made to carry the position by front attack; but skirmish firing and the forming of lines were kept up to attract attention, while General Crook, with the Eighth Corps, retired to the rear about three miles and crossed to the right side of the valley, which lies between two chains of mountains covered with brush. Here his men ascended the side of the mountain, and crawling through the brush, reached the left flank of the Confederates about sunset. Descending from the mountain, the Confederate line was flanked and being charged from in front at the same time, broke and fled.

The regiment was about the only cavalry present at this time, and the want of more was seriously felt. Devin's Brigade joined in the pursuit that followed through the entire night, beyond Woodstock, and captured many prisoners. The 23d was spent in picking up prisoners who had become separated from their organizations the night before. The valley at this point is a little more than one mile wide, and perfectly open. The enemy was driven on up the valley, the regiment reaching Harrisonburg on the 24th, where it remained for some days.

When on the return march down the valley, everything in the shape of forage, wheat, corn, etc., was destroyed, and live stock driven along with the column. This was for the purpose of placing the valley in such a condition that the Confederate army could no longer depend upon it for supplies. The decisive cavalry battle known as "Tom's Brook" was fought October 9th, the rest of Sheridan's army halting while Torbert defeated Rosser.

The regiment went into camp near Cedar Creek on October 12th and remained until attacked on the morning of October 19th, 1864. About 4 a. m., the army was surprised in camp and there was considerable confusion owing to the darkness. The regiment saddled in haste and got into line. At break of day it was discovered that the left had been taken by surprise and involved the whole line, which doubled back from left to right. Shortly after daylight the Confederates were in possession of the camps and all they contained. The troops retired to the Sixth Corps, which was less demoralized than the others, stubbornly contesting the ground. A new line was selected about two miles to the rear of the first position on Cedar Creek. The advance of the Confederates here ceased, and a line was being established to resist further advance, when General Sheridan arrived on the field about three o'clock, from Winchester. The command in his absence had devolved upon General Wright, of the Sixth Corps.

Soon after General Sheridan's arrival the advance was ordered; the tide of battle turned and the

Confederates were routed with the loss of their captures of the morning, much of their own artillery, trains and fifteen hundred prisoners. Captain Lowell, of the Sixth, who led the reserve brigade to the charge in this battle, was killed. The regiment camped that night on its old camp ground and remained there until the middle of November, when it withdrew to Kernstown, three miles south of Winchester.

Early in December the regiment marched to Stephenson's station and formed a part of General Merritt's command on his raid into Loudoun Valley, returning on the 10th. December 19th the regiment went with General Torbert's command on the raid to Gordonsville, and returned December 31st, when it went into camp for the winter at Kernstown. The weather was intensely cold during these operations and both men and horses suffered severely.

February 27th, 1865, the camp was broken up and the regiment marched from Winchester with the cavalry corps, under General Sheridan, up the valley on the way to rejoin the Army of the Potomac, near Petersburg. It was supposed that the Shenandoah Valley and Virginia generally had been devastated before, but the brigade commander's report shows that it was still possible to find a few things upon which the Army of Northern Virginia might rely in its dying struggle with the mighty host closing around it:

"Headquarters Cavalry Reserve Brigade,
Camp near White House, Virginia,
March 21st, 1865.

MAJOR:—In compliance with instructions from headquarters, First Cavalry Division, of this date, I have the honor to make the following report of the operations of this brigade since leaving Winchester, Virginia, on the 27th ultimo:

The brigade, consisting of the Sixth U. S. Cavalry, Lieutenant McLellan commanding; Sixth Pennsylvania Cavalry, Major Morrow commanding; First Rhode Island Cavalry, Captain Capron commanding; Second Massachusetts Cavalry, Colonel Crowninshield commanding, left camp at Winchester on the morning of the 27th of February last; marched thirty miles to camp, one mile beyond Woodstock. The Sixth U. S. Cavalry and Sixth Pennsylvania Cavalry were sent under command of Major Morrow to Edenburg; drove the enemy's pickets from the town and secured the bridges at that place. On the 28th, marched to Laurel (Lacey's) Spring, thirty miles; arrived at 3.30 a. m., on the 1st instant. On March 1st marched through Harrisonburg to within five miles of Staunton, twenty-nine miles. Marched on the Waynesborough road eleven miles, and camped on Christian's Creek on the 2d of March. On March 3d, marched to Waynesborough; destroyed iron bridge over North Fork, South River; destroyed one light steel 3-inch ordnance limber and caisson; also 100 wagons, forges, battery and ammunition wagons; threw ammunition into river; also a large quantity of muskets, small ammunition and other ordnance stores, previously captured same day by the Third Cavalry Division under Brevet Major-General Custer. Moved through Rockfish Gap and camped two miles beyond Brooksville, fifteen miles; weather cold and rainy; roads execrable. On the 4th, marched eight miles and camped at Ivy Depot, on the Virginia Central Railroad; burned the depot, water-tank and warehouse containing Confederate tobacco and commissary stores; roads and weather worse. March 5th, marched seven miles; camped near University of Virginia, at Charlottesville. Joined the command, drew rations, burned the tents and lightened the loads. On the 6th, marched without transportation to Scottsville, twenty-one miles; worked till midnight destroying James River Canal, locks, boats, with subsistence stores, and bridges; 7th, burned woolen factory with a large quantity of cloth, candle factory with a large amount of candles, lard-oil, etc.; large five-story flouring mill, with flour, corn and wheat; a large manufactory, machine-shops and tobacco warehouses.

I regret that a few private dwellings, close to the mill, were more or less charred by the intense heat. No accident or loss of life, however, occurred. Same day marched towpath to New Market, thirty-two miles, destroying canal locks, bridges, stables, storehouses, tobacco, etc. Halted and burned large mill at Warren. Stopped at Howardsville; destroyed large wagon and plow factory, wagon-shop, forge; also railroad bridge, and tobacco and subsistence warehouses. On the 8th, marched up towpath to Bent Creek bridge, on the James, opposite Duguidsville, and returned to New Market, twenty-five miles. Returned by bridge road. Weather rainy, and return road dangerous and deep in mud. On the 9th, moved back to Howardsville; thence on towpath to Scottsville, which place was reached at noon on the 10th; thence moved same day to Fluvanna Institute and Columbia; camped about midnight; distance marched, fifty-six miles in thirty-six hours. March 11th, moved across the viaduct and camped two miles beyond Columbia. March 12th, marched twenty-four miles to near Tolersville; thence to Frederick's Hall Station, fifteen miles, destroying sections of Virginia Central Railroad, twisting rails, burning cross-ties, &c.; camped two miles beyond the station near Army Headquarters. March 14th, marched to Taylorsville, on Richmond and Potomac Railroad, twenty-seven miles. Burned railroad bridges (three) on Richmond and Potomac Railroad and Virginia Central

Railroad, over the Little and South Anna River, respectively, 1000, 600 and 700 feet long. Captured three pieces of artillery (3-inch ordnance guns) by a few men of the Fifth U. S. and Second Massachusetts Cavalry; turned the guns and fired upon the enemy. Marched on the 15th across the South Anna; remained in position all day; deployed Sixth U. S. Cavalry as skirmishers. Sent squadron of Second Massachusetts Cavalry to Hanover Court House; marched back to Oxford, across the North Anna and bivouaced, ten miles. On the 16th, rejoined wagons; marched through Chesterfield Station on Mangohick Church, eighteen miles. March 17th, marched via Aylett's to King William Court House; camped at 2 p. m. On the eighteenth moved slowly to White House, where arrived at 2 p. m. Found forage and stores awaiting us. Marched on 19th across the river, and camped on Hill's plantation. Weather last three days warm and pleasant; road sandy and much better.

* * * * * * * * * * * * * * *

Total casualties in this brigade, 3 killed and 2 wounded.

I am, Major, very respectfully,

Your obedient servant,

ALFRED GIBBS,

Brigadier-General of Volunteers,

Commanding, Cavalry Reserve Brigade.

Major A. E. DANA,

Assistant Adjutant-General,

First Cavalry Division."

The cavalry joined the Army of the Potomac, near Petersburg, March 27th, 1865, and, on March 29th, proceeded to Dinwiddie Court House. Here the cavalry corps engaged the enemy on the 30th, and drove them into their works at Five Forks, holding the position for three hours against repeated attacks and until the ammunition was exhausted.

The enemy got in on the right flank of the regiment under cover of dense woods, and when the line was withdrawn for ammunition the Confederates charged the flank, capturing Lieutenant Nolan and eighteen men. On March 31st, their infantry having come up, the enemy attacked and drove the cavalry corps back to Dinwiddie. Next morning the regiment occupied the extreme right in the memorable battle of Five Forks and connected with the Fifth Corps when it came into action during the afternoon, the regiment wheeling to the left and resting the right on the enemy's works. About 3 p. m. an advance was ordered which never ceased until sunset, when the battle was won.

The cavalry corps went in pursuit, April 2d, and came up with the Confederates and engaged them at 3 p. m., but they retreated. The pursuit was continued incessantly and with great loss to the enemy until April 6th, when they were compelled to make a stand to save their trains. The cavalry corps pressed hard on their flank and awaited a favorable opportunity to capture the trains. Their infantry was forced to form, enabling the Sixth Corps to arrive during the delay. The Third Cavalry Division was now ordered to charge, the other two divisions supporting, and this, the battle of Sailor's Creek, resulted in the capture of about 10,000 Confederates.

During this action the regiment was ordered to take possession of some log huts. It is recorded in the regimental archives that the few men now left in the ranks hesitated, believing it was sure death; but Lieutenant McLellan, a veteran of the old army, faced them and said, "Men, let us die like soldiers." Every one of the little band rushed for the huts under a shower of bullets, and gained the cover with a loss of but three men wounded.

The pursuit was pressed until 9 p. m. While trying to force a passage across the creek after dark, a shell burst in the midst of the little remnant bearing so bravely the standard of the Sixth, and wounded three, one of whom died next day. The march was resumed on the 7th, and on the 8th, after a forced march to Appomattox station, a charge was made resulting in important captures. April 9th, 1865, the Confederates made a desperate attack upon the cavalry at Clover Hill, but the arrival of infantry supports about 9 a. m., relieved the cavalry, which immediately proceeded at a gallop to the enemy's left with a view to charging upon that flank. On nearing the Confederate lines a flag of truce was met requesting a cessation of hostilities as it had been decided to surrender. The surrender was announced at 4 p. m.

Sheridan's cavalry led the advance of the army to the Wilderness; again led it to Cold Harbor;

by its raid to Trevilian it caused the enemy to withdraw its cavalry during the march of the Army of the Potomac to the James river and Petersburg; then transferred operations to the Shenandoah Valley, clearing up that region in time to rejoin the army near Petersburg, and to earn in the final campaign fame which will endure for all time.

From the 5th of May, 1864, to the 9th of April, 1865, the day on which the Army of Northern Virginia surrendered, the cavalry corps sent to the War Department two hundred and five battle-flags, captured in open field fighting; this nearly equals the number sent by the combined Union armies during the whole period of the war.

As soon as General Lee's army surrendered the cavalry was started for Petersburg, and after a brief rest resumed the march for North Carolina to join General Sherman's army. When near Danville, the news that Johnston's army had surrendered was received and the cavalry turned back and proceeded to Petersburg. From here the regiment marched to Washington via Richmond and Alexandria, arriving May 21st, 1865, where it was reviewed by General Sheridan and then proceeded to camp near Bladensburg, Maryland.

The regiment, although depleted to a mere shadow of the full organization which so proudly marched down Pennsylvania Avenue three years before, turned out and participated in the historic Grand Review, which took place in Washington, May 23d, 1865. No finer or more seasoned body of men ever passed in review before a sovereign than the array which filed before the President and his assembled grand commanders on that day.

The salient features of the regiment's history during this most eventful period of our nation's existence have now been traced from the date of its first service, in the Peninsula campaign, until formed for the last charge at Appomattox. The history of the regiment is that of the regular brigade, than which none brighter appears upon the records of the Army of the Potomac. The regiment was fortunate at the beginning of its career in having General Emory present as its lieutenant-colonel to organize it. The talent and courage of the squadron leaders, who so materially aided in establishing a reputation for the regiment, caused the early loss of these officers, who were soon selected for higher commands. Brave Sanders, a southerner and West Pointer, who remained loyal, was promoted to brigadier-general and was killed at the siege of Knoxville, Tennessee. Lowell was killed while leading the brigade to the charge, he being then colonel of volunteers serving in the same brigade with his own Sixth. There were many other officers of the regiment holding high

CAVALRY OFFICER, FULL DRESS, 1865.

commands, like Generals Hunter, Emory, Carleton, Kautz, the two Greggs, and others, who rendered good service commensurate with the increased rank held by them.

Subsequent to the close of hostilities, the Adjutant-General's office not having given proper credit to the regiment for its services in battle, General Sheridan sent to the War Department the following communication, which is cherished as a manly and characteristic action on the part of that great leader:

"I take this occasion to strongly urge that justice be done the Sixth Cavalry, and that the battles as given in the within order issued by me * * * be credited to this regiment on the next Army Register, so that its record, or so much of it as is permitted in the Army Register, may be in a measure correct and complete. In the following battles the Sixth Cavalry fought under my personal supervision, viz.: Wilderness, Todd's Tavern, Furnaces, Spottsylvania Court House, Yellow Tavern, Meadow Bridge, Winchester, Fisher's Hill, Cedar Creek, Five Forks, Dinwiddie Court House, Clover Hill, Sailor's Creek and Appomattox Court House."

The records of casualties during the Civil War show eight officers killed; 53 men killed in action, and 53 other deaths; 122 wounded in action, and 17 killed by accident; 438 missing, most of these being captured at Fairfield and in other charges; making a total of 689 enlisted men.

The regiment participated in the following actions during the war:

Date.	Place.	Companies Engaged.
April 5th to May 4th, 1862	Siege of Yorktown, Va.	Regiment.
May 4th and 5th, 1862	Williamsburg, Va.	A,B,D,E,F,G,H,I,K,M.
May 9th, 1862	Slatersville, Va.	A,E,K.
May 20th, 1862	New Bridge, Va.	A,B,D,E,F,G,H,I,K,M.
May 23d and 24th, 1862	Ellison's Mills, Va.	A,B,D,E,F,G,H,I,K,M.
May 25th to 29th, 1862	Hanover Court House, Va.	A,B,D,E,F,G,H,I,K,M.
June 26th, 1862	Black Creek, Va.	A,B,D,E,F,G,H,I,K,M.
June 27th, 1862	Gaines' Mills, Va.	Detachments.
June 30th to July 2d, 1862	Malvern Hill, Va.	A,B,D,E,F,G,H,I,K,M.
August 4th to 6th, 1862	Malvern Hill, Va.	A,B,D,E,F,G,H,I,K,L,M.
September 4th, 1862	Falls Church, Va.	A,B,D,E,F,G,H,I,K,L,M.
September 10th, 1862	Sugar Loaf Mountain, Md.	A,B,D,E,F,G,H,I,K,L,M.
Sept. 16th and 17th, 1862	Antietam, Md.	A,B,D,E,F,G,H,I,K,L,M.
October 7th, 1862	Charlestown, Va.	A,B,D,E,F,G,H,I,K,L,M.
November 1st, 1862	Philomont, Va.	A,B,D,E,F,G,H,I,K,L,M.
November 2d, 1862	Union, Va.	A,B,D,E,F,G,H,I,K,L,M.
November 3d, 1862	Upperville, Va.	A,B,D,E,F,G,H,I,K,L,M.
November 5th, 1862	Barbee's Cross Roads, Va.	A,B,D,E,F,G,H,I,K,L,M.
November 8th, 1862	Little Washington, Va.	A,B,D,E,F,G,H,I,K,L,M.
November 10th, 1862	Corbin's Cross Roads, Va.	A,B,D,E,F,G,H,I,K,L,M.
Dec. 11th to 15th, 1862	Fredericksburg, Va.	Regiment.
February 14th, 1863	Richard's Ford, Va.	B.
Apr. 29th to May 7th, 1863	Stoneman's Raid, Va.	Regiment.
June 9th, 1863	Beverly Ford, Va.	Regiment.
June 17th, 1863	Benton's Mill, Va.	Regiment.
June 21st to 22d, 1863	Upperville, Va.	Regiment.
July 1st to 3d, 1863	Gettysburg, Pa.	Regiment.
July 6th, 1863	Williamsport, Md.	Regiment.
July 7th, 1863	Funkstown, Md.	Regiment.
July 7th to 12th, 1863	Boonsborough, Md.	Regiment.
July 9th to 11th, 1863	Near Funkstown, Md.	Regiment.
Sept. 12th to 15th, 1863	Brandy Station, Va.	Regiment.
October 11th, 1863	Culpeper and Brandy Station, Va.	Regiment.
Nov. 26th to Dec. 2d, 1863	Mine Run Campaign, Va.	Regiment.
May 5th to 7th, 1864	The Wilderness, Va.	Regiment.
May 7th and 8th, 1864	Todd's Tavern, Va.	Regiment.
May 9th to 12th, 1864	Sheridan's expedition from Todd's Tavern to James River, Va.	Regiment.
May 11th, 1864	Yellow Tavern, Va.	Regiment.
May 12th, 1864	Meadow Bridge, Va.	Regiment.
May 12th, 1864	Mechanicsville, Va.	Regiment.
May 22d to June 1st, 1864	On North Anna, Pamunkey and Totopotomoy Rivers, Va.	Regiment.

DATE.	PLACE.	COMPANIES ENGAGED.
May 27th and 28th, 1864	Hawes' Shop, Va.	Regiment.
May 30th, 1864	Old Church, Va.	Regiment.
May 31st and June 1st, 1864	Cold Harbor, Va.	Regiment.
June 11th to 13th, 1864	Trevilian Station, Va.	Regiment.
June to August, 1864	Before Petersburg, Va.	Regiment.
June 29th, 1864	Dabney's Mill, Va.	Regiment.
July 27th to 29th, 1864	Deep Bottom, Va.	Regiment.
August 16th, 1864	Berryville, Va.	Regiment.
September 19th, 1864	Winchester, Va.	A,B,C,D,F,G,H,I,K,L,M.
September 20th, 1864	Fisher's Hill, Va.	A,B,C,D,F,G,H,I,K,L,M.
Sept. 20th to 30th, 1864	Sheridan's expedition in the Shenandoah Valley, Va.	A,B,C,D,F,G,H,I,K,L,M.
October 19th, 1864	Cedar Creek, Va.	A,B,C,D,F,G,H,I,K,L,M.
November 29th, 1864	Loudoun Valley, Va.	A,B,C,D,F,G,H,I,K,L,M.
March 14th, 1865	Taylorsville, Va.	A,B,C,D,F,G,H,I,K,L,M.
March 31st, 1865	Dinwiddie Court House, Va.	A,B,C,D,F,G,H,I,K,L,M.
April 1st, 1865	Five Forks, Va.	A,B,C,D,F,G,H,I,K,L,M.
April 2d, 1865	Southerland Station, Va.	A,B,C,D,F,G,H,I,K,L,M.
April 6th, 1865	Sailor's Creek, Va.	A,B,C,D,F,G,H,I,K,L,M.
April 8th and 9th, 1865	Appomattox Court House, Va.	A,B,C,D,F,G,H,I,K,L,M.

This is a goodly array of actions, many of them historic battles, in which the regiment took part. For each battle fought there are weeks and months of outpost duty, weary marches and fruitless scouts, that try the strength and spirit of every command. It is a marvel that any regiment could keep up its organization at all, under such service conditions, without a depot squadron from which to recruit its depleted ranks. All honor is due to the brave men who constantly rallied to the standard from dismounted camps, hospitals and southern prisons. The cavalry officer must ever lead the way, but in a civil war no regiment can hope to have its guidons always with the advance guard, as were those of

9

the Sixth Cavalry, unless the men in the ranks are filled with esprit-de-corps, born of loyalty, faith and courage.

NOTE.—As originally organized, the regiment was divided into three battalions, two squadrons to each battalion and two companies to each squadron. The Act of July 17th, 1862, changed the designation of company to troop. General Order No. 5, Headquarters of the Army, June 20th, 1873, provided that the word company should be used in official orders and communications. This designation was continued up to May, 1881, when the Secretary of War directed that the legal designation—troop—should be used instead of company.

The terms battalion, squadron and company have been retained in the chapters relating to the period of the Civil War. In the subsequent chapters squadron and troop have been used to conform to present practice. The tactical use of two-company squadrons practically disappeared after the Civil War.

CHAPTER VII.

REGIMENT ORDERED TO TEXAS.

REORGANIZATION AFTER WAR—SCARCITY OF OFFICERS—VALUE OF SUBALTERNS FROM THE OLD ARMY—EMBARKATION FROM NEW YORK—STORM OFF HATTERAS—HORSES THROWN OVERBOARD—NEW ORLEANS—REGIMENT REACHES TEXAS—VARIED DUTIES OF RECONSTRUCTION PERIOD—CHOLERA—INDIANS ATTACK GARRISON BUFFALO SPRINGS—FIGHTS WITH COMANCHES—SCHREYER'S—SERGEANT AHRBERG'S—CHAFFEE'S, NEAR PAINT CREEK—MCLELLAN'S, NEAR NORTH FORK LITTLE WICHITA—RAFFERTY'S FIGHT WITH KEECHIES—TUPPER'S, NEAR BIG WICHITA—SERGEANT STRUPP'S—CHAFFEE'S, NEAR BELKNAP ROAD—MELLEN'S RIDE.

WHILE the volunteer regiments were being sent to their homes as rapidly as the available transportation could move them, the regulars were ordered into camps to prepare for service on the western frontier. After a few days' encampment at Cloud's Mill, near Alexandria, Virginia, the Sixth was sent to Frederick, Maryland, where it arrived on June 14th, and a general reorganization of the regiment began.

It should be remembered that the losses of the regular regiments could not be made up by recruitment during the war. This arose principally from the fact that enormous bounties were paid for volunteers in various States. At one time volunteers were transferred quite freely to fill up the regiment, but this source of supply soon failed. The result was that the strength of the troops steadily declined, and at one period, after a succession of heavy losses, the men were consolidated into two provisional companies, the records of each organization, however, being kept separate. The incomparable Reserve Brigade of the cavalry corps, to which the Sixth belonged, mustered less than five hundred sabres during the closing scenes of the grand drama enacted near Appomattox.

Some of the difficulties of reorganizing the regiment may be understood by an examination of the list of officers, showing what duties they were engaged upon. It will be observed that there was not a second lieutenant in the regiment at this time.

STATIONS AND DUTIES OF OFFICERS OF THE SIXTH CAVALRY, JUNE 30TH, 1865.

Colonel.
David Hunter ....Major-General Volunteers.
Lieutenant-Colonel.
S. D. Sturgis ....Brigadier-General Volunteers.
Majors.
J. H. Carleton ....Brigadier-General Volunteers.
R. M. Morris ....Commanding regiment.
S. H. Starr ....On leave.
Captains.
A. V. Kautz ....Brigadier-General Volunteers.
A. W. Evans ....Colonel, 1st Maryland Cav.
W. S. Abert ....Colonel, 3d Mass. Artillery.
J. H. Taylor ....Lieutenant-Colonel, A. A. G. Vols.
J. I. Gregg ....Brigadier-General Volunteers.

G. C. Cram................On leave.
J. S. Brisbin..............Colonel, 5th U. S. Colored Cav.
I. W. Claflin..............Inspector Cav'y Dept., W. Va.
B. T. Hutchins............Lieutenant-Colonel, 1st N. H. Cav.
H. T. McLean.............With regiment.
T. Paulding...............Recruiting service, N. Y. City.
J. B. Johnson.............Recruiting service, Cincinnati, Ohio.

1st Lieutenants.
J. F. Wade................Colonel, 6th U. S. Colored Cav.
J. C. Audenried...........Captain, A. D. C. Vols.
Henry Tucker.............En route to regiment.
J. W. Spangler............A.A.Q.M. at Hdqrs., Middle Mil. Div.
C. B. McLellan............With regiment.
Albert Coats..............Lieut.-Colonel, 6th U. S. Colored Cav.
Joseph Kerin..............Mustering duty.
S. M. Whitside............Commissary of musters.
Daniel Madden............With regiment.
Nicholas Nolan............With regiment.
J. A. Irwin................With regiment.
T. C. Tupper..............Recruiting service, Carlisle Bks., Penna.
L. H. Carpenter..........Lieut.-Colonel, 5th U. S. Colored Cav.
J. H. Wood...............Lieut.-Colonel, 2d N. Y. Mtd. Rifles.
A. R. Chaffee.............With regiment.

2d Lieutenants. None.

The regiment received hundreds of recruits during the summer, the majority of them having seen some service in the volunteers. Many officers joined also, including a number of newly commissioned second lieutenants. It was very serious work for the few officers present to reorganize and drill the new companies at a time when every one was tired of war and the volunteers were being welcomed home in every village and town of the north.

Now, again, was shown the wisdom of the course adopted in the original organization of the regiment, in which it was provided that a certain percentage of the officers should be appointed from the ranks of the army. This brought in as subalterns a body of well instructed drill-masters from the old cavalry regiments, who having adopted the army as a career, remained habitually for duty with the regulars. Their courage and capacity as squadron leaders were tested, not only on many hard fought battlefields, but in the rehabilitation necessary after every raid or campaign under such leaders as Pleasanton, Stoneman, Buford, Merritt and Sheridan.

The regiment broke camp at Frederick, Maryland, October 15th, 1865, and proceeded by rail to Battery Barracks, New York, where it embarked, October 19th, on board the steamship "Herman Livingston" for New Orleans. The steamer sailed early next morning, and when off the coast near Hatteras, during the 23d and 24th, encountered a violent storm. One of the sad incidents of this trying voyage was the loss of horses, thrown overboard to lighten the ship. The ship weathered the severe gale which sent many vessels to the bottom, and reached Key West on the night of the 27th, and New Orleans on November 2d.

The regiment remained in camp near New Orleans until the 10th, when it sailed on the steamer "Clinton" for Galveston, arriving there on November 12th. Austin, Texas, was reached on November 29th, and Camp Sanders established half a mile west of the town. The headquarters remained here for nearly three years, when on August 24th, 1868, it was moved to Fort Richardson.

The regiment performed not only the usual frontier service, but, in addition, much of a character not strictly military. The troops were seldom employed together; in fact they were not infrequently scattered all over the State. During the period 1865 to 1871, the duties in Texas were of the most varied and dangerous kind. After the close of the Civil War the country was over-run with desperadoes and outlaws who were even worse than the hostile Comanches, and the officers and men were continually called upon to guard the courts of justice, assist revenue officers, aid in executing convicted criminals, supervise elections, pursue outlaws and murderers, and in general to institute lawful proceedings where anarchy reigned. Many soldiers were assassinated for their devotion to law and order, and nothing but incessant vigilance and unflinching courage prevented the guerrilla community from controlling the border counties of that State.

Owing to the scattered condition of the troops the records of this period are very meagre and unsatisfactory, and important actions in the light of to-day are entirely omitted or remain only as traditions in the regiment. This difficulty is one met with in all regimental records where those making the history are usually so overworked that they seldom have time or deem it important to record current events.

On June 12th, 1866, G troop was sent from Austin to New Orleans, for reconstruction duty, and remained there for more than two years during a most critical period of the city's history, performing duty at General Sheridan's headquarters, as the regiment had done during his more active career in the Army of the Potomac.

A detachment of the regiment marched from Fort Belknap during the month of July, to Maxwell's celebrated ranch on the Clear Fork of the Brazos river, and established Fort Griffin which was subsequently occupied by a portion of the regiment.

During September, 1866, F troop was sent to Spring Creek to escort recruits for the regiment to Austin. Upon arriving at Onion Creek, September 15th, on the return journey, cholera broke out and the command went into camp. Lieutenant Adam Kramer was sent from Austin, took charge and endeavored to stamp out the much dreaded disease. Ten of the men died before the command could move on to Austin.

Under instructions dated June 5th, from Headquarters, District of Texas, Captain Ira W. Claflin left Austin with H troop on a tour of inspection of the posts at Jacksboro, Fort Belknap, Phantom Hill, Chadbourne, and other places, marching nearly fourteen hundred miles.

A vast amount of scouting was done in Texas by the regiment, sometimes merely as patrol duty, but not infrequently resulting in overhauling war parties of the roving, restless Indians who inhabited Texas and Mexico, and who had developed ordinary horse and cattle stealing into a fine art.

On July 21st, 1867, while Captain Hutchins with a greater part of the garrison from Buffalo Springs was trailing a party of Indians, who had committed depredations in Jack County, the post, which had been left with a small detachment and quartermaster employees, under Lieutenant Majtheny, was attacked by Indians who were repulsed with a loss of one horse killed and one Indian wounded. When Captain Hutchins abandoned the pursuit because the Indians scattered and the trail was lost, he returned to find that they had evidently re-assembled at a preconcerted rendezvous and endeavored to capture the post before the garrison could get back. There were a number of families at the post during the attack and the small number of enlisted men present made Lieutenant Majtheny's task a difficult one. Fortunately, however, the efforts of the Indians were frustrated, but they hovered about the vicinity until the approach of the returning troops was discovered, when they disappeared.

Lieutenant Gustavus Schreyer, with Troop F, encountered a band of Indians near Fort Belknap, Texas, August 30th, 1867, and lost two men killed.

The following commendatory order speaks well for the enlisted men of the regiment:

"Headquarters, District of Texas,
Austin, Texas, November 21st, 1867.

General Orders
No. 40.

The Brevet Major-General Commanding takes pleasure in commending the energy and courage displayed by Sergeant W. A. F. Ahrberg, Troop 'L,' 6th U. S. Cavalry, and the detachment under his command, in their recent encounter with a party of Comanche Indians; whereby three Indians were killed, one captured, nineteen animals and some arms recovered, and the Indians completely routed.

By command of Brevet Major-General J. J. Reynolds.

C. E. Morse,
1st Lieutenant, 26th Infantry, A. A. A. G."

The captured horses were restored to the citizens from whom they had been stolen.

March 5th, 1868, Captain A. R. Chaffee with Troop I left Fort Griffin, Texas at 8.30 a. m., on a scout after Indians. He marched on the day mentioned to Leobetter's Ranch and from thence in the night to Dead Man's Creek. Crossed Clear Fork of the Brazos, about twelve miles below Phantom Hill, on the 6th, and soon after found an Indian trail which he followed throughout the day. On the 7th, about 10 o'clock, he came upon a party of Indians camped near Paint Creek. The Indians were charged and seven of them killed. The commanding officer issued the following complimentary order, on the return of the troop to the post:

"Headquarters, Fort Griffin, Texas,
March 10th, 1868.

General Orders
No. 19.

The Commanding Officer takes pleasure in openly announcing to the troops of this command the complete success of the expedition which left this post on the 6th instant, under command of Captain A. R. Chaffee, 6th U. S. Cavalry. This short and decisive campaign has resulted in the killing of five Indians and one Mexican and one Mulatto (both of whom were leaders), the capture of five horses, together with a large number of shields, bows, arrows, etc., and the total breaking up of an Indian camp, which has been for a long time a scourge to the people of the frontier. The casualties on our side were three men wounded, viz.: Privates John F. Butler and Charles Hoffman, of I troop, and Private James Regan of F troop. With the exception of the wounds of these men, the result is extremely gratifying; yet, of course, not more so than the soldierly manner in which the troops bore their deprivations throughout the pursuit, suffering from the want of water and want of shelter from the cold storm that raged throughout the entire march, without a murmur of discontent. In all campaigns where important results are achieved, and especially in operations against Indians, where the nature of the country is not well known, troops must expect to undergo hardships and deprivations, which cannot be foreseen or obviated; yet it is only the true soldiers who accept these inconveniences as necessary and unavoidable, and who, like men, maintain their spirits in spite of these.

(Signed) S. D. STURGIS,
Lieutenant-Colonel, 6th Cavalry, Commanding."

About this time the desperadoes previously mentioned, organized into bands of outlaws in many parts of Texas, one of the most notorious being Lee's band. On March 7th, 1868, Corporal Henhold, Troop D, left Sherman, Texas, with 13 enlisted men and some citizen guides, to break up this band. The pursuit carried the detachment to Read Creek swamp, where the band was effectually broken up by killing two and capturing five of their number. One troop marched more than a thousand miles in pursuit of outlaws during the last three months of 1868.

The year 1869, was not uneventful, although there were no fights with the Indians, who, while engaging in petty depredations and preparing for more deviltry on a large scale, managed to avoid actual collision. Matters drifted along, but by constant activity and scouting the troops succeeded in preserving peace along the frontier assigned to them.

The Indians grew more bold in 1870, and began to operate over a wide extent of country. Lieutenant I. M. Walters, who was out with a detachment, encountered a band of marauding Indians on May 30th and fought them with a loss of one soldier and two citizens killed. During July they made attacks along the mail stage route, and troops were hurried from all the camps to reopen the line and drive the Indians back to the reservations. Captain McLellan was the first to come in contact with them, and his report gives so thorough an idea of the scouting for Indians on the frontier, that it is quoted in full:

"Fort Richardson, Texas, July 16th, 1870.

Lieutenant SUMNER H. BODFISH,
Adjutant, Sixth U. S. Cavalry, Post Adjutant.

LIEUTENANT:—I have the honor to submit the following report: In obedience to Special Orders No. 131, dated Headquarters, Fort Richardson, Texas, July 6th, 1870, I left this post with a detachment of two commissioned officers, one acting assistant surgeon and fifty-three enlisted men from Troops A, C, D, H, K and L, 6th U. S. Cavalry, in pursuit of a party of Indians who were reported as having attacked the Overland Mail party and captured the mail at Rock Station, about sixteen miles west of this post; on arriving at that point I found the mail wagon a short distance from the road. I also found a small package addressed to the quartermaster of this post, also the bottom of the mail-bag, but could discover no indication of a large party of Indians or of one hundred and fifty head of horses as reported by the mail driver. I, however, discovered a trail of not more than eight or ten horses, leading in a northwesterly direction. Owing to the lapse of time in reaching this point, the rough character of the country, and the impossibility of following so small a trail with prospect of overtaking the party, I proceeded to Flint Creek, twenty-two miles from this post, at which point I overtook Lieutenant Sands, in command of F troop, 6th

U. S. Cavalry. This officer reported to me that he had found the mail emptied into the bottom of the mail-wagon; on examining the mail, I found but few of the packages had been disturbed.

I encamped with Lieutenant Sands for the night, and on the morning of the 7th, dispatched a courier to Fort Richardson with the mail, then proceeded in a westerly direction, passed to the foot of Flat Top Mountain, and thence in a northwesterly direction to the headwaters of Salt Creek, where I encamped for the night. In consequence of a heavy rain storm on the night of the 6th, all traces of Indians which may have existed were entirely obliterated.

On the morning of the 8th, I marched in a northwesterly direction, a distance of sixteen miles, and encamped at water holes in Mesquito prairie, and could still discover no signs of Indians. On the morning of the 9th, I marched in a northwesterly direction, crossing the headwaters of the West Fork of the Trinity River, where I discovered the trail of a party of five or six Indians. Believing this to be the trail of a portion of the party who robbed the mail, I followed it in an easterly direction along the West Fork of the Trinity, a distance of eight miles, where the trail became very indistinct owing to the heavy rain of the morning. I then marched in a northerly direction, crossing the headwaters of the South Fork of the Little Wichita, where I found the whip belonging to the mail driver and a very indistinct trail leading in a westerly direction. The trail not being sufficiently distinct to warrant my following it, I proceeded in a northwesterly direction until I struck the headwaters of the Middle Fork of the Little Wichita, where I encamped for the night on a high bluff on the south side of the North Fork of the Little Wichita. In consequence of the heavy rains for some days previous, the creek was impassable, but was falling rapidly. I remained in camp on the 11th, with a view of crossing on the morning of the 12th, or as soon as the creek should fall sufficiently to enable me to do so. Before daylight on the morning of the 12th, a severe rain storm set in, rendering the creek entirely impassable.

At 10 o'clock a. m., I marched in a westerly direction with the view of scouting the country around the headwaters of the North Fork of the Little Wichita and between that point and the Brazos River. I had proceeded about five miles when the advance guard reported four Indians in sight moving in a southerly direction. I immediately closed up the command and moved in the direction the Indians had taken at a smart trot, and had proceeded at that gait for a distance of about half a mile when I came in sight of a column of Indians, larger than my own, and about a thousand yards distant. I immediately formed in line with a view to charging this column.

After arriving within five hundred yards of the Indians, I discovered two other bands about equal in numbers to those first discovered, and also a number of scattered Indians on both my flanks. A large band of the Indians on my left immediately started towards my pack mules, which, with the rear guard, were about four hundred yards in rear of my line. Thinking it impracticable to charge the Indians, owing to their greatly superior force and the risk of having the rear guard and pack mules (which composed a little more than one-third of my command) cut off, I halted and opened fire, which was promptly returned by the Indians. After maintaining my position for about half an hour, being completely surrounded by the Indians and exposed to a galling fire from all sides, and finding it utterly impossible to make any impression upon the enemy, I became convinced that the only hope of extricating my command from their dangerous position, without great loss and perhaps total annihilation, was to retreat to some strong point where I could act on the defensive without the danger of again being surrounded. I dismounted the command and fell back slowly in a southerly direction, maintaining the crest of the rolling prairie, closely followed by the Indians, who kept up a rapid fire from every available point.

I continued falling back for four hours and a half, being exposed during the entire time to a hot fire from the rear and both flanks, and in very many instances being obliged to dislodge the enemy from commanding points in my line of retreat. My retreat lay for the most part over a rolling prairie, the remainder over a marshy and broken country, which was rendered much more difficult of passage by the recent heavy rains. About 3 p. m., I forded the Middle Fork of the Little Wichita, still closely followed by the enemy. About 4 p. m., I forded the South Fork of the same stream, where the enemy abandoned the pursuit.

After resting the command for a brief period, I marched in a southeasterly direction, crossing the West Fork of the Trinity and continued my march until midnight, when I went into camp about 10 miles northwest of Flat Top Mountain. On the morning of the 13th, I dispatched couriers to Fort Richardson, requesting that ambulances might be sent me for the transportation of my wounded. My intention was to remain in camp until the arrival of the ambulances, but about 8 a. m. my pickets were driven in by a party of about forty Indians. Fearful that they might be the advance party of the band I had fought on the 12th, and not being in a condition to renew the fight against so largely superior numbers, I burnt all the property that I was unable to transport and mounted my command and marched in a southeasterly direction, and struck the Belknap road about 23 miles west of Fort Richardson, and from thence marched along the road to Rocky Station, where I rested for three hours. I then moved forward again and after about two miles I met the ambulances from Fort Richardson and went into camp. On the morning of the 14th I marched to Fort Richardson, which post I reached about 12 m.

My object in making this apparent forced march during the night of the 12th was for the purpose of removing the wounded as rapidly as possible to this post.

The casualties during the engagement were two enlisted men killed, one acting assistant surgeon and ten enlisted men wounded. The wounded were all brought off the field, but I regret to state that the killed were left in the hands of the enemy, it being utterly impossible to carry them off the field. I had eight horses killed and twenty-one wounded. The loss of the enemy was fifteen killed and a large number wounded.

I captured one horse, and am happy to state that nothing fell into the hands of the enemy except one pack containing the baggage of the officers.

It gives me pleasure to bear testimony to the gallantry displayed by Brevet Captain C. H. Campbell and Lieutenant H. P. Perrine, 6th U. S. Cavalry. During the engagement both of these officers had their horses shot under them early in the fight. Acting Assistant Surgeon G. W. Haldi was wounded early in the fight and had his horse shot twice during the engagement.

I would make especial mention of the following enlisted men who made themselves conspicuous in acts of bravery during the engagement:

1st Sergeant Stokes, Sergeant Kerrigan, Corporals Smith and Connor, of Troop H; 1st Sergeant Kirk, Sergeant May, Corporal Watson, Bugler Winders, Farrier Porter and Private Neal, of Troop L; Sergeant Winterbottom, of Troop A; Sergeant Eldridge, of Troop C, and Corporal Given, of Troop K.

The citizen guide, Mr. Dozier, deserves great credit for the cool manner in which he performed his duties during the fight; in fact, I am proud to state that the entire command acted in the most creditable manner, nobly contesting every inch of ground during the retreat and falling back slowly and in perfect order. There were not less than two hundred and fifty warriors opposed to my small command, and all well mounted and armed with Spencer carbines, rifles and revolvers, with an abundance of ammunition and without incumbrance of any kind, not having any squaws or children, and but few pack animals. I am impressed with the belief that this band of Indians were Comanches, from the reservation, for in my experience of twenty-one years' service on this frontier, and being my sixth engagement with hostile Indians, I have never before met a party so well appointed in every respect. I captured some red flannel, perfectly new and unsoiled, which, in my opinion, gives evidence beyond a doubt that they could not have been long from some point of civilization.

I regret that I cannot claim a victory, but at the same time will state that it was one of the most important engagements that ever took place in northern Texas, and taking all into consideration, I regard the expedition a perfect success. I found the Indians in force and fought them with my small command for four and a half hours, and taught them a lesson which they will not soon forget. In conclusion I extend to the entire command my heartfelt thanks for the gallant manner in which they behaved during the engagement; nobly and with alacrity did they perform the duties assigned them. Total distance marched during the expedition, about two hundred miles.

Appended please find list of killed and wounded.

Very respectfully,

Your obedient servant,

C. B. McLellan,

Captain 6th Cavalry, Brevet Major, U. S. A.,

Commanding Troop L."

This action called forth the fighting qualities of the individual members of the command, and so gallantly did they respond that the War Department conferred medals of honor upon nine of the enlisted men for specific acts of bravery. The Department Commander publicly complimented the command in a general order, as follows:

"The Department Commander has the pleasure of commending the gallantry displayed by a detachment of the 6th U. S. Cavalry, under command of Captain Curwen B. McLellan, 6th U. S. Cavalry, on the 12th and 13th of July, 1870,

INDIAN WARRIOR WATCHING CAVALRY COLUMN.

in Baylor County, Texas, against a greatly superior number of Indians. This engagement doubtless saved the frontier counties in northwestern Texas from a most destructive raid from a band of 250 Indians."

The Indians became very bold immediately after their fight with Captain McLellan, and under date of July 17th the colonel of the regiment, General James Oakes, reported from Fort Richardson that all that part of Texas was infested with Indians, well mounted and clothed, and armed with repeating carbines and rifles. The Indians belonged to the Fort Sill reservation.

Captain T. C. Tupper, with his Troop G, left Fort Richardson June 1st, 1870, to escort cattle to Kansas, en route over the trail to California. On his return march he passed through Indian Territory and found the conditions at Fort Sill and along the Texas border anything but satisfactory. In his report he mentions in detail numerous murders and outrages committed in that region, and says:

"It seems to be generally impossible to ascertain anything of a reliable nature of the depredations committed by these Indians. They constantly accuse each other, trade arrows, steal horses and carry away women and children, and perhaps take an occasional scalp, and that they make no concealment of it, but when remonstrated with by their agents, excuse themselves upon the plea that the theft or murder was committed in Texas, which State they evidently consider not a portion of the United States. Many of them already acknowledge having been with raiding parties in Texas."

In a report from Fort Sill, dated August 2nd, 1870, Brevet Major-General B. H. Grierson says:

"Two raiding parties have been reported as having been in Texas, and an engagement occurred between them and the 6th U. S. Cavalry in which three Indians were killed and a number wounded. The Indians report that Kiowas have in their possession seven captives, one woman and six children, who were lately captured in Texas. They agree to bring them in and deliver them up, as well as captured property, and state they had just held a general council and had decided to cease all hostilities and would be here soon, and that the balance of the Cheyennes, now with the Kiowas, would return to their agency."

This intolerable state of affairs continued along the Texas border for some years, in fact the condition was so bad that even after the regiment had moved to Kansas for station, the only change in its duties was to scout south to the border instead of north, from its former posts in Texas.

September 26th, 1870, Captain W. A. Rafferty left Fort Richardson, with twenty-two men of his Troop M and five Tonkawa Indians, on a scout towards the headwaters of the Trinity river, and encamped the next night where Captain McLellan bivouacked with his command after his fight in the preceding July. On September 29th, after going into camp on a branch of the Little Wichita, two Indians were discovered about a mile from camp. A part of the command saddled up and pursued them for several miles when they escaped in the underbrush and could not be trailed because of the rocky ground.

At daylight, on October 4th, the guide, Mr. Dozier circled the camp and discovered a trail across the Fort Belknap road, two miles to the eastward, which had been made the previous night, and led north to the Wichita mountains. The trail was followed over wooded mountains for twenty miles, and upon emerging on the prairie the Indians were not in sight. The prairie was crossed, principally at a trot, for about twenty-five miles, making the day's pursuit fifty miles.

The command bivouacked, and at daylight took up the trail again. After following across the Little Wichita six or seven miles, the Indians were overtaken and immediately attacked. Two Indians were killed and one was wounded, but by abandoning his horse the latter escaped in the underbrush. The remainder of the party, eight or ten in number, escaped; two horses were killed and eighteen captured. The pursuit was abandoned when the Indians scattered towards the mountains. One of the Indians killed was Keech-Quash, chief of the Keechies. He had a hunting-pass on his person. A saddle, some female clothing and other articles were captured, which indicated that the Indians had been recently raiding a settlement.

Captain T. C. Tupper left Camp Wichita, Texas, October 3d, 1870, with Troops A and G on a scout. On the night of October 6th, while in camp between the Big and Little Wichita rivers, the camp was charged by a body of forty or fifty mounted Indians. The charge was made with yells and firing, evidently to stampede the animals which were double lariated to picket lines, except the more spirited animals which were tied to mesquite trees. There was an outer camp-guard of ten men and the entire squadron was bivouacked in couples, at intervals of fifteen or twenty yards, surrounding the horses.

The charge of the Indians was checked within about twenty yards of G troop by the fire which was promptly opened on them from that side. The charging party divided into two columns and rode off into the darkness. During the firing twelve horses broke loose and stampeded. Stable call was sounded at the first alarm, and the men, except those stationed on the outskirts of the camp, returned to their horses.

A quarter of an hour after the Indians withdrew, Captain Mauck with thirty-five mounted men went in pursuit, in the effort to recover the horses. Soon after their departure the camp was again fired into by some of the Indians. Captain Mauck made a circuit of about twelve miles around the camp, but could discover no regular trail and returned about 2 a. m. At daylight the search for the trail was taken up again, but as the command had neither guide nor Indian scouts, the scattered renegades could not be traced. A wounded pony, some lances and a few arrows were all that was left to indicate the recent presence of hostiles.

Captain Tupper concluded that the Indians had gone toward the Big Wichita river and proceeded in that direction. The dismounted men whose horses had been lost, twelve in number, were provided with three days' rations and ordered back to Camp Wichita, under charge of Sergeant Louis Strupp. On the second day's march towards the post the sergeant saw a party of fifteen Indians approaching. He concealed his detachment and the Indians came up and went into camp about a quarter of a mile away. The Indians were riding large American horses and driving a herd of about thirty horses and ponies along with them. Sergeant Strupp thought the horses were those which had been stampeded from Captain Tupper's command and determined to recapture them. Leaving two with the pack pony, he took the other ten men and proceeded down a small ravine and up the creek to where the Indians had halted in the brush. When within about eighty yards his party was discovered and firing began on both sides. The

Indians ran to their horses, mounted, and continued fighting from horseback for a short time. Sergeant Strupp's party captured five American horses and other property, but did not kill any of the Indians so far as is known.

When the Indians discovered how small his party was, they followed and harassed him all the next day. He reached the post after four days' march and the captured horses were turned in and subsequently delivered to citizens who claimed them.

On October 12th, 1870, Lieutenant W. J. Reese was sent with a detachment of the regiment in in charge of Indian prisoners to effect an exchange for white captives in the hands of Indians on the Fort Sill reservation, and who had been carried off from Texas. This was a shameless species of transaction but one the army was compelled to adopt, from time to time, to save unfortunate women who had fallen into the hands of savages and whose lives would have been sacrificed in any attempt at rescue.

Captain A. R. Chaffee left Fort Richardson, November 12th, on a scout, and on the 14th, soon after going into camp near the Belknap road, some cattle were observed running as though being chased. The troops stood to the lariats while a Tonkawa scout jumped on his horse and went to ascertain what was causing the commotion in the cattle herd. The scout, Anderson, had scarcely disappeared behind a slight elevation when a shot was fired. The troop commenced saddling at once and Anderson came back on a run and announced that he had seen five Comanches on the other side of the hill. Captain Chaffee started immediately with two Tonkawas, two guides and seven of the men, who had saddled quickly, and in a few minutes struck the trail. The pursuit was at a gallop for about fifteen miles until the Indians were overtaken, but unfortunately this did not happen until dark. The five Indians had been joined by seven others. The running fight which took place was of short duration, the Indians, as usual, scattering.

The detachment returned to camp about nine o'clock at night. Next morning the troop marched to the scene of the fight and found seven ponies and two saddles which had been abandoned by the Indians but which could not be located in the darkness the night before. The trail was followed to Post Oak Creek and then abandoned, as all indications showed the Indians were hastily leaving the country. Several other trails, not many days old, were crossed during the pursuit.

During the month of December, 1870, a number of officers were ordered from Camp Wichita to Fort Richardson for duty as members of a general court-martial. Lieutenant B. H. Mellen made the trip alone on horseback. The journey required a ride through a country infested with Indians. The weather was extremely cold, but everything went well until towards evening on the first day when he reached the river, which was swollen by recent floods and filled with floating ice. He was forced either to accept a plunge into the icy flood or return to the post with his duty unperformed.

He plunged into the stream and the brave horse struck out and swam to the opposite shore, where, in endeavoring to ascend the bank, he slipped and fell backwards into the river. Lieutenant Mellen was encumbered with his overcoat, riding boots, and pistols. As he arose to the surface he saw that his only chance for life was to float with the current until he found a more favorable place to reach the shore. He succeeded finally in grasping an overhanging limb and drew himself out of the stream to the bank.

He was so overcome by the shock and exertion that, when safely ashore he fell insensible. He remained unconscious until late in the night when, upon recovering, he found his horse had also come out of the river and was standing by his side. He attempted to rise and mount, but learned to his consternation that his feet were frozen in his boots and he could make no use of his limbs whatever.

He attempted again and again to rise, but his efforts were unavailing. The patient horse remained by his side all through the night, the next day, the second night and the second day, while the benumbed sufferer made fruitless efforts to mount.

At last toward evening of the second day he was able to grasp the stirrup and drag himself into the saddle. His faithful horse bore him out from the river bottom on to the prairie where he discovered a light and made towards it. As he approached the light he was met by the click of rifles and the demand of "Who's there?" He was confronted with Winchesters in the hands of hunters, camped near the river. He announced his name and destination and told of his condition. The hunters at once took him off his horse and carried him into the hut. A hasty examination showed that his legs were frozen in his large cavalry boots and that immediate professional assistance was necessary to save his life. The thermometer at this time registered ten degrees below zero. One of the hunters hastily mounted and hurried off to Fort Richardson for assistance. The surgeon started at once with the ambulance, and upon reaching the hunters' camp found Lieutenant Mellen's condition so much worse that it was necessary to return immediately to the post with him to save his life.

Upon arriving at the post hospital his boots were

cut off and his limbs were found frozen so solid that it was necessary to amputate both feet. He still grew worse, and a second operation had to be performed, taking off more of his legs. His condition was critical for some time, but a naturally strong constitution enabled him to pull through the terrible ordeal, only to find his career as a cavalryman terminated forever. He was shortly after placed on the retired list of the army.

CHAPTER VIII.

On the Plains—Kansas and Indian Territory.

Lawlessness in Texas—Cattle Thieves—Camp at Fort Hays—Indian Depredations—Tupper overtakes Cheyenne Raiders—Sergeant Kohn recovers Stock from Indians—Mail Party attacked—Major Compton's Escort attacked Twice—Indian Territory Expedition organized—Fight near Red River—Sergeant Woodall's Gallant Defense—Supply Train attacked—Surrender of Satanta and Big Tree—Horse Thieves—Overton's Fight, Staked Plains—Rescue of Germain Girls—Sergeant Ryan's Fight, North Fork, Red River—Cheyenne Outbreak—Henely overtakes Cheyennes, Sappa Creek—Over the Santa Fé Trail to Arizona—Exchange Horses.

IN the spring of 1871, the regiment was ordered to change station to the Department of the Missouri, having been subjected to more than five years of duty such as seldom or never has fallen to the lot of civilized soldiers in any country. Ordered direct from the scenes of the great civil conflict to the distant frontier to combat a savage foe unexcelled in ability, cunning and cruelty by any other tribes, save perhaps the Apaches, the officers and men found themselves confronted with all the hatred and bitterness left by the Civil War in the hearts of a people, who had not been called upon to suffer as those of many of the other southern States had done. Many of the ex-Confederate soldiers had succumbed to the inevitable with bad grace, and the more lawless of them encouraged a hostile feeling towards the very men who were daily exposing their lives in protecting the settlements. It was enough to contend against the Indians, but when, by ill-treatment and assassination of comrades, the men were finally made to recognize the contempt in which the community held them, there was short shrift for the lawless guerrillas who were frequently encountered.

There was not much regret in the regiment when the headquarters and troops which had been assembled at Fort Richardson, moved out on March 20th, 1871, for the north. The command arrived at Fort Sill, April 1st, and within a few days the troops destined for stations in Indian Territory and Kansas started to their various posts.

During 1871, '72 and '73, the troops were constantly scouting in the vicinity of their stations, but no serious encounters took place. Occasional mail, or other escorts, were attacked and many acts of savagery were committed at widely separated points on the great plains, by the various tribes inhabiting the country between British America and the Gulf of Mexico.

On October 25th, 1873, Lieutenant J. B. Kerr, with a detachment of twenty-five men, attacked and captured a party of eight cattle thieves near Little Cabin Creek, Texas, recovering seventy horses and two hundred head of cattle which had been stolen.

A large portion of the regiment was assembled in camp near Fort Hays, from which point the country in the vicinity of the Saline, Solomon and Republican rivers was kept thoroughly patrolled with scouting parties. Two troops had been sent to Mississippi and Louisiana for the much despised reconstruction duty in January, 1872, but they returned in 1873 and participated in the active scouting which preceded the general campaign against the hostiles the next year.

Settlers were pushing into Kansas far beyond the safety line, and daring and unprincipled buffalo hunters were constantly endangering the peace of the community at this period. The pressure of the advancing settlers, coupled with the rapid disappearance of the buffalo herds, rendered the preservation of peace a difficult matter during 1871, '72 and '73, but the regiment labored faithfully with the delicate question. To sit idly by and witness the disappearance of their meat supply at the hands of the heartless skin-hunters was beyond the endurance of the Indians.

The war parties became more bold, and once

more "bleeding Kansas" was called upon to suffer the consequences of the inevitable conflict between advancing civilization and the doomed Indians; a conflict, the tides of which have rolled back and forth across plain and mountain for nearly three centuries, with here and there a success for the red men, but with the ultimate result always the same from the days of the brave Wampanoags of New England, and Powhatans, of Virginia, down to the Sioux at Wounded Knee.

Even before the grass began to grow in the spring of 1874, the Indians on the reservations became very restless. Up to this time a custom had existed amongst the great tribes of paying extended visits to one another. On March 12th, a party of Southern Cheyennes, who had been on a six months' visit to the Northern Cheyennes and Arapahoes, passed west of Fort Dodge en route to their reservation, and before reaching Camp Supply, Indian Territory, some white men stole between thirty and forty of their ponies. As soon as this occurrence was reported, troops were ordered out as a precautionary measure, for, judging by past experience, it was certain that the Indians would retaliate.

Captain T. C. Tupper, with G troop, left Fort Dodge April 6th, and on the 10th learned that the Indians had just stolen from settlers, near Sun

PLAINS INDIAN, 1875.

City, Kansas, twenty horses and mules and fifty-two head of cattle. The trail was immediately followed, and, after a pursuit of more than fifty miles, the party was overtaken and all the stock recovered. In the fight which occurred, a son of Little Robe, Chief of the Cheyennes, and another Indian were wounded.

On June 14th nine Indians made a dash on a ranch in the Medicine Lodge country and ran off some stock. Sergeant S. M. Kohn, Troop G, Sixth Cavalry, who happened to be in the vicinity with a scouting party, took up the pursuit immediately, recovered the stock and captured one Indian pony in a running fight of two miles.

On June 19th the Camp Supply mail party was attacked and the non-commissioned officer in charge wounded.

Major C. E. Compton, Sixth Cavalry, accompanied by the Medical Director of the Department, and an escort of fifteen men, left Fort Dodge, Kansas, on June 20th en route to Camp Supply, Indian Territory. At the crossing of the Cimarron river, the party was joined by the mail escort which had been attacked the preceding day. At the crossing of Buffalo Creek on June 21st, while passing from the bottom through a gulch to the high prairie land, a war party of twelve or fifteen Indians opened fire on the detachment. The fire was promptly returned and the men advanced in skirmish line, drove the Indians from the hills and cleared the road to the open ground. The Indians withdrew, and the party proceeded to its destination.

Returning from Camp Supply, Major Compton's party, increased to twenty-two men, was passing through Beaver Creek hills on the 24th, when a volley was received from behind a knoll at a distance of about fifty yards. Every one was on the alert and a skirmish line was quickly formed facing the fire. The order to charge was given, and the men made a gallant rush for the crest of the hill, which they gained, and drove twenty-five or thirty Cheyennes from their position. The Indians retreated into the neighboring ravines, where their ponies were secreted, but were finally driven out on to the open ground where they continued for some time to fire from long range. Four Indians were killed and five ponies captured without the loss of a soldier.

On July 5th, 1st Lieutenant L. A. Abbott, with a detachment, scouting from Fort Dodge, chased a small party of Indians about twelve miles.

From day to day reports came from widely separated localities of theft, rapine and murder by the Indians. Trains were attacked, ranches looted, and women and children carried away into captivity. It had now become evident to the authorities that desultory scouting and chasing war parties, which had knowledge of pursuit, were equally unprofitable. Expeditions were organized all over the west, and this was the beginning of the final collapse of Indian power for sustained hostilities. For the work on the southern plains, expeditions were organized in Texas, New Mexico and Kansas. Active scouting began with large columns and the Indians were pursued without intermission until the campaign of 1874-5 so completely paralyzed the hostiles that they abandoned their belligerent attitude, fled from their familiar hiding places in the Pan Handle and sought the protection of the agencies.

During the month of August, 1874, the expedition with which the Sixth operated, took the field. Troops A, D, F, G, H, I, L and M were organized into two battalions under the command of Majors C. E. Compton and James Biddle, and joined Colonel N. A. Miles' command.

On the evening of August 26th, a large trail was found near the Sweetwater. The trail constantly grew larger through accessions of Indians, presumably from the agencies. Being delayed by the inability of the train to move rapidly through the sand, rations and reserve ammunition were issued and the command pushed ahead, leaving the wagons to follow.

On the morning of the 30th, when moving over

a plain about twelve miles from Red river, the advance guard was charged by about two hundred Indians, who came so close that one scout was wounded by a spear thrust. When driven off, the Indians retreated to a line of hills and joined their main body. The Indians numbered from four to six hundred warriors and took up a position along a broken line of bluffs, interspersed with deep ravines. The troops were deployed in line, with but a small reserve, and moved forward to the attack, advancing from crest to crest and driving the Indians from every position they took up.

Captain Chaffee led his troop in a gallant charge, using pistols, and later Major Compton's battalion charged up a hill, the crest of which was about two hundred feet high, and carried the position. The Indians at first showed some bravery, but the determined nature of the attack whenever they made a stand, caused a change of tactics, and they drew back to very long range.

They made a final stand on the right bank of Red river, on a high bluff. The location was very strong, as only two men could advance up the trail abreast. Captain Tupper led his troop up the rugged ascent, the bugles sounding the charge, and the Indians again fled. The fight had lasted over five hours and from the first to last position had extended over twelve miles. As they abandoned the field, the smoke of their burning villages could be seen in the rear of their line. Immediate pursuit began across Red river and up the Tulé, through the deserted villages, and for over a hundred miles their trail was strewn with broken-down ponies and abandoned property.

The Indians killed buffaloes to obtain water-sacks and made for the Staked Plains. The dead Indians, lodges, arrows and moccasins found along the trail indicated that the Kiowas, Comanches and Cheyennes had come together in this campaign.

The command, including both men and horses, suffered from the heat as well as thirst; there was little water to be had, and that obtained was generally so alkaline as to be unfit for use and caused much sickness. It was determined, however, to continue in the field, and supplies were ordered to be forwarded.

Two parties were sent from the battle-field to Camp Supply, Indian Territory, with dispatches for supplies, one of which was under the charge of Sergeant Z. T. Woodall, of Troop I, Sixth Cavalry.* This one was attacked by Indians, and the following letter, written by General Miles, tells the story of this remarkable fight:

* Sergeant Woodall continued to render valuable service for many years as 1st Sergeant of I Troop, and only recently (1899) died at his post of duty as Ordnance Sergeant, in Havana, Cuba.

"Adjutant-General, U. S. Army.

GENERAL:—I deem it but a duty to brave men and faithful soldiers, to bring to the notice of the highest military authority an instance of indomitable courage, skill, and true heroism on the part of a detachment from this command, with the request that the actors be rewarded, and their faithfulness and bravery recognized by pensions, medals of honor, or in such way as may be deemed most fitting.

On the night of the 10th instant a party consisting of Sergeant Z. T. Woodall, Troop I; Privates Peter Roth, Troop A; John Harrington, Troop H, and George W. Smith, Troop M, 6th Cavalry; Scouts Amos Chapman and William Dixon, were sent as bearers of dispatches from the camp of this command on McLellan Creek, Texas, to Camp Supply, Indian Territory. At six a.m., on the 12th, when approaching Washita River, they were met and surrounded by a band of 125 Kiowas and Comanches, who had recently left their agency, and at the first attack all were struck, Private Smith mortally, and all the others severely wounded.

Although enclosed on all sides, and by overwhelming numbers, one of them succeeded, while they were under a severe fire at short range, and while the others with their rifles were keeping the Indians at bay, in digging with his knife and hands a slight cover. After this had been secured they placed themselves within it; the wounded walking with brave and painful efforts, and Private Smith, though he had received a mortal wound, sitting upright in the trench to conceal the crippled condition of their party from the Indians.

From early morning till dark, outnumbered twenty-five to one, under an almost constant fire, and at such short range that they sometimes used their pistols, retaining the last charge to prevent capture and torture, this little party of five defended their lives and the person of their dying comrade, without food and their only drink the rain water that collected in a pool, mingled with their own blood. There is no doubt but that they killed more than double their number, besides those that were wounded. The Indians abandoned the attack at dark on the 12th.

The exposure and distance from the command, which were necessary incidents of their duty, were such that for thirty-six hours from the first attack their condition could not be known, and not till midnight of the 13th could they receive medical attendance or food; exposed during this time to an incessant cold storm. Sergeant Woodall, Private Harrington and Scout Chapman were seriously wounded; Private Roth and Scout Dixon were struck but not disabled.

The simple recital of their deeds and the mention of the odds against which they fought; how the wounded defended the dying, and the dying aided the wounded by exposure to fresh wounds after the power of action was gone, these alone present a scene of cool courage, heroism and self-sacrifice, which duty as well as inclination prompts us to recognize, but which we cannot fitly honor.

(Signed) N. A. MILES,
Brevet Major-General."

Lieutenant Frank West with 20 men of the Sixth, was sent with Captain Lyman, Fifth Infantry, and his company, from camp with a wagon train to meet the out-coming train and bring the supplies to the front. The train was found September 7th, when Lieutenant West's detachment was increased by seven men coming out to join the regiment. The stores were transferred in a violent storm, and the return march begun, when the Indians appeared and killed and scalped a teamster who had wandered off a short distance. The train was followed, and on the 9th the attack of the Indians, about 250 in number, commenced.

The train had just emerged from a deep ravine

when the Indians charged the rear fiercely, riding to within 100 yards and shooting down Lieutenant Lewis and Sergeant Armour, Fifth Infantry. The train was corralled a mile or more north of the Washita river for the ensuing fight, which lasted four days. A scout was sent through to Camp Supply, being chased on the way, and returned with Troop K, Sixth Cavalry, and medical assistance for the wounded, who had endured great suffering during the four days' fighting and exposure without food or water.

Whilst the attack on the train was in progress, a misty rainstorm came on, during which the Indians withdrew from one flank, and soon after a column of mounted men were discovered moving by. Scouts were sent out and returned saying the column was a body of Indians, but it subsequently developed that it was Major Price's battalion of the Eighth Cavalry, which had come towards the sound of the firing and passed by in ignorance of its proximity to the besieged train.

About this time the Indians made a raid and carried off a white boy from the vicinity of Buffalo station, west of Fort Hays. Lieutenants J. B. Kerr and J. A. Rucker, with twenty men, took the trail and pursued for six days, crossing the Solomon, Saline and Smoky Hill rivers, compelling the Indians to abandon much of their plunder. Before the Indians scattered, they shot the boy through the heart and left his body on the trail.

On October 10th, Major Compton, with two troops, intercepted a body of Indians fleeing north before troops advancing from Texas, pursued them through the sand hills for more than a hundred miles and drove them back south of the Canadian river.

On October 4th, 1874, Colonel Neill reported the surrender of the celebrated chiefs Satanta and Big Tree, with many lodges of Kiowas, but they gave the unwelcome information that a part of the tribe had gone with the Comanches to the Staked Plains. These latter were the Indians who attacked the supply train September 9th.

Horse thieves took advantage of the unsettled condition of affairs to ply their nefarious trade, and Lieutenant Hanna with ten men of Troop B was sent from Fort Dodge on November 4th in pursuit of a band. It was overtaken on the 9th and in the fight which lasted two hours, Private Skelton was wounded, Lieutenant Hanna's horse killed, two thieves wounded and twelve horses and mules recovered.

On November 8th, 1874, Lieutenant Overton with Troop D, Sixth Cavalry, and Company D, Fifth Infantry, all under Lieutenant Baldwin, struck a large village of Cheyennes north of McLellan's

Creek and drove them out on the Staked Plains. Major Compton went with Troop H, Sixth Cavalry, to the assistance of these troops, but the pace was so rapid he did not arrive until the fighting was practically over. Two captive white girls, Adelaide and Julia Germain, were rescued during this engagement.

The story of the Germain family is a most pathetic one, and, as the regiment was instrumental in the recovery of the four girls, the tale of their capture and rescue may properly find a place here.

This family was travelling through Kansas, en route from Georgia to Colorado, when they were attacked by Cheyennes near Smoky Hill river. The father, mother, brother and one sister were killed. Two young girls, five and seven years of age, and two grown girls, were carried off to the Cheyenne village. A knowledge of these facts was obtained from the two little girls recovered in the fight of November 8th. The two children were taken to Fort Leavenworth, and Congress directed, in the appropriation act for support of the Cheyennes, that $2500 be deducted for each child and placed to their credit in the Treasury at five per cent, and that the interest be used for their support until they should reach twenty-one years of age, when the principal should be paid to them.

Lieutenant-Colonel Thomas H. Neill, Sixth Cavalry, commanding a camp near Cheyenne agency, sent an Indian runner to Stone Calf's village with this note on January 20th, 1875:

"To Katherine Elizabeth or to Sophia Louisa Germain, white women now in the hands of the hostile Cheyennes with Grey Beard or Stone Calf. I send you these few lines to tell you that your younger sisters, Juliana and Nancy, are safe and well and have been sent home to Georgia. Your sad captivity is known all over the country and every effort to obtain your release will be made. Read this note to Stone Calf or Grey Beard, and say to Stone Calf that his message asking peace has been received, and that I will receive him and his band upon condition that he shall send you and your sister in first, and then he can come in with his band and give himself up to the mercy of the Government, and I will receive him. I send you with this, pencil and paper. Write me Stone Calf's answer, and anything else you may desire; I think the Indians will make no objection."

Stone Calf's village had been located on the Staked Plains, near the Pecos river, but on February 14th, 1875, he moved to near Custer's old battle-ground. Two more troops were added to Colonel Neill's command in order that he might force a surrender, but, by the exercise of patience, the unhappy captive girls were rescued without a fight, and this was followed, on February 26th, by Stone Calf's surrender with 1600 Cheyennes.

The condition of the two Germain girls was pitiable in the extreme. They declined being sent to Georgia, stating that they had no relatives or associations there to take them back, and desired to go to school somewhere in Kansas. They were sent to Fort Leavenworth, where they were taken charge of by a worthy family. Their subsequent history is unknown.

On December 1st, Captain Chaffee made a night march to surprise a party of Indians reported to be on a branch of the North Fork of Red river, but the Indians received warning and decamped in great haste. 1st Sergeant Ryan, Troop I, with a detachment, pursued and overtook them at daylight, December 2nd, attacked and routed them, capturing their ponies, about seventy in number, which were mostly saddled and packed.

The campaign was continued far into the winter, the last movement on the Staked Plains being executed in intensely cold weather, the thermometer registering at times twenty-five degrees below zero, and "Northers" prevailing almost incessantly. The Indians were fought in nine engagements, and were so harassed during this campaign that they were unable to commit their usual depredations. After continuous pursuit they went into the agencies and surrendered in a greatly impoverished condition, and have never regained their old war spirit.

The experience derived in this campaign, found expression in the following words from General Miles :

"For long and rapid pursuit of an enterprising enemy, frequently without grazing, with poor water, the strength of the cavalry and animals must be preserved, or it results in a few weeks campaigning and several months remounting and recuperating. Hence, I would prefer for effective and continuous compaigning, two companies of cavalry, supplied with the regulation allowance of short forage, to eight companies, starved for want of grain or weighed down by a superabundance of grass, especially when the command is expected to capture or exhaust the thousands of hardy ponies that afford the Indians convenient and valuable relays. Desultory scouting, often made without positive design and with less result, has a tiresome, exhaustive and injurious influence upon the cavalry. Friendly Indians or daring scouts can be more economically employed to hunt for the hostile camps, discover trails or movements of Indians, and cavalry saved for the direct march, resistless dash and rapid pursuit for which that arm of the service is so well adapted."

Peace prevailed until spring, but on April 6th, 1875, Captain Rafferty's Troop M was engaged near the Cheyenne agency from 3 p. m., until dark with about 150 Cheyennes. Nine Indians were killed, four soldiers wounded, and nine troop horses killed or wounded.

A party of Cheyennes took the trail for the north, and, having been seen crossing the railroad, Lieutenant Austin Henely with forty men of Troop H, Sixth Cavalry, was sent by rail to Wallace, Kansas, and left there April 19th to strike the trail southeast of the post. The trail was followed rapidly for over a hundred miles to Sappa Creek, in northern Kansas, where the Indians were overtaken at daylight on April 23d. A portion of the Indians escaped, but the others took cover in some holes and fought to the bitter end. Nineteen warriors were killed and one hundred and thirty-four ponies captured, with a loss of two men of Troop H, Sergeant Papier and Private Theims.

A commendatory order was published a few days later which contains this paragraph:

"The Department Commander feels justified in saying that no better managed affair has occurred in this Department for many years, and he commends it to the emulation of all as a brilliant example of intelligent enterprise, rare zeal and sound judgment in the discharge of duty."

After a brief period of active scouting, the regiment proceeded to relieve the Fifth Cavalry in Arizona, the order having been issued the preceding year and suspended on account of the Indian troubles. The order relieving the regiment from duty in the Department of the Missouri contained the following:

"The Sixth Cavalry entered this Department from the Department of Texas in the summer of the year 1871, and since that time has been actively employed in patrolling the country, protecting the frontier settlers, and scouting against hostile Indians.

Its patrol duty has been such as required great judgment and discrimination to keep the peace between the settlers and the Indians, and its scouts have been attended with great hardship, exposure and suffering.

The Department Commander is glad to have this opportunity to say that these duties have been performed by the regiment with much skill and efficiency, to their own honor and to the best interests of the service."

The first half of the regiment, with the headquarters and band, assembled during May and marched under the command of Captain McLellan from Fort Lyon, Colorado. The march was made in a leisurely way over the route known as the old "Santa Fé trail," to Santa Fé, New Mexico, where the first half of the Fifth Cavalry was met. The headquarters of the Eighth Cavalry was at Santa Fé at this time, and the three bands made the Plaza of this ancient town attractive for several days. It required more than music, however, to lighten the hearts of the Sixth cavalrymen, for they were subjected to the pangs of exchanging their handsome American horses for the "broncos," brought from Arizona by the Fifth. Before the regiment completed its long tour of service in Arizona, however, the men learned to respect the tough little horses that were able to keep in the field indefinitely, living on such grazing as they could obtain while in the night herd, and during the halts along the trail.

When Albuquerque was reached, two troops took the road for northern Arizona, and the others continued down the Rio Grande valley and across through Apache Pass to stations in southern Arizona. Upon arrival of troops at their new stations, the remaining troops of the Fifth Cavalry were relieved and proceeded east, meeting the second half of the Sixth at Fort Union, New Mexico, where a similar exchange of horses was effected as that which took place at Santa Fé between the troops of the first half of each regiment.

CHAPTER IX.

ARIZONA—THE LAND OF THE APACHES.

NATURE OF COUNTRY—METHODS OF WARFARE—USE OF SCOUTS—NARROW ESCAPE—ATTACK ON FORT APACHE—CHIRICAUHUA OUTBREAK—INDIAN SITUATION—CONCENTRATION OF REGIMENT—REMOVAL TO SAN CARLOS—SCOUTS AFTER TONTOS—RUCKER'S FIGHT, LEIDENDORF RANGE—CAPTURE OF GERONIMO'S NEPHEW—RAID ON SAN CARLOS—WARM SPRINGS INDIANS LEAVE RESERVATION—PURSUED AND RUNNING FIGHT—CONSTRUCTION OF MILITARY TELEGRAPH LINES—RUCKER OVERTAKES RAIDING PARTY—CONCENTRATION OF INDIAN SCOUTS, MEXICAN BORDER—NOT PERMITTED TO CROSS—DROWNING OF LIEUTENANTS HENELY AND RUCKER—MORE ARMY THAN NAVY OFFICERS DROWNED—PERRINE'S FIGHT—VICTORIO—TROOPS SENT TO AID IN NEW MEXICO—McLELLAN RESCUES TROOP NINTH CAVALRY—LOST IN DESERT—VICTORIO'S RAID TOWARD SAN CARLOS—KRAMER'S FIGHT—RENEGADES DRIVEN FROM ARIZONA—MADDEN FINDS MANY MURDERED SETTLERS—CHIRICAUHUAS DEFIANT—COMBINED ACTION AGAINST VICTORIO—DRIVEN TO CHIHUAHUA—SURROUNDED—ANNIHILATED BY MEXICAN TROOPS—WHITE MOUNTAIN TRIBE DISPLAY FANATICISM—CIBICU FIGHT—ATTACK ON FORT APACHE—OPENING COMMUNICATION—REINFORCEMENTS—ACTIVE SCOUTING—DRIVING MALCONTENTS TO RESERVATION—CHIRICAUHUAS LEAVE RESERVATION—CEDAR SPRINGS FIGHT—PURSUIT TO MEXICAN BORDER—LOCO'S BAND LEAVES RESERVATION—TUPPER'S PURSUIT AND FIGHT—AMBUSCADE OF MEXICANS—EXTERMINATION—WHITE MOUNTAIN OUTBREAK—DIFFICULT FIGHT, BIG DRY WASH—REMARKABLE CONCENTRATION OF SCOUTING COLUMNS—GENERAL CROOK'S EXPEDITION SIERRA MADRE—MARCHES.

UPON arrival of all the regiment in the Department of Arizona the troops were widely distributed, B going with headquarters to Fort Lowell, near the old town of Tucson; A and D to Fort Apache, on the reservation of the White Mountain Apaches; C, G and M to Fort Grant; E and I to Fort Verde; H to Fort Bowie; L to

Camp San Carlos, this being the location of the Indian agency for the Apaches, Apache-Mojaves and Apache-Yumas; K to Fort McDowell, and F to Fort Whipple. A glance at the map will show what a very thin spreading of protection this distribution afforded the people of Arizona from the raids of the Apache—a name synonymous in the southwest with all that is cunning and devilish.

Arizona is an immense expanse of country, much of it covered with rough and broken mountain chains—the southern spurs of the Rockies. The western part contains immense deserts, and neither Indians nor settlers undertook to extract a living from such parched and uninviting sand wastes.

The history of the Apaches is shrouded in much uncertainty. The whole face of the country is filled with the remains of villages occupied by a people of an entirely different nature, and, in all probability, akin to the scattered Pueblo Indians of to-day. The cliff-dwellers left many strange abodes in almost every watered cañon and the foundations and walls of many of their valley locations indicate a large population in olden times. All settlers well acquainted with the habits of the various tribes, unite in the belief that the disappearance of the old dwellers in Arizona is traceable to the incessant warfare of the Apaches. It was against these absolutely wild Indians that the regiment was destined to be pitted for more than ten years.

The records of the War Department show that between January 1st, 1866, and May, 1875, when the Sixth was ordered to duty in Arizona, two hundred and seventeen fights had occurred between troops and Indians within the limits of the territory. The number of attacks made upon ranches, wagon trains, stage coaches and travelers, can only be conjectured.

The character of Arizona was entirely in favor of the Apaches, whose lives had been devoted to overcoming the natural obstacles of an inhospitable country. The Indians had learned to utilize much in nature that was unknown to the whites, and they were so accustomed to exposure that sudden changes from snow-covered mountains to parched sand deserts affected them but little, if at all. Travelling without baggage, and able to cover when hard pressed, from fifty to seventy miles on foot within twenty-four hours, they constituted most formidable enemies. Their food consisted of game, baked mescal root, which is very palatable and not unlike sweet potato, grass seed and other wild productions of that strange land.

With a supply of food which would not furnish a meal for a soldier, an Apache would go upon a distant raid, trusting to luck and his knowledge of nature's foods that he might not suffer. His ability to crawl stealthily upon his enemy, to conceal himself with a few handfuls of grass, to deliver his fire and disappear as from the face of the earth, characterizes him as an enemy who must be guarded against incessantly. Often the watchful traveler, with gun in hand, has been allowed to pass safely through an Apache ambuscade, for they rarely attacked unless they could do so without injury to themselves.

The manner in which Apaches concealed their rude "wicky-ups," consisting of bent boughs covered with brush, together with their wary and watchful natures, made their capture almost impossible to white men. Success was only attained ordinarily when Indian scouts were sent out to locate the hiding places in advance. Then the scouts, with a detachment of soldiers and a pack train, would proceed by night marches to the vicinity. The train would be concealed and food prepared after dark when the smoke of fires would not rise in the usually clear atmosphere to give warning. With rations on their backs, the scouts and dismounted cavalrymen would then walk and crawl to positions surrounding the "rancheria" and wait for daylight. On the approach of dawn, at the first sign of life, the firing would begin and be continued until every "buck" or warrior was killed. The scouts never took prisoners except women and children. As all Indians understood this there was always a break for cover and a fight for life. There were occasional escapes, but usually if the "rancheria" was surrounded before discovery, annihilation of the "bucks" followed.

It was the opinion generally of those most experienced in Apache warfare, that, if the government had failed to take advantage of tribal animosities, Arizona would have remained as undeveloped to-day as it was when acquired by the United States. The fighting propensities of the Apaches were turned to account by first employing one tribe against another, and later on the development of the Indian scout system reached such a point that they were frequently employed against their own people. These scouts pursued their own kindred with the unerring instincts of the bloodhound, and when overtaken killed them as remorselessly as they would have done their white enemies. It was only through the presence and influence of officers and soldiers that women and children were spared. Their savage natures may be comprehended when it is known that in one instance a scout, having learned that his father had been proclaimed an outlaw, went into the mountains and killed him, hoping to secure a reward.

Comparative quiet reigned during the summer while the regiment was marching in, but it was not long before the marauding bands began their usual deviltry, which continued at intervals during all the years the regiment was stationed in that country.

During the early part of December, 1875, a party of White Mountain Apaches made a raid in the immediate vicinity of Fort Verde, destroying a sheep herder's camp in the valley below, and then struck the stage road between the post and department headquarters, at the head of Copper Cañon, just after an ambulance, containing the Adjutant-General, Inspector-General and Medical Director, had passed into the cañon on the way to the post. It was a narrow escape, for the officers were entirely unprepared for the attack.

Soon after an ox train belonging to a government contractor arrived at the entrance of the cañon and the oxen had just been unyoked for the night, when the Indians appeared, killed nearly all the cattle and drove off the remainder. Apache-Mojave scouts were put on the trail but failed to overtake the renegades. The cattle were found killed along the trail.

When sufficient time had elapsed to allow the Indians to consider the trail abandoned, a detachment and thirty scouts, was sent out, this being the first scout of the regiment in Arizona, and followed the trail through the cañons of Tonto Basin to the line of the reservation, upon which returning renegades were at that time accorded protection.

During December, Major James Biddle was ordered out to the Mexican border with a squadron from Fort Grant, to drive back Mexican soldiers violating neutrality laws.

On January 9th, 1876, Troops A and D were in garrison at Fort Apache. The Indians, living in the vicinity, for some fancied grievance jumped into the timber and rocks and opened fire on the post. The firing continued for several hours; the Indians were finally driven from their position with a loss of one killed.

Scouting parties were constantly out from the various posts during the winter and spring, more as a precautionary measure than for any apparent necessity. It had become evident, however, at the New Mexican agencies and the Chiricauhua agency in Arizona, that the Indians were preparing for depredations. They declared that the government had acted in bad faith, that no meat had been issued for four weeks, that many of their young men were away on raids for horses and mules, and it would be better for them all to go than to remain and starve.

Two white men, Rogers and Spence, owned a well-known ranch on the overland stage road at Sulphur Springs in southern Arizona. They were known to have constant intercourse with the Chiricauhuas and were believed to be trading in whiskey and other illicit supplies. Much surprise was caused, early in April, 1875, when their whilom friends killed them and ransacked the ranch. Lieutenant Austin Henely, with thirty men, went in pursuit of the Indians as soon as the murder was reported at the agency, which was located a few miles away at Fort Bowie. The Indians were overtaken in the San Pedro mountains, where they were found strongly entrenched, and in such numbers that Lieutenant Henely withdrew, with the loss of one man, as soon as he had developed their position and saw the futility of fighting with his small force.

The killing of Rogers and Spence might have been the result of a drunken brawl, but so many indications of unrest and discontent were evident that investigations were made to determine what conditions must be met. The trail of blood which blighted southern New Mexico and Arizona for ten years following this period, renders necessary a few remarks of explanation.

As the Indians living in New Mexico were practically the same as the Chiricauhua Apaches, General Hatch was ordered at once to the southern agencies to investigate. He found some conditions, concerning which his report may be profitably quoted:

"These Indians have not advanced in any manner since placed upon reservations. They plant less than when wild and seem to have devoted their energies in preparing for the warpath by theft of horses and purchase of arms and ammunition. The reservation furnishes a place of concealment for stolen property, and draws near it a disreputable class of traders. There is no discipline among these Indians; they come and go when it pleases them, raid with impunity on the neighboring settlers in small stealing parties, and make extensive raids into Mexico.

Eventually the settlers will be strong enough to resist successfully. In the meantime a sense of insecurity will pervade the community, and I believe it is economy for the government to settle the matter at once."

While General Hatch was there the Indians were greatly excited, for some of the Arizona Indians who had engaged in the massacres of Rogers and Spence, and a party of Mexicans, had arrived to stir up the other Indians. Victorio, Loco and other chiefs, openly announced their policy of making peace with Sonora and then raiding inside of the United States, and all the young men favored this arrangement. The timely arrival of troops was all that prevented a general outbreak.

While the general and his troops were on the spot, a young warrior, Lopez, with his raiding party, came in with mules run off from the Clifton copper mines, in Arizona, and openly asserted that they intended keeping what they had captured. It was learned that this was one of six raiding parties then out, one of which contained nearly forty bucks.

The troops made a bold showing and recovered

nearly all the mules, but it was apparent that the garrisons of Arizona and New Mexico had an herculean task cut out for them if they were to preserve the peace and protect the scattered ranchmen and miners without strong reinforcements.

The proximity of the Chiricauhua Reservation to Sonora made it impossible to prevent raids in Arizona, so an immediate removal of the agency to San Carlos was determined upon. The troops of the regiment were scattered over the territory but they were promptly put on the march to southeastern Arizona and rendezvoused at Forts Lowell, Grant and Bowie.

One squadron, under General James Oakes, marched from Fort Lowell to the agency at Fort Bowie; Major Compton proceeded to the eastern side of the reservation from Fort Grant, with a squadron and a company of Apache scouts; Captain Brayton, Eighth Infantry, proceeded from Fort Grant, in command of a squadron of the regiment and a company of Indian scouts, along the western side of the reservation.

Lieutenant Henely went into the mountains from Fort Bowie and assisted about two hundred friendly Chiricauhuas to the agency adjoining the post.

As the various columns began to close in around the little range, in which the tribe had always lived, many of the disaffected fled to the rocky fastnesses of the almost inaccessible mountains of northern Mexico, only a few miles away, and remained for years as a scourge to the settlers and miners along the border.

While A and E troops and a few scouts were in camp in the Chiricauhua mountains awaiting the return of D troop from scouting for trails, four Indians came to the mouth of the cañon on the way in from a raid in Sonora. The scouts discovered them, when two dashed towards the agency and were allowed to go in; the other two started on the back trail to the valley and were killed, together with one horse, before the troops could mount and reach the scene.

A round up of those who reported at the agency was made and they were sent to San Carlos about the 15th of June. For many years the numbers on this reservation had been reported at about one thousand, yet the count disclosed only three hundred and twenty present. Those who fled to Mexico did not number nearly that many, if their outgoing trails were to be taken as evidence.

Soon after the arrival of the Chiricauhuas at San Carlos Agency, the troops were sent back to their posts, and the entire country vacated by the Indians was filled with daring prospectors, who were aware of the existence of fine mines in the vicinity. Many of these hardy miners paid with their lives for the privilege of prospecting that section.

The young Indians were very resentful at the loss of their old mountain homes, and soon became so bold in their raids that another company of scouts was organized for the special purpose of guarding that portion of the border. 2d Lieutenant John A. Rucker, than whom no officer in the army was better qualified for the work before him, was assigned to the command.

On August 15th, 1876, a detachment of E troop and Indian scouts had a fight in Tonto Basin, in which eight Indians were killed and two wounded. Between January 9th, and February 5th, 1877, a detachment of E troop and Indian scouts killed eighteen Indians and captured twenty in three fights, while scouting in Tonto Basin from Fort Verde.

During December, Indians ran off some stock, and Lieutenant Rucker with a detachment of H and K troops and thirty-four scouts, took up the trail near old Camp Crittenden and followed it more than two hundred miles, to the summit of Stein's Peak range. At this point the command temporarily abandoned the pursuit, went into Fort Bowie for supplies, returned and took up the trail January 7th.

The scouts discovered the camp of the hostile raiders next day in the Leidendorf mountains. During the night the scouts and soldiers surrounded the camp, and at daylight opened fire; the hostiles took cover in the rocks and the fight continued for about two hours, when the soldiers and scouts charged and carried the position. Many of the Indians escaped; Geronimo's nephew, a boy of five or six years of age, was captured, and ten bodies of the dead remained upon the field. Forty-six horses and mules were captured, also a large quantity of blankets, calico, manta and other goods, stolen from a wagon train which had been recently jumped. About $1200.00 in Mexican silver was found in the camp.

This was the first severe chastisement the Chiricauhuas had ever received, and when it is considered that they were so well armed that ten modern breech-loaders were left on the field, all the more credit is due Lieutenant Rucker and his men. In former years the Indians had used bows and arrows to a great extent, together with old muzzle-loaders and nondescript arms; the Chiricauhuas were the first to acquire up-to-date breech-loaders, and it was not long before all the other Apaches were similarly armed.

Early in February, 1877, the Chiricauhuas ran off stock from the San Pedro valley in southern Arizona, and Lieutenant Rucker followed the trail, in snow storms of unusual severity, to the vicinity of the Warm Spring Reservation in New Mexico. The trail was abandoned at the reservation line, but information was obtained that the raiders had arrived safely at the agency with the stolen stock. Lieutenant Henely visited the Warm Spring agency, and on March 17th, telegraphed to General Kautz, the Department Commander:

"I saw Geronimo at the Warm Spring Agency yesterday; he had just returned from a raid with one hundred horses. Was very indignant because he could not draw rations for the time he was out."

About the middle of August, several parties of Indians crossed the Mexican border at various places and concentrating at a preconcerted rendezvous, proceeded to the San Carlos reservation. Lieutenant Robert Hanna started in pursuit with a cavalry detachment and company of Indian scouts, and followed from Fort Huachuca to near Fort Bowie, when he learned that the mail driver had been killed by another party, east of the post. Lieutenant Rucker, with his cavalry detachment and company of scouts, joined Lieutenant Hanna's pursuing party and the united commands followed the gradually increasing trail into a rough country, almost destitute of water. While in the Stein's Peak range the men soon exhausted their canteens and many were almost crazed before water was found. The trail turned west and led into the San Carlos reservation; Lieutenants Hanna and Rucker dropped the pursuit and reported their commands at Fort Thomas, on the edge of the reservation.

The renegades went into the camp of the Warm Springs Apaches who had been moved from New Mexico against their will and induced them to leave the reservation. A considerable number started out by Ash Creek Tanks, where a detachment from the various posts, under Lieutenant Carter, was camped with a band of friendly White Mountain Apaches under Alchise. The detachment had been for some weeks building a telegraph line across the reservation, to connect the southern posts with Fort Apache; the construction parties worked without arms and were only saved from massacre by running out of rations and moving on over the mountain towards Black river the same day that the Indians broke out. When the renegades reached the abandoned camp, they stole some of Alchise's horses, and his band pursued and fought them near the head of Ash Creek.

Captain T. C. Tupper, with his troop and the commands of Lieutenants Hanna and Rucker, were ordered in pursuit. The Indians were followed from daylight until dark each day, the pursuing troops camping on the trail wherever darkness overtook them.

On the evening of September 8th, the fleeing Indians were overtaken near the San Francisco river, in New Mexico, and a running fight took place for about ten miles, and until darkness put a stop to it. The following day the pursuit and fight continued. The renegades numbered about fifty, of whom twelve were killed and thirteen captured. The prisoners admitted that the Indians had been leaving in small parties for some time, and this was verified, on October 5th, when Chief Loco went in to Fort Wingate, New Mexico, and offered to surrender with nearly one hundred and fifty Indians, who had left San Carlos. Lieutenant Hanna's command marched more than seven hundred miles on this scout; the others a little less.

The route taken by these Indians in their flight was through such a broken and rough country that the cavalrymen were constantly on foot, leading up and down precipices almost impossible to anything but sure-footed pack mules and goats. The regiment was called upon frequently to pursue over this country in after years, and it did not improve on acquaintance.

The necessity for telegraphic communication in Arizona had become apparent before the regiment arrived in the department, and troops had begun the construction of a military line. The duty was taken up by a number of lieutenants in charge of detachments, and a really great work completed by connecting the Pacific Ocean at San Diego with the Gulf of Mexico, with lateral branches to all semi-permanent military posts. The line followed the overland mail route, which was in turn followed by the "Sunset" railroad construction parties some years later.

The magnitude of this work can only be appreciated by an examination of the map and a knowledge of the country over which the material had to be shipped. The difficulty of supplying working parties with water was, alone, enough to discourage any corporation, yet this great public improvement was accomplished without any blare of trumpets by the men of the regular army, working in such harmony in Texas, New Mexico and Arizona, that when the moment arrived for the last connection to be made on the high plains of southern New Mexico, the instruments in all the modest frontier offices acknowledged the call through several thousand miles of wire.

The completion of such a difficult piece of public work in a civilian community, would have been heralded by invitations to governors and public officials, special trains, speeches and banquets, yet the simple life of "the regular" led him to expect exactly what he got—orders to rejoin his troop and be ready to use the knowledge he had obtained to go out and repair the line whenever raiding parties or the elements caused a break. A number of men were killed in the performance of this lonely and thankless duty.

13

During the autumn of 1877, the pack-trains were much improved, and, by the addition of competent packers, it was made possible for troops to conduct sustained operations against the hostile Indians without necessity for going to a post every few days for supplies.

On November 27th, 1877, Lieutenant J. A. Rucker left Fort Bowie with detachments from C, G, H and L troops, and his company of scouts, with forty days' rations, to make a search for renegades in the Sierra Madre mountains of Mexico, from which direction most of the trails appeared to have come in the past.

When on the San Bernardino river, in Sonora, a company of Mexican soldiers was met, returning from the pursuit of Apaches who had been raiding in Chihuahua and Sonora, and who had gone north on the east side of the Guadaloupe mountains and crossed the border.

Lieutenant Rucker returned at once to the American side of the line, found and followed the trail through incessant rains, north into New Mexico, where on December 14th, three hostiles were discovered on Ralston Flat, preparing dinner and endeavoring to dry out their plunder, which was spread about near the water-hole. One Indian was killed and one badly wounded. The two hostiles returned the fire vigorously and escaped while the scouts delayed to secure the plunder, which consisted of two mules, a horse, three saddles, and merchandise of all kinds.

Lieutenant Rucker concluded that these Indians belonged to a larger party returning from a raid in New Mexico. He immediately crossed to the Las Animas mountains, to cut the trail, and found it, quite fresh and leading back to the Sierra Madres.

It was while following this trail south that the troops noticed the renegades had adopted the plan of making their camps on top of hills, which they carefully fortified. With modern arms, behind fortifications, they had become a power to be reckoned with most seriously.

The "rancheria" was discovered during the afternoon of December 17th, and the safety of the pack-train having been provided for, the command toiled forward all night, on foot, over the roughest country imaginable. The "rancheria" was surrounded as completely as possible and the attack began at daylight. The Indians fought desperately for a time, but finally dashed into the ravines and fled in all directions. They were pursued for several miles when the exhausted command was recalled. The Indians left fifteen dead upon the field. Sixty horses and mules, fifty saddles, and all their food, clothing and property were captured. The command traveled more than five hundred miles on this scout.

While Lieutenant Rucker's command was absent, Indian Agent Hart reported, December 12th, that the Chiricauhuas had jumped Ramon Sell's wagon train at Ash Springs and carried off liquors and stores of all kinds. Such troops as were available were sent out, and the detachment from Fort Bowie found the mail-driver killed and mail destroyed. This showed they were moving south towards Lieutenant Rucker's command, whose encounter with them has just been described.

On April 5th, 1878, a detachment of E troop, with Indian scouts, while scouting west of Bill Williams' Mountain, in northern Arizona, killed seven Indians and captured seven squaws and children.

During the latter part of April, Lieutenant Dravo, while scouting with a detachment of I troop, from Fort McDowell, captured seventeen Indians at Smith's Mills, near Wickenburg, Arizona.

The incessant raiding parties from Sonora, Mexico, were rapidly making a desert of southern Arizona. The mail-drivers were being constantly waylaid, and travelling, except at night, was extremely dangerous. Information was obtained that the Indians had a rendezvous in Sonora, from which the Mexicans had been unable to dislodge them.

The commanding general determined, if possible, to break up this band, and orders were issued for three companies of scouts, with selected cavalry detachments, under Lieutenants Hanna, Rucker and Carter, to concentrate from Forts Huachuca, Bowie and Apache. Lieutenants Rucker and Carter joined commands near the Chihuahua-Sonora line, but were stopped by orders issued in consequence of objections to crossing the border, filed by the Mexican commander. The treaty only admitted of crossing while on a hot trail. The mixed command withdrew through Guadaloupe Cañon and established a supply camp near the border, in the Chiricauhua Mountains, to which point Captain Madden had been ordered with his troop.

Lieutenant Henely, who had been placed in command of Lieutenant Hanna's scouts when that officer broke down, was ordered to the camp relieving Lieutenant Carter's scouts, whose time of service was about to expire. A few days after Lieutenant Henely joined the supply camp, a waterspout struck the head of the cañon and in a few minutes made a raging torrent of the hitherto little rivulet, along which the troops were camped. Both Lieutenants Heneley and Rucker mounted their horses and assisted in packing the rations, which were being rapidly submerged, to high ground.

On the last trip out of the stream, Lieutenant Rucker made a safe landing, but Lieutenant Henely's horse was knocked down by the torrent and rolling boulders. The horse got out safely, but, as Lieutenant Henely rose to the surface, he was dashed against a stump and evidently rendered insensible. Lieutenant Rucker quickly uncoiled his lariat and riding close to the bank threw it across his friend, who made no effort to catch it. Without a thought of self this noblehearted, generous fellow leaped his magnificent and willing horse off the high bank ahead of Henely, and as the animal rose to the surface endeavored to save the drowning man. The torrent was such now that no human being could strive successfully against it, and when those who had followed along the bank saw Rucker's horse reach shore without him, they realized that he, too, had been sacrificed to the fury of the waters.

Thus died together, at an untimely age, two classmates and comrades, who had given evidence of the highest order of ability in Indian warfare by success in battle, which is the only true test of the soldier. Their loss was sincerely mourned, not only by the regiment, but by all the frontier community from Kansas to Arizona.

The water subsided as rapidly as it had risen, and the bodies were found upon the ground a short distance below the camp, by the anxious watchers. Every effort at resuscitation failed and their bodies were carried by the sad and simple funeral cortege to Fort Bowie, in Apache Pass, where they were interred side by side in a cemetery, the headboards of which almost invariably bore the inscription "killed by Apaches."

Strange as it may seem, it is nevertheless a fact, that during a period of ten years, more deaths by drowning occurred amongst line officers of the army than amongst those of the navy, including the "Huron" disaster, in which nearly all on board were lost. This is probably due to the sudden and terrible nature of western floods on the one hand and the naval life-saving appliances on the other.

Lieutenant H. P. Perrine, with a detachment of B and M troops and Indian scouts, struck a party of three renegade Chiricauhuas at the Clifton Crossing of the Gila river, on September 13th, 1878, but was unable to get within range of them before discovery. Their trail was followed to New Mexico where they were overtaken, September 17th, on Bear Creek, northwest of Fort Bayard, and two were killed and four horses and one mule captured.

During this same month Major A. P. Morrow, Ninth Cavalry, was pursuing that wily chief, Victorio, in New Mexico, and Captain C. H. Campbell with Troop A joined the command and accompanied it to Mexico, where the Indians were overtaken in the Guzman Mountains, near Corralitas river. In the fight which followed one private of A troop was killed.

There was comparative peace in Arizona during 1879, owing to the active pursuit of all raiders during several years immediately preceding. From their concealment in Mexico, raiding parties continued to harass districts further east, and the regiment frequently entered New Mexico to assist troops in that department. During April, 1879, several officers of the regiment with detachments and Indian scouts went to the Mescalero Agency, east of the Rio Grande, where Generals Hatch and Grierson made an attempt to disarm the Indians who had been surreptitiously leaving the agency and joining Victorio's raiding parties, and subsequently returning to their camps with the plunder. A part of the Indians resisted and broke away, but were instantly pursued and a number killed.

During this same month General Hatch ordered a squadron of the Ninth Cavalry to concentrate in the San Andreas Mountains, to oppose Victorio, who was reported in that vicinity. Through some mistake in orders Captain Carroll reached the mountain pass one day ahead of time. He was attacked at San Andreas Springs by the Indians, who had every advantage of position and controlled the only available water. Captain Carroll fell twice wounded, and eight of his men were shot down early in the attack. The command was making a good fight under many disadvantages, but matters had reached such a critical stage that the savages had the troops completely at their mercy.

Captain C. B. McLellan, Sixth Cavalry, after a vigorous march all night, arrived on the scene with Troop L and detachments of F, G, and M, of the Sixth Cavalry, and two companies of Indian scouts, the various detachments being under Lieutenants Touey, Gatewood and Cruse. Upon approaching the pass firing was heard, but it was some time before the actual condition of affairs could be ascertained. As soon as the desperate plight of the Ninth Cavalry was discovered, Captain McLellan secured his pack trains and put every available man on the firing line. The action continued from 7.30 a. m., to 3.30 p. m., when the Indians were finally driven from the pass in the direction of the Mescalero Agency. About forty horses and mules were captured and three dead Indians were found on the field. The rugged character of the ground and the length of time the Indians held out enabled them to remove their dead and wounded.

About two hours after the Indians had been defeated, General Hatch and Major Morrow arrived separately at the pass, with their respective commands, as originally planned. The next day, after a foot scout over the mountains, General Hatch ordered Captain McLellan's command through the

"White Sands" to Tulerosa, without an experienced guide. The command got lost in the desert and was seventy-two hours without water.

Only those who have known the pangs of thirst can comprehend the suffering of men and animals wandering through such deserts as the Jornado del Muerto, where this command operated for the next two weeks. Weary and foot-sore, dragging tired and thirsty animals, all the surroundings tended to discourage and depress, yet this fine, old commander, who had penetrated this Indian country soon after the Mexican war, conducted his command throughout its arduous campaign with such skill and judgment, that, after marching more than one thousand miles, he rejoined the regiment in Arizona without the loss of a man or horse. It is the experience which such men brought to the regiment in its formative period which always enabled it to perform its full share of duty without unnecessary loss or disaster.

Victorio evidently reckoned that the presence of troops from Arizona in New Mexico had left the former country open, so he proceeded toward the San Carlos Reservation early in May, with fifty warriors and attacked peaceable Indians living on Eagle Creek, killing twelve of them. The party then proceeded towards the head of Ash Creek, on which a scouting camp was located.

Information having been received of the affair on Eagle Creek, Captain Kramer moved rapidly from the camp with the available men of D and E troops, numbering only about twenty, and a like number of Lieutenant Blocksom's Indian scouts. The scouts being on foot, the cavalry passed rapidly to the front and while hurrying along the narrow trail, the column received a volley from the hostiles concealed in a gulch, at a distance of about fifty yards. Sergeant Griffin, a magnificent specimen of the old-time cavalryman, was mortally wounded and died soon after. The troops engaged the hostiles until the scouts came up, when the Indians broke under the fire and rushed to their horses, which they had concealed near by in the timber. They were pursued about nine miles when they made a stand in a strong position. The scouts were sent around to the rear, and when the attack was pushed home, the hostiles broke again and were pursued until dark.

Captain T. C. Tupper, after a forced night march of nearly fifty miles, arrived on the scene with his troop at daylight. Soon after a wounded Mexican and the bodies of two unknown white men, prospectors, were found near the bivouac. Captain Tupper assumed command and took up the trail, which led, as straight as a deer can travel, across the same rough country he had passed over when he pursued the Warm Spring renegades two years before.

Victorio's party traveled sixty miles before they made a halt. They abandoned many worn-out horses along the trail, but upon debouching into the valley of the San Francisco river they ran into a bunch of cattle and killed eighteen or twenty, and obtained rawhides to shoe their horses. The pursuing troops took as much of the meat as they needed for immediate use. All this occurred within five miles of General Hatch's command, consisting of eight troops of cavalry and a large number of scouts.

The Indian trail became much larger by accretions from the mountains to the east, and as a fight was anticipated by General Hatch, Captain Tupper, who had joined him, continued on the trail with his command, in advance, for several days. The horses were much run down and as there did not appear to be any prospect of overtaking the Indians, the Arizona contingent was withdrawn from the pursuit and returned to the regiment, leaving the Ninth Cavalry on the trail.

Captain D. Madden, with his Troop C, had been patrolling the country from the Arizona line on the overland stage route as far east as the Rio Grande. On his way back from the river he heard of the Indian depredations in the San Francisco valley, telegraphed for and obtained authority to move north. He abandoned his wagon transportation at Silver City, and marched with two days' hard bread and such bacon, sugar and coffee as could be carried on the saddles. He found the trail on the east side of the San Francisco river on the morning of May 7th, and pursued it with much vigor.

The presence of the troops in that vicinity encouraged the settlers, who had become greatly depressed by the raids and the wide path of destruction made by the elusive savages. Captain Madden found that seventeen settlers had been murdered by the raiding parties just ahead of him. There were many fresh trails in the country, and conditions indicated that these parties were committing the acts of deviltry to cover Victorio in his San Carlos raid, which has just been described. Captain Madden ran out of supplies, and, being unable to buy more than two days' rations in the sparsely settled country, was compelled to return to his transportation, after sending word to General Hatch, whose command had arrived in the vicinity, as to the direction taken by the Indians.

The Chimehuevis, a band of Pah-Utes, living on the Colorado river, for some fancied neglect or grievance, defied the authorities at the agency during the summer. They took up a stronghold in an almost inaccessible mountain about fifty miles away. No cavalry had been kept in that vicinity during the peace of many years' standing. Lieutenant-Colonel Price was sent in command of an expedition, consisting of Troops H, I and K, of the Sixth, a troop of the First Cavalry and a battalion of the Eighth Infantry, from California.

Good management and a display of force, which cut off all hope of aid from the Pah-Utes and Shoshones, of California and Nevada, averted an Indian war which would have been attended with difficulties beyond calculation. The Grand Cañon and the multitude of smaller cañons along the Colorado river would have afforded these Indians safe places of concealment, and perhaps years would have been required to close a war, once hostilities had begun.

Throughout the department constant vigilance and active scouting were maintained, with a view to aiding the troops in New Mexico, who had their hands full with Victorio and his tireless raiders, whose success had made their destruction necessary to prevent the enforced abandonment of the whole frontier.

Troops in Texas, New Mexico and Arizona were given the task of making Victorio's further raids an impossibility, and Mexican troops were sent to the Chihuahua and Sonora frontiers to aid in the operations. Nearly all the regiment was assembled at Fort Bowie, with several companies of Indian scouts, and additional pack-trains were organized to carry sufficient rations to enable the regiment to continue in the field until the campaign could be brought to a successful termination.

While waiting for definite news from New Mexico as to Victorio's movements, resulting from the campaign being waged there, the relay driver came into camp with the sad news that the Apaches had jumped the overland stage, near Fort Cummings, New Mexico, killing the driver and passengers, including the young son of Captain D. Madden, who was then present with his troop, about to take the field. Young Madden had been in the east at college and was on his way to the regiment to spend his vacation with his family.

General Carr started with his column and covered the western flank along the New Mexican line, while the Texas and New Mexican columns pushed steadily south. The Sixth passed through the northeast corner of Sonora and then into Chihuahua, Mexico. On October 14th, Victorio was surrounded by Mexican troops, commanded by Colonel Joaquin Terrasas, in the Castillo mountains, Chihuahua, and after a desperate fight the band was almost annihilated. Victorio, sixty warriors and eighteen women and children were killed. Sixty-eight women and children were captured, and two Mexican boy captives were rescued. About thirty warriors were absent, which was a matter for regret. Nearly two hundred horses and mules and all the camp plunder were captured.

The trail of murder and rapine which marked all the movements of these Apaches, made their extermination a cause for general rejoicing throughout the Mexican border, and enabled nearly all troops of the regiment to return to their posts for recuperation and refitting.

While some chiefs have become more widely known, it was the opinion of many well-informed officers that Victorio was possessed of courage unsurpassed by that of any living Indian; that his was a master mind, superior to Cochise, Geronimo, Ju, Natches, or any other of that famous branch of Apaches which contained warriors equal to any on the continent. Victorio came nearer to forming a coalition of Apaches, Comanches and Navajos, against the whites, than any other chief, and for several years prior to his death in Mexico, at the hands of Colonel Joaquin Terrasas' command, he laid waste the country from the Pecos river, west, to the San Carlos, in Arizona, and to the south far across the Mexican border, in Chihuahua and Sonora. Troops from three departments—Missouri, Texas and Arizona—as well as those of the Mexican army, were kept constantly in the field in the effort to defeat him. Men and animals were literally broken down in merely endeavoring to neutralize his power.

During the summer of 1881, there appeared amongst the White Mountain Apaches a rising star in the guise of a Medicine Man, named Nockay det Klinne. This oracle gradually inflamed the minds of the Indians, and became so infatuated by his success that he doubtless believed the truth of his own weird dreams. So long as he confined himself to ordinary incantations there was no special cause for anxiety. In common with more civilized charlatans, however, he had gradually mulcted the faithful believers of much of their limited wealth, and it became necessary for him to make a bold stroke to conceal the falseness of his prophecies.

Considering the length of time the White Mountain Indians had been associated with the whites and their general intelligence, it is inexplicable how this fanatic imposed upon the tribe so seriously as to make large numbers of them believe that if they would rise and murder the whites, he would restore to life all their ancestors. He had been promising to raise the dead for some time, and he was growing rich through the largesse of his foolish patrons. When he announced that all the dead Apaches were risen, except that their feet were held down waiting for the whites to be driven from the Indian country, the time for interference had arrived.

It is neither expedient nor profitable to enter into a discussion of an aimless Indian policy, which permitted license to run riot on reservations until Indians grew impudent in brooding over racial wrongs, and then threw upon the small and inadequate garrisons the work of restoring order and enforcing obedience.

Fort Apache is an isolated post in the midst of the White Mountain Reservation. General E. A. Carr, the colonel of the Sixth, had been ordered there for temporary duty during the early part of the summer when there was no indication of Indian trouble. As dissatisfaction amongst the Indians became daily more apparent, its source was located and General Carr had an interview with the Medicine Man and several chiefs, in which he explained how futile would be their efforts to rise successfully against the white race. Nockay det Klinne was repeatedly summoned to report to Agent Tiffany at San Carlos, but ignored all orders and retired to his camp on Cibicu Creek, about forty miles from Fort Apache. Agent Tiffany's police having failed, he requested General Carr to arrest the Medicine Man.

Recognizing the very serious turn of affairs, General Carr telegraphed the department commander recommending that additional troops be sent at once to Fort Apache, to overawe the

Indians and prevent an outbreak, by convincing them of the folly of an uprising. Troops were not sent, but General Carr temporized with the Indians who were growing more bold and insolent day by day, hoping to impress upon the authorities the absolute necessity of reinforcements to prevent an Indian war, expensive alike in blood and treasure. Orders were ultimately issued for more troops to proceed to Fort Apache, but through some strange mischance, or ill advice, they were not allowed to proceed over the mountains from the Gila river, seventy miles away from the scene where soldierly diplomacy was arrayed against Indian fanaticism and wily cunning. The hours for parleying reached their limit when the agent made a formal demand that the military arm should be set in motion and the recalcitrant Medicine Man be brought before him dead or alive.

During the excitement of the dances inaugurated by the Indian Messiah, the craze became widespread and involved the Apaches in nearly all the camps in the White Mountain Reservation. The Indians brewed "tizwin," a frightful intoxicant made from corn, and added to their weird madness.

As soon as the department commander telegraphed the order for General Carr to comply with the agent's request, the Indians cut the line and occupied the only practicable road and mountain trails, thus completely isolating the garrison. Warning had been received that the scouts, hitherto of unblemished character for fidelity, were strongly fascinated with the uncanny doctrines of the plausible and silver-tongued Medicine Man.

Upon receipt of his orders to arrest or kill Nockay det Klinne, General Carr sent a runner to his camp with a message that no harm was intended toward him, but he must come in and report as desired by the agent. An evasive answer was received. It was learned he was to visit the camps adjacent to the post for another big dance and arrangements were made to secure him, but he grew suspicious and failed to put in an appearance.

On Monday, August 29th, General Carr paraded his little command, consisting of two troops of his regiment, D and E, with a total strength of seventy-nine men and twenty-three Indian scouts, and marched on the trail to Cibicu Creek. There was but one officer for duty with each organization. One small infantry company was left for the protection of the garrison. The command moved leisurely and camped in a deep gorge at the crossing of Carizo Creek.

Some days prior to this time it had been deemed advisable to withdraw the ammunition in the hands of the scouts. General Carr now thought that it was more judicious to have a plain talk with them and assume an air of confidence. No overt act had been committed by any of them, and in past years they had accompanied the troops on innumerable scouts, exhibiting at all times courage, untiring energy and vigilance. The object of the expedition was explained and the ammunition restored to all the scouts.

Sergeant Mose was selected to precede the command and notify the Indians that no hostile action was contemplated, and that the only purpose was to have Nockay det Klinne come to the post. Mose carried out his instructions faithfully.

Next morning the command toiled slowly up the narrow trail to the top of the cañon, and crossed the divide. Upon arriving in the valley of the Cibicu, the scouts took the trail leading along the creek, but General Carr chose the fork leading along the high open ground. While still several miles from the Medicine Man's camp, Sanchez, a well-known chief, rode out of the creek bottom, shook hands with the officers at the head of the column, and then calmly and deliberately rode down the column counting the men. He then turned his pony and galloped back to the creek which, at this point, ran in between low bluffs and hills. This was the first and only suspicious act noticed by any one.

The column marched steadily forward and turned into the bottom, crossing the stream not far from the Medicine Man's "wicky-up." Officers and men had all been cautioned to be in readiness for treachery, but the Medicine Man surrendered so readily that the warning seemed unnecessary. General Carr directed the interpreter to state plainly that Nockay det Klinne and his family would be taken to the post and no harm was intended to them, but if any attempt at rescue was made, the Medicine Man would be killed.

Lieutenant Cruse, who commanded the scouts, was directed to take charge of the prisoners with the guard, and follow in the column between D and E troops. General Carr, with his staff, then led the way across the creek by a different trail from the one used in going over. This trail led through high willows and underbrush, and it was not discovered, until too late to rectify the mistake, that Lieutenant Cruse had missed the entrance to the crossing and was going down the opposite side to the lower crossing, followed by E troop.

General Carr selected an excellent camp site and the packs were taken off, D troop horses turned out under the herd guard and the usual preparations made for camping in a country where tents were seldom used.

At this time it was observed that mounted Indians were coming up the creek from the gulches which the column had avoided, and that they were collecting around the Medicine Man's guard. When the guard crossed the creek and was about entering the limits of the camp, General Carr told Captain E. C. Hentig to quietly warn the Indians away from the camp and directed Lieutenant W. H. Carter, regimental quartermaster, to separate the scouts and put them in camp. These two officers walked only a few paces to where the Indians were. Lieutenant Carter called the scouts and directed Sergeant "Dead Shot" to put them in camp. The scouts left the other Indians, but appeared uneasy and demurred about camping because of numerous hills of large red ants, common to all parts of Arizona. The scouts arranged themselves at intervals along the crest of the "mesa" or tableland, which had been selected as a camp ground.

Captain Hentig passed a few yards beyond the scouts and called out to the Indians, to all of whom he was well known through his five years of service at Camp Apache, "Ukashe," which means "go away." As he raised his hand to motion to them, a half-witted young buck fired and gave the war cry. The long-delayed explosion took place at a moment when the men on foot had been warned not to show any signs of expecting a fight.

Captain Hentig and his orderly, who was between him and Lieutenant Carter, fell at the first volley. The dismounted men of D troop seized their arms;

the small headquarter guard, engaged in putting up a tent for General Carr, advanced on the scouts with brave Sergeant Bowman in the lead, and opened fire. At this time there were more than a hundred Indians besides the scouts in camp, and less than forty dismounted men engaged in a hand-to-hand conflict.

General Carr walked calmly towards the position just vacated by the mutinous scouts, and called firmly to the guard, "Kill the Medicine Man!" Sergeant McDonald, who was in charge of the guard, fired, wounding Nockay det Klinne through both thighs, but the sergeant was immediately shot by the scouts. The Medicine Man and his squaw endeavored to reach the scouts, the Messiah calling loudly to the Indians to fight, for if he was killed he would come to life again.

Lieutenant Carter's orderly trumpeter was going towards the guard with the saddle kit, and when General Carr called, he drew his revolver, and while the Medicine Man was yelling, this young boy thrust a pistol muzzle into his mouth and fired. The squaw was allowed to pass out of the camp chanting a weird death song in her flight.

The scouts and other Indians were promptly driven from the immediate vicinity. Lieutenant Stanton, whose troop had been at the rear of the column, was just forming line mounted, when the fight began and as the scouts drew off into the underbrush, the troop was dismounted and charged through the bottom, driving the Indians out on the other side of the creek.

Sanchez and a few followers shot the herder nearest the stream, and with wild yells, stampeded such horses as had been turned loose. The mules still had on their aparejos and remained quietly standing in the midst of all the turmoil around them until the packers were ordered by the quartermaster to take them to the bottom for protection.

There was but a moment's respite during the retreat of the Indians to the neighboring hills. The command was immediately disposed to resist the attack, which commenced as soon as the Indians had gotten to cover in their new positions.

An incident happened during the early part of this fight which well illustrates the training and discipline of the men. A detachment of D troop had been sent back with a pack mule to a gulch where some dry wood was observed as the column passed. The mule was being packed when the fight began. Instead of seeking safety in flight or waiting to see the result, the mule was abandoned, the men mounted, dashed back into the melee and shared with their comrades the chances of desperate battle.

General Carr had but three officers, Lieutenants

Stanton, Carter and Cruse, and the small size of the command required every one on the firing line. Assistant Surgeon McCreery was kept busy with the wounded, whom he attended under fire with perfect composure and courage. The loss in this fight was Captain Hentig and six men killed. That the loss was no more was due in a great measure to the coolness and courage of General Carr.

A situation better calculated to try the mettle of a command could scarcely be imagined. Having effected the object of the march,—the arrest of a notorious and mischief-making Medicine Man,—without difficulty, and with no resistance on the part of his people, the troops had set about making camp for the night, when suddenly they were fired upon, not alone by the friends of the Medicine Man, but by their own allies, the Indian scouts, who had hitherto been loyalty itself. The confusion and dismay which such an attack at such a time necessarily caused, might well have resulted in the annihilation of the entire force, and constituted a situation from which nothing but the most consummate skill and bravery could pluck safety.

When darkness settled over the field the dead were buried in a single grave, prepared inside of General Carr's tent. The burial party and a few men who could be spared from the firing line, stood about the grave with bared heads while General

Carr recited the burial service. As the last sad notes of "taps" died away, the column prepared to return to the post toward which small parties of Indians had been seen going all through the afternoon.

Before leaving the field General Carr sent Lieutenant Carter to examine the body of the Medicine Man and determine if life was extinct. Strange to say, notwithstanding his wounds, he was still alive. The recovery of this Indian, if left in the hands of his friends, would have given him a commanding influence over these superstitious people, which would have resulted in endless war. General Carr then repeated the order for his death, specifying that no more shots should be fired. Guide Burns was directed to carry out the order with the understanding that a knife was to be used. Burns, fearing failure, took an ax and crushed the forehead of the deluded fanatic, and from this time forward every person murdered by these Apaches was treated in a similar manner.

The column then started and marched all night, arriving at the post during the next afternoon. Many of the Indians had preceded the command and all night they were haranguing in the vicinity. They covered the roads and trails, and killed a number of citizens, the mail carrier and three soldiers coming in from duty at the ferry on Black river.

On the following morning, September 1st, the Indians burned some buildings in the vicinity, and in the afternoon attacked the post but were driven off. Captain Gordon was wounded during this attack while at the corner of the main parade.

There was much in the situation to produce gloomy forebodings, not for the safety of the post, but for that of the scattered settlers. There were not enough troops in Arizona to handle a general outbreak, and it could not be determined just what tribes were implicated in the revolt. The first thing necessary was to open communication. This was accomplished by sending Lieutenant Stanton, with thirty-three men, to Fort Thomas. That part of the road which was in the mountains was covered in the night, and the balance of the seventy miles was made during the following day. General Carr's command had been reported, for several days, as massacred and the papers of the entire country were filled with dire forebodings as to the results of this outbreak. The news carried by Lieutenant Stanton was the first to lift the cloud from the grief-stricken relatives and friends of the Fort Apache garrison.

Troops were hurried towards Arizona from east and west, and the available portion of the regiment was moved promptly to the reservation, in the vicinity of which the Indians in revolt were lurking. Lieutenant G. E. Overton was ordered from Fort Thomas to overtake B, C and F troops and a company of scouts which crossed the Gila, September 1st, and go to the relief of Fort Apache. Troop A crossed to go with the column but was recalled and sent to the agency at San Carlos. On September 3d the department commander became uneasy and ordered Major Biddle to join this column and halt it until enough force could be brought up to make a sure fight. He started with M troop and arrived at Black river during the evening of September 16th, but could not cross for three days on account of high water, the Indians having destroyed the ferry.

Lieutenant Overton's column reached Fort Apache and enabled General Carr to relieve the strain created by the feeling of being in a state of siege. To do this he sent out troops each day to scout the surrounding country and to bury the dead along the roads. Lieutenant Overton had some doubts about the loyalty of the scouts attached to his command, and on September 5th was given this order by General Carr:

> "After your statement of yesterday evening, the Colonel Commanding directs that you take out to-morrow part of your Indian scouts, say five. Take Lieutenant Clarke with guide and soldiers, and have the scouts carefully watched and killed if treacherous, but caution the men not to kill them unjustly. The rest will be left in camp and watched here."

Lieutenant Overton went out on the road through the cañon to Turkey Creek, and his men buried three soldiers and five civilians, who had been killed when the Indians had attacked the post, and before the people had become aware of the outbreak. The fact was developed that when the Indians cut off communication, they fortified various places along the road with a view to preventing relief from reaching Fort Apache. Overton's column, in going to the post, left the road at Black river and crossed the mesa in a direct line, avoiding the usual route.

The revolting Indians undoubtedly made their attack at Cibicu under the spur of the Medicine Man's harangue, and the excitement incident to his arrest, but they had counted for some time upon a general uprising of several thousand Apaches, as well as the Navajo nation. The failure of the other Indians to join them in revolt, left them powerless to confront all the troops marching into the country, and they withdrew into the almost inaccessible mountains surrounding their reservation.

Columns were started towards the Cibicu country from various posts, but as this region was a part of the reservation, it was necessary to draw a peace line near the agency in order to avoid any conflict with friendly Indians. When the line was announced, five days were given for the Indians to remove their families within the safety limits. When the time expired, September 21st, not only friendly Indians, but the main body of the hostiles themselves slipped in, and Sanchez and other chiefs began negotiating for surrender.

The column under General Carr proceeded first to the scene of the fight at Cibicu Creek, and found the Indians had decamped, leaving two squaws behind who were too old to travel. The bodies of the dead had been exhumed and were reburied by the troops. This column then marched, under orders, for the head of the San Carlos river, to drive in a band of Indians which had failed to come within the prescribed peace limits. After a rough march through a difficult country, the Indians were discovered located on a range of hills, and were promptly charged and sent scampering towards the agency.

This column stopped outside the peace lines, but received orders in the night to move to the vicinity of the agency and be ready to arrest the hostiles in their camp at daylight, in conjunction with two troops of the First Cavalry, under Major Sanford. The column arrived at the Indian camp, and when daylight appeared, and while waiting for Major Sanford's command, the Indians were observed stealing away—one or two at a time. General Carr gave the order to surround the camp. This was promptly done, and an interpreter sent to order all the Indians to come out and fall in. The operation resulted in the capture of forty-seven warriors. Major Sanford arrived with his command soon after, when the Indians were confined in a school building.

Major Biddle had been ordered with a column from Fort Thomas to the sub-agency, to arrest hostile Coyoteros, but the movement resulted in an outbreak of the Chiricauhuas, who had been moved to that point in 1875 and had been made desperate by their treatment since.

At this juncture General MacKenzie arrived from New Mexico with part of the Fourth Cavalry, and assumed command of field operations, relieving the department commander.

Lieutenant Overton, with A and F troops, was ordered from Fort Thomas on the Chiricauhua trail, which led straight south, on account of their knowing that all the troops were north of them. Major Sanford, with two troops of the First Cavalry in charge of the Indian prisoners, was started on the main road in the same direction. The fleeing Indians met a contractor's train near Cedar Springs, killed the teamsters and a fine young Mexican, Samaniego by name, and who had had charge of the transportation of the regiment from Santa Fé, New Mexico, to Tucson, six years before.

Lieutenant Overton, with his small command following the trail, reached Cedar Springs just as the presence of the Indians had been discovered by the two troops of the First Cavalry, escorting the Indian prisoners from Fort Thomas. Major G. B. Sanford assumed command and, detaching one troop of the First to guard the prisoners, proceeded at a trot on the trail.

After passing the pillaged wagon train, Lieutenant Overton asked permission to move ahead more rapidly, because the trail was following the main road, direct to Camp Grant, where the families of the officers and married soldiers had been left without adequate protection. Major Sanford approved the request, and the two Sixth Cavalry troops took the gallop, and a short distance beyond the pillaged wagon train, discovered the bodies of a detachment which had come out to repair the telegraph line and had just been killed. While examining to see who the dead men were, the Indians opened fire from the front and left, where they held a very strong position in the rocks and timber.

The two troops of the Sixth were dismounted and moved against the Indian position. The troop of the First moved, mounted, against the Indians' right flank, which was posted on a hill, and drove them back. The entire line pushed forward, driving the Indians toward Mount Graham, where they took up a strong position which they held until about 9 p. m., a heavy fire being kept up all the time. Captain R. F. Bernard had assumed command because of Major Sanford's illness, which compelled him to withdraw to the train. About 8 p. m., the Indians charged the left flank, but withdrew under heavy fire.

The Indians went up on the mountain and passed around the right flank in the darkness. The command was withdrawn and moved into Camp Grant, arriving after midnight. Lieutenant Blocksom joined the command about 8 p. m., with fifteen men from Camp Grant, and participated in the latter part of the engagement.

Captain Bernard marched to Willcox station next day and left there on the following morning, October 4th, 1881, to cut the trail of the still fleeing Indians. During the day the column overtook Captain Carroll and two troops of the Ninth Cavalry which had been brought by rail from New Mexico, and were then on the east side of the dragoons following the fresh trail of the Chiricauhuas, who were but a short distance ahead. The six troops took up a gallop over the rough hills, attacked the Indians and drove them to the mountains, where they took up a very strong position in the rocks near the South Pass. The troops were placed, just before dark, in a semi-circle around the mountain position.

At daylight the troops pushed up to the position and found the Indians had escaped over the mountain. The troops followed into the San Pedro Valley, passing about six miles from Tombstone, then east through Mule Pass, across Sulphur Spring Valley, thence through the southern end of the Chiricauhuas, over the plains of San Bernardino, and through the Guadaloupe Mountains into Mexico.

This pursuit was conducted through heavy rains, which caused the Indians to abandon many horses and mules, and much plunder, but as they were able to change horses, it was impossible for troops to overtake them. Four Indians were captured, one killed and a few wounded. This band reached the Sierra Madre Mountains, their old hiding place in Mexico, and lived to harass the border for many years. The escape of these Indians seemed miraculous, for, besides the troops hot on their trail, other commands were sent down on both sides of the Chiricauhua Mountains, through which the whole band passed. The Indians had been pushed so hard, and had lost so much stock, it was concluded they would not require watching for some time, so the various columns returned with a view to aiding in settling with the other tribes.

The rapidity with which reenforcements had been brought into the department, and the failure of the revolt to enlist any but a few White Mountain and

Chiricauhua adherents, resulted in the surrender of most of those engaged in the Cibicu affair, except the scouts. Three of these surrendered at San Carlos, Sergeant Dead Shot, Sergeant Dandy Jim and Corporal Skippy. Their immediate confinement and subsequent trial by court martial, made renegades of all the others. The three were tried, found guilty of mutiny, murder and desertion to the enemy in battle, and were hung at Fort Grant, Arizona, March 3d, 1882.

The movement of all the troops of the regiment in this short and sharp campaign, have not been followed. All were kept constantly active, but some did not meet the Indians in battle although their service was as arduous as that of the troops which did. The events leading up to the Cibicu fight, and subsequent operations, have been described quite minutely because of the after controversy and ridiculous charges made concerning the conduct of affairs at that time.

The year following the Cibicu outbreak, was one filled with much hard scouting. The Chiricauhuas, under Chief Loco, made one of their periodical outbreaks from the reservation in the spring, and starting for Mexico, left a trail of blood almost unprecedented. Troops at once started from all the posts, and Lieutenant G. H. Sands, with a few men from Fort Thomas, overtook the rear guard before they were well clear of the reservation and exchanged a few shots.

Many troops were on the trail, but Captain T. C. Tupper, who was sent by rail to the San Simon Valley and was joined next day by Captain W. A. Rafferty, was the successful pursuer. The two troops and two companies of scouts, all much reduced in numbers, moved out on the scattered trails, which were very confusing, and followed southeast towards the Mexican line. On April 27th the column reached a cañon on the east side of the Animas Mountains, when it became apparent the Indians were not far ahead. Guide Al. Sieber, with some selected scouts, was sent forward at dusk, followed later by the other scouts. About 8 p. m., the cavalry left the camp, leaving the pack trains on herd and with orders for the guard to keep up the fires for the usual length of time, to deceive the Indians.

The Indians were found about eight miles away, camped in a strong, natural fortification. Scouts crept in to make sure they were there, and then all the Indian scouts were sent up the mountain side above the hostiles. The cavalry led their horses by a circuitous route around the lower side of the position, with the understanding that at dawn the scouts should open the fight and the cavalry then close in from below. The plan was carried out, and as the cavalry moved nearly a mile at a charge up to and through the Indian herd, it passed over ground swept by fire from both sides. A volley was poured into Captain Rafferty's troop at close range, but the Indians fired high. Both troops were in a similarly exposed situation and had to be quickly withdrawn. A large number of Indians occupied a spur of rocks and controlled the open ground for several hundred yards.

Lieutenant Touey was sent to cut out the herd and succeeded, losing one man killed, in the dash for the animals. The fight was kept up until noon when it became apparent that the small command could not dislodge twice their numbers from one of nature's strongholds. Instead of riding the Indians down, it became a serious question as to how to withdraw. The scouts succeeded in getting around to the pack trains, and as the lines fell back, the hostiles swarmed out of the rocks and began catching up stock.

About this time it was discovered that two boxes of ammunition had been left on the ground less than six hundred yards from the Indian position. G troop was deployed and moved up again in skirmish line, when the ammunition was recovered and packed on a mule.

The command was in Mexico and now moved back toward the border, about ten miles, to water. Colonel Forsyth was met here with a number of troops of the Fourth Cavalry and Gordon's troop of the Sixth, which had been picked up on the trail. The following day the united command moved back to the scene of the previous day's fight and found the enemy had abandoned the position, leaving twenty saddles, much plunder, and even ammunition. About twenty horses had been killed, besides the herd of seventy-four captured. Twelve warriors and several squaws were killed in the fight, and eight more dead were found who had died along the trail from wounds received in the action.

The hostile Indians had started from their stronghold about dark, and early next morning, April 29th, while crossing a level plain in their flight, encountered a regiment of Mexican infantry, under Colonel Garcia, which happened, through accident, to be in that vicinity changing station. A fight to the death ensued; the Indians were at a great disadvantage, being not only exhausted by their long flight from the reservation, but further crippled by their wounded and recent loss of horses in the fight of the previous day. The Mexicans killed seventy-eight and captured about thirty squaws and children. A great many squaws were killed in the melee. About thirty or forty warriors escaped. Chief Loco's son was killed in the Tupper fight. The Mexicans lost about twenty men killed and nearly forty wounded. This recalls the fate of

Victorio's band, which, after several years of magnificent strategy, that kept twenty times its numbers employed constantly in the field, fleeing from the cordon of troops from Arizona, New Mexico and Texas gradually closing around them, sought safety across the border only to rush into the arms of Mexican troops, who avenged their long-suffering borderers by annihilating the Indians.

The extermination of Loco's band released the troops temporarily from the field and they made their way back to their respective posts by easy stages, for the animals were so much run down by constant marching without forage that many were barely able to drag themselves along the trail.

Serious trouble arose on the San Carlos Reservation early in July, resulting on the 6th in the killing of Colvig, chief of the agency scouts, and three Indian policemen. Colvig was the civilian sent with despatches to overtake General Carr's command on the trail to Cibicu Creek, and subsequently was known as Cibicu Charley. For several days it was not known whether it was an outbreak of the usual kind or merely one of the murderous affrays common on the reservation. All doubt was removed, on July 8th, when the Indians attacked McMillenville, an isolated mining village north of the reservation. The renegades were led by Nantiatish and Sanchez, and included a number of the scouts who mutinied at Cibicu creek. They made a dash across Tonto Basin in the direction of the Black Mesa, and it was rumored that they were taking the trail towards the Navajo country.

Troops were immediately ordered from Forts Apache, McDowell, Thomas and Whipple, widely separated posts, with a wilderness of cañons and rough mountains intervening. Captain A. R. Chaffee, Sixth Cavalry, struck the trail first, but the other columns were not very far behind, although they had been several days marching over extremely difficult country, guided only by occasional reports of outrages and thefts committed.

On the morning of July 17th, Captain Chaffee arrived at General's Springs, at the summit of the Black Mesa, and found the Indians had camped there the previous night. Sending a courier back and leaving a note on a bush at the spring to notify other troops, he pushed rapidly on the trail. The courier on the back trail soon encountered the column from Fort Apache, consisting of E and K troops of the Sixth, and two troops of the Third. Major Evans, who was in command, immediately detached the advanced troop of the Third, under Lieutenant Converse, to move forward rapidly as a reenforcement, in case the Indians should be overtaken before the column could arrive.

Captain Chaffee overtook the Indians about 3 p. m., and had just formed his skirmish line when the column under Major Evans arrived. Although the senior officer of all the troops in the field, Major Evans generously placed his own command at Captain Chaffee's disposal, and directed him to proceed with the attack as planned.

The Indians occupied a strong position across a deep cañon with numerous small cañons running back on the side occupied by them. The cañon was covered with a growth of heavy timber. A party of scouts was sent around to get in rear of the hostiles and the fight opened in single shots and then volleys. The reverberation from the rock walls of the cañons added to the noise of battle. The hostiles fired from behind breastworks and trees, and the troopers were compelled to fight dismounted, from cover to cover.

Captain Abbot, with a small squadron, consisting of K troop of the Sixth, Lieutenant Hodgson, and D troop of the Third, both troops much reduced by pack-train guards and horse-holders, was sent across the ravine to the left, and after a spirited movement effectually covered the right flank of the Indians. Lieutenant Converse, in leading I troop of the Third down the trail to join this movement, was seriously wounded. Captain Abbot gradually worked this flanking command to the left, driving the hostiles from their rifle-pits and connected his line with that of the scouts. Lieutenant West was sent across the cañon on the right flank with I troop. This force being unable to accomplish the object, Captain Kramer was sent across with E troop to reenforce this part of the line. Finally, about dark, after very heavy firing, Captain Abbot succeeded in joining his line to that of Captain Kramer, which crossed on the other flank, and thus hemmed the Indians in a ravine where they had sought refuge after abandoning the position about their camp.

Captain Kramer advanced on the right and drove the Indians from their rifle-pits on that flank. The camp was across and partly in a side ravine which was charged and captured by Lieutenant Cruse with E troop. The Indians now retreated to the central ravine, leaving their herd in the hands of the troops. At this time a party of Indians who had gotten out opened fire on the rear of the troops.

The conditions were now such that there was grave danger of the troops firing into one another. The voice of a chief was heard loudly giving orders to the hostiles. There were many breaks in the line, and the wounded troopers were being removed with great difficulty. Under the circumstances the lines were drawn back across the cañon, except Lieutenant Johnson and a few men who, through some oversight, were left all night on the Indians' side of the field.

Other troops arrived during the night, and next morning there were twelve cavalry troops assembled on the scene from four posts—a remarkable concentration of scouting columns all in search of the same marauders.

The scouts crossed the cañon and found the hostiles had fled, abandoning everything and leaving six prisoners in the hands of the troops and sixteen dead upon the field. A severe hail storm set in, lasting four hours, which covered the trail so completely as to prevent pursuit. The troops remained two days near the scene of the fight. Litters were made and the wounded transported by hand eight miles, back to the open country where ambulances could reach them.

The fight took place at the Big Dry Wash, a branch cañon of Chevelon's Fork of the Little Colorado river. Seventy horses, fifty saddles and much camp plunder were captured. Among the dead were two of the renegade scouts who mutinied in the Cibicu fight. Forty-two horses and mules were returned to owners, who reclaimed them as having been recently stolen. The troops lost one man killed, seven wounded and two officers of the Third Cavalry, Lieutenants Converse and Morgan, wounded. The rugged nature of this part of the Mogollon mountains prevented the hostiles from being again brought to bay, and they escaped to the various Indian camps about the reservations, where they were secreted by their kindred.

Throughout 1882 and 1883, the Chiricauhuas raided incessantly from their safe retreats in the Sierra Madre, in Mexico, and this condition of things kept the whole border country in a state of turmoil, notwithstanding many towns of considerable size had grown up around the rich mines, which had been recently discovered and developed after the removal of the Chiricauhua tribe from their old reservation on the border.

General George Crook, who had commanded the Department ten years before and to whose skill and knowledge of Indians the country owed its first taste of peace, as a result of his operations against the Apaches during 1871–'72 and '73, was again assigned to command. He made a tour through the Apache reservations in the unostentatious way which characterized everything he did. He sent for the renegade White Mountain Apaches, who had been outlaws since the Cibicu trouble, and again took them into his confidence. As a result of his tour he concluded that there was only one way to end a condition which kept the reservations perpetually in turmoil, and that was to go to the fountain source and crush the Chiricauhuas or bring them in.

During the winter he caused a large force of Indian scouts to be enlisted and had supplies prepared for extended field operations. The Indian scouts were assembled at San Bernardino Ranch, under Captain Emmet Crawford, Third Cavalry, and Lieutenant C. B. Gatewood, Sixth Cavalry. Captain A. R. Chaffee was ordered to report there also with his Troop I, this being the only force except scouts.

General Crook took command of the expedition and started across the Mexican line May 1st, 1883. The command arrived on the Bavispe river on May 12th, when Captain Crawford and Lieutenant Gatewood went ahead with the scouts and struck the hostiles on the 15th, killing nine, capturing five and wounding a number. Captain Chaffee was ordered forward to cooperate, but the fight was practically over before the troop could reach the field. The Indians subsequently sent in word that they wished to surrender. Upon doing so, the command returned slowly to the border and rejoined the supply camp at Silver Creek, June 10th, and one month later I troop returned to its post. The command had marched nine hundred miles and brought in four hundred hostile Indians who had surrendered to General Crook.

Upon the grave of this loyal, sincere, unassuming and accomplished soldier, whose body lies in honored rest at the crest of the "Distinguished Generals' Hill" in beautiful Arlington, there is a tombstone, erected by his loving comrades, upon the face of which appears in bronze a group consisting of General Crook, the officers, guides and chiefs who accompanied him on this campaign into Mexico.

During the ensuing year there was a state of comparative peace, which simply means that all the troops were not in the field all the time.

During its nine years service in Arizona—the usual tour for a cavalry regiment on that station is three years—the hardest service was the incessant detached duty. This was good training for the men, however, for it developed a large number of self-reliant and courageous frontiersmen amongst them, which immensely increased their value as soldiers.

The difficulty of keeping the regiment supplied with recruits in that far-away country, together with the necessity for many small detachments, caused the troops to take the field habitually with an average strength of less than forty men.

Not including the long journeys with Indian scout companies, escorts with public funds, mails, paymasters and other officers, the average distance marched by all the troops of the regiment for the nine years, was 6,419 miles; the greatest number of miles marched during the period was 8,514, by troop A.

CHAPTER X.

New Mexico.

Change of Station but not of Duties—Distribution of Regiment—Improving Posts—Chiricauhuas again leave Reservation in Arizona—Enter New Mexico—Pursuit—Crawford's First Expedition—Josanie's remarkable Raid—Guarding the Border during Crawford's Second Expedition—Death of Crawford—Renegades seek Conference—Surrender to General Crook—Prisoners sent to Florida—Geronimo and Natchez Stampede—Pursuit—General Miles relieves General Crook—Gatewood enters Geronimo's Camp and induces Surrender—Hardships, scouting for Apaches—Special Mention—Inaugurating New Methods of Cavalry Instruction—Skeleton Troops.

ORDERS were issued during the spring of 1883 for the regiment to exchange stations with the Fourth Cavalry in New Mexico, a very slight change considering that the regiments occupying these two stations habitually scouted over each other's territory. The troops left their Arizona stations during June, and marched to New Mexico, two troops going by rail to Colorado.

Upon arrival in New Mexico, the headquarters were located at Fort Bayard, some troops going to Forts Wingate, Stanton, and Cummings, New Mexico, and Fort Lewis, Colorado.

The regiment settled down to garrison life, building quarters, putting in water-works, and improving the posts generally, which continued until the spring of 1885, when nearly all the troops were hurried to the field in May, to head off their old enemies, the Arizona Apaches, who broke away from Fort Apache and fled towards Mexico.

The wildest and most savage element on the Arizona reservations included the Chiricauhua bands. On May 17th, 1885, without reasonable grievance, Geronimo, Nana, Mangus, Natchez and Chihuahua, with nearly forty bucks and ninety-two women and children, fled from the reservation near Fort Apache in Arizona. The outbreak was preceded by a general "tizwin" debauch. The renegades started for New Mexico, and within an hour after they left their camp at Turkey creek, two troops of the Fourth Cavalry, under Captain Smith, and Indian scouts under Lieutenants Gatewood, of the Sixth, and Davis, of the Third Cavalry, started in pursuit. Notwithstanding the promptness with which the pursuit was inaugurated and the vigor with which it was maintained, it was impossible to overtake the fleeing renegades, who traveled one hundred and twenty miles before halting for rest or food.

Immediately after the outbreak was made known, troops were put in motion from all available posts, in the effort to intercept the hostiles before reaching Mexico.

The Indians directed their course toward New Mexico and entered the Black Range, northwest of Fort Bayard, where the headquarters and four troops of the Sixth were then stationed. These troops, as well as those of the regiment from other New Mexican posts, were hurried to the field. Within a few days no less than twenty troops of cavalry were scattered through the country, yet the hostiles eluded them and crossed into Mexico on June 10th, notwithstanding the pursuers, men and animals, had been pushed to the limit of endurance. The hostiles left more than a hundred and fifty dead or abandoned horses and mules along the trail.

Captain Emmet Crawford, Third Cavalry, who had reported to General Crook at Fort Bayard, the headquarters of the Sixth Cavalry, was ordered to the border with A troop of the Sixth, and a large detachment of Indian scouts. Two small parties split off from the main body of the hostiles, and one of these struck Captain Lawton's camp and killed four men out of seven, composing the camp guard, during the absence of the troop.

Captain Crawford took up the main trail with ninety-two scouts and A troop, with which were Captain Kendall and Lieutenant Hanna. The trail was followed to the Sierra Madre, in Mexico, a distance of over five hundred miles.

Lieutenant Gatewood, Sixth Cavalry, enlisted a hundred more scouts at Fort Apache and went back to scout the Black Range and Mogollon country and then joined the expedition to Mexico.

During the pursuit of the renegades in the Mexican mountains, every known water-hole along the border was guarded by troops and small detachments of scouts. Depots for supplies and reserve camps, in the nature of a second line, were established. Heliograph stations were put in operation to communicate rapidly along the border, which was patrolled incessantly. A number of troops of cavalry were stationed near settlements far back from the border, to give protection in case any hostiles succeeded in eluding the frontier cordon.

Captain Crawford discovered a fresh trail, June 22d, 1885, leading into the Bavispe Mountains, and sent Chatto and a body of selected scouts forward to overtake and hold the hostiles until A troop and the other scouts could come up. Chatto discovered the rancheria next morning in such a position that it was impracticable to surround it, so he made the attack at once, and in a running fight of several miles, captured fifteen women and children. Five horses, some saddles, revolvers, belts and other property, taken from Captain Lawton's camp in Guadaloupe Cañon when the guard was attacked, were recovered. One Indian was killed and a number wounded. The band was under Chihuahua, whose family was captured.

All through the summer the indefatigable pursuit of the hostiles went on in Mexico. Early in November a party of eleven renegades scattered and slipped through the cordon of frontier patrols in New Mexico, a part of them only being encountered by two scouts patrolling between water-holes, one of whom was killed. Much of the preceding story has been given to show existing conditions when this small party of hostile raiders entered our borders. Their marvelous career, covering a period of a few weeks, reads like improbable romance.

As soon as they crossed the border, despatches were sent to warn all detachments and the whole country was immediately on the alert, for the raiders began their murderous career soon after crossing to the American side.

While being pursued by troops from Fort Bayard and from a camp of the Eighth Cavalry, farther east, the renegades killed a Mexican boy, on the Mimbres River, and carried off his brother, a lad of about twelve years of age. This child was taken on one of the most successful, difficult and dangerous raids ever made by Apaches and then carried as a prisoner far down into Mexico. He was subsequently rescued by troops and restored to his parents.

Pursuit was never relaxed, yet this band of dare-devils went as far as the White Mountain reservation where one of their number was killed by a friendly Indian, this being the only loss sustained by them. They then returned to New Mexico, waylaying and murdering with impartiality. They actually lay in ambush for a troop of the Eighth Cavalry scouting for them, and killed Assistant Surgeon Maddox and four men, riding at the head of the column, in Dry Creek Cañon, New Mexico.

This party of renegades, under the leadership of Josanie, a brother of Chihuahua, crossed the border early in November and passed back into Mexico before Christmas, carrying several captives with them, and leaving thirty-eight known murders to mark their bloody trail. The difficulties of the situation can scarcely be comprehended by those not familiar with the country.

This campaign of 1885 enforced upon the authorities the absolute necessity of ending these periodical outbreaks. General Crook's labors had always been regarded by him as wanting fulfillment, because many years before, when he had the situation in his grasp and the well-organized machinery ready to strike a fatal blow at the power of the Chiricauhuas, he was halted in his career by a peace commission, a species of mistaken interference which has been frequently met with because of the vacillating Indian policy which has always characterized the dealings of the Government towards these wards of the nation. Later, upon his return to Arizona, as before shown, he went into Mexico and brought about four hundred hostiles back to our border. They had not been whipped, however, and it required but little to send them scurrying back to the Sierra Madres, like a pack of coyotes.

The troops continued at their field stations, extending from El Paso westward along the border, to guard the water-holes and follow every raiding party. The Sixth and Eighth Cavalry guarded the New Mexican frontier, while the Fourth and Tenth occupied the Arizona portion. Several infantry regiments also participated in the campaign, giving protection to many isolated and exposed points. Pursuing columns were incessantly on the trail, thus giving the hostiles no opportunity to establish themselves with any degree of safety.

On the night of January 10th, Captain Crawford attacked the main camp near the Arras river, in Mexico, and captured all the stock and supplies of the hostiles. The Indians asked for a conference next morning, and in anticipation of this the command, consisting almost entirely of scouts, laid down for much needed rest and did not exercise the usual vigilance.

Before daylight the scouts, while asleep, were attacked by one hundred and fifty Mexicans. The scouts immediately jumped for cover and opened fire. It required all the exertions of Captain Crawford and his officers to stop the firing. Every effort was made to show the Mexicans the true status of affairs. Captain Crawford took an exposed position on a rock, without arms, and had an interpreter explain the situation. Suddenly, and without warning, a Mexican who had approached within about thirty yards, fired, shooting Captain Crawford through the head. The firing at once became general and was only stopped when the Mexicans had lost their commanding officer and second in command. The conduct of the Mexicans throughout this affair was reprehensible in the extreme, and filled the whole army with a feeling of bitterness.

Captain Crawford was a modest, brave and efficient soldier, a staunch friend and a typical manager of men, either white or Indian. His assassination was a crime, and the act was promptly disavowed by the Mexican government.

The hostiles again asked for a conference, and they were met by General Crook in the Cañon de las Embudos, south of the border, a day's march from San Bernardino. The Indians were very suspicious and demanded that the "Gray Fox" should pledge his word to restore them to the reservation as if no outbreak had occurred. Throughout the negotiations the Indians were kept in an excited state by a miserable wretch named Tribolet, who sold them whisky and boldly bragged about the profits of his illicit traffic. General Crook finally induced the hostiles to surrender without acceding to their demands to be returned to the reservation, and he started back at once, leaving the Indians to be escorted on their journey by officers and scouts. Geronimo and Natchez stampeded with about thirty-five followers. The remainder arrived at Fort Bowie where, on April 7th, 1886, they were put aboard a train and sent to Fort Marion, Florida. The party included Chihuahua, Josanie, the leader of the celebrated raid through New Mexico the previous autumn, and seventy-five bucks, women and children.

This was the entering wedge of the final collapse of Apache hostilities which had so long ravaged the border. Although only about twenty-five bucks were know to be still on the warpath, the troops were kept in the field and the pursuit continued relentlessly.

General Miles was assigned to command, relieving General Crook, and continued the field operations with great vigor. After being incessantly pursued and harassed for more than two thousand miles, the Indians were finally induced to come in by Lieutenant C. B. Gatewood, Sixth Cavalry, who, at the imminent risk of his life and without any assurance of a peaceable reception, rode into the hostile camp accompanied by two friendly Apaches, and demanded their surrender. He was personally well known to the hostiles through having had charge of them at Fort Apache, on the White Mountain reservation. Realizing that troops were always on their trail and that there was no hiding place to which the unerring eyes of the scouts would not lead their pursuers, they agreed to surrender. They took up the trail to Arizona, Captain Lawton, Fourth Cavalry, marching parallel with them for eleven days to Skeleton Cañon, where, on September 4th, 1886, they surrendered formally to the department commander, and with others of their tribe were sent east for confinement.

Scouting for Apaches has always been attended with more labors and difficulties than honors and successes. When the question of brevet promotions for Indian service was before the War Department, and recommendations were called for, one of the old officers of the regiment expressed officially these views:

> "Relative to the creditable and successful service against Indians in Arizona during Apache outbreaks, I am of the opinion that such service involved greater hardship, privation, endurance, more unremitting and unceasing vigilance, and more harassing difficulties of the march, and generally for longer periods of time than any service experienced by me during the Civil War, with the possible exception of the Gettysburg campaign; this, too, with the chance of irretrievable disaster, immeasurably greater, and the hope of reward infinitely less."

At the period when the Sixth entered on duty in Arizona, the Indians had very generally been put on the reservations, but small parties were always running away. General Crook had introduced Indian allies as an element in the warfare, and they were invaluable to the troops. Soon, however, it dawned upon the cavalrymen that the six-months enlistment periods had been gradually educating a large body of fine warriors to the accurate use of firearms, and that at each outbreak the Indian scouts were less willing than before to "go in" without plenty of soldiers. They were smart enough to see the marked difference between rushing at daylight on a rancheria, which contained bows and arrows and old-fashioned guns, and an attack on a well-planned camp where Winchester magazine rifles in the hands of expert marksmen peeped out from every stone and outlying breastworks guarded every practicable approach.

The command of the companies of Indian scouts usually devolved upon the young lieutenants of the regiment, and while developing self-reliance, coolness and woodcraft, the incessant exposure resulted disastrously to many of them.

Two of these young officers deserve special mention—Lieutenant John A. Rucker, whose station was always "in the field," and who, during his service with scouts followed nearly every hostile trail between the Gila river and the Sierra Madre in Mexico, within a few hours after it was made, and who finally laid down his young life in a seething mountain torrent in which no being could live a moment, in an unsuccessful effort to save the life of his friend and classmate, Henely.

The other—Lieutenant Charles B. Gatewood—who entered upon duty with the Apaches within a few months after joining the regiment. He saw much active service during the Victorio and other Apache outbreaks, taking part in several engagements in New Mexico. He was commended later by the Major-General commanding the Army, for his conduct in the surprise and defeat of Chatto and Bonito, and the rescue of five captives near the headwaters of the Bavispe river, in the Sierra Madre, Sonora, Mexico. An act which has made him known throughout the army and the country generally, and which Ned Casey probably had in mind when he was so foully murdered by the Sioux, is thus mentioned in the recent general order of the War Department commending him "for bravery in boldly and alone riding into Geronimo's camp of hostile Apache Indians in Arizona, and demanding their surrender."

Victorio and Geronimo were types of the Apache warriors who, under various local names, Chiricauhuas, Mescaleros, Coyoteros, etc., scourged the southwestern territory for nearly three centuries. Predatory, brave, cruel and rapacious, they would have been anomalies amongst Plains Indians such as Red Cloud and Spotted Tail; and Chief Joseph, the Nez Percé, appeared knightly in his warfare in comparison with the average Apache chief.

That portion of the regiment, near the reservation of the Mescaleros, was frequently called out to keep these Apaches in order, for whenever any of the other Indians went on the warpath, they could always count upon receiving encouragement and recruits from this tribe.

Those troops stationed at Fort Wingate, on the contrary, were more often called to the field to prevent the white men from encroaching upon the rights of the Navajos, Moquis, Zunis and other semi-civilized Indians located in the vicinity of the post, and some of whom occupied lands by right of inheritance, dating back before the Spanish Conquest. Some of the Spanish columns penetrated this section in their northward march, for it was here that the "Seven Cities of Cibola" were supposed to be located.

Captain H. P. Perrine, with Troops B and F, which went to Colorado when the regiment marched to New Mexico, took the field from Fort Lewis in pursuit of hostile Utes, and engaged them July 15th, 1885, at Wormington Cañon. One packer and one volunteer were killed.

There were numerous changes of stations between troops while in New Mexico, but taken as a whole—after Geronimo's band was exiled—the regiment never before had so little scouting and marching as during the period it occupied that Territory. The time was profitably employed, however, for the regiment had been so continually engaged in field operations in Arizona, that recruits were habitually sent to troop duty long before they were properly instructed, and squadron and regimental drills were known only by tradition to most of those in the regiment.

Prior to leaving Arizona, General McDowell had published orders with a view to encouraging target practice, mounted as well as on foot, and had directed that the training of the horses should be made a special feature of drills, particularly the application of the Rarey system to refractory "bronco" horses. The regiment took up the work in earnest, and the four troops on duty at regimental headquarters at Fort Bayard, soon mastered the system so thoroughly that nearly all the horses in the squadron would lie down on the line and allow the carbines to be fired over their bodies. Many photographs were taken of the drills at this time for use in illustrated papers, and it is believed that this was the first development of what afterwards became the practice throughout the cavalry arm.

During the lull in active operations against the

Indians, the troops from distant posts were ordered to simulate raids by pursuing one another. Considerable hard riding resulted from the practice, and doubtless the experience in the saddle was profitable, especially to the young officers. At all events, some of the work performed on this duty will rank creditably with the long-distance rides frequently indulged in by European officers.

The regiment, like all others, suffered a reduction through the "skeletonizing" of two troops. The men and horses were distributed amongst the other troops, and two very efficient organizations of the most expensive kind were lost to the country. There has never been but one opinion in the line of the army as to "skeletonizing" of organizations in the regular service, and that was not favorable to the idea.

CHAPTER XI.

BACK TO THE PLAINS AND THE BAD LANDS.

ORDERED TO CHANGE STATION—HURRIED DEPARTURE—INCIDENTS—EIGHT DAYS' RAILROAD JOURNEY ENDS IN BLACK HILLS—OUT-FITTED FOR WINTER CAMPAIGN—PATROLLING BAD LANDS—EFFORT TO HEAD OFF BIG FOOT'S BAND—MERRY CHRISTMAS—NEWS OF WOUNDED KNEE FIGHT—CONCENTRATION OF TROOPS—K TROOP ATTACKED ON WHITE RIVER—REGIMENT TO THE RESCUE—CLOSING IN AROUND AGENCY—INDIANS SURRENDER—GRAND REVIEW—ESCORTING BIG FOOT'S BAND—ASSIGNMENT TO STATIONS—BLIZZARDS—SERVICE IN YELLOWSTONE PARK—RUST-LER WAR—REGIMENT PRESERVING PEACE—INDIAN TROOP—DEDICATION WORLD'S FAIR—CHICAGO STRIKES—COXEY ARMY—CHANGE OF STATIONS—NEW DUTIES—CHARACTER OF ARMY INSTRUCTION—MODERN EXERCISES—INDIAN FIGHTS—DISAPPEAR-ANCE OF THE FRONTIER.

DURING 1890 the Plains Indians caught the Messiah craze, and Ghost Dances were taken up by many tribes from the Indian Territory north to the Canadian border. The regiment heard of all these things, as from a far away land, little dreaming that the danger would grow to such proportions as to demand a call for troops from distant stations. On November 23rd, a telegraphic order came, as from a clear sky, for the regiment to prepare at once for a change of station and to take the field in Dakota.

Cars could not be procured readily, for the posts occupied by the regiment were not in the vicinity of railroad centers. Travel rations were not to be had, so that bread was baked and beef cooked for the journey, but the latter spoiled and had to be thrown away en route, and the food for the men provided out of their own troop funds. The final notice to move arrived after midnight, December 1st, and all through the night the wagons were rumbling to the station and everything was ready to load before the cars arrived. The sections pulled out during the day, and after a long journey through New Mexico, Colorado, Kansas and Nebraska, the regiment unloaded at Rapid City, South Dakota, on the eastern slope of the Black Hills, on December 9th.

During the journey one of the lieutenants was married, a child was born on the train to the wife of one of the sergeants, and another sergeant, who had been brutally attacked near the railroad station at La Junta, was left at Fort Logan, Colorado, and died in the hospital before the regiment reached its destination.

The regiment found supplies awaiting at Rapid City, and also a telegram saying the command was to be prepared for field service as soon as possible. One squadron started next day and the others followed as fast as the men could be equipped with winter clothing. Only those who have experienced the rigors of winter on the northern plains and in the Bad Lands of Dakota, can appreciate the necessity of guarding well against disaster. To enable troops to remain in the field and accomplish their work in midwinter, special clothing becomes a prime necessity. To meet these conditions the men were supplied with fur caps and gloves, blanket-lined canvas overcoats, heavy German oversocks of felt or wool, and Arctic overshoes. The horses were provided with blanket-lined canvas covers and calked shoes.

To the regiment was assigned the duty of patrolling the Cheyenne River country, but the necessary transportation had been delayed and it was several days before the supplies and the pack and wagon trains were ready for the field. The squadrons were at first distributed along the Cheyenne river, but, under instructions from General Brooke, were assembled to meet a threatened attack from the large hostile village to the south, and about which a number of regiments were drawing closer and closer a cordon calculated to bring on battle or cause a surrender.

When Sitting Bull was killed and some of his followers made their way to Big Foot's village, near the Belle Fourche, about forty miles to the northeast, Lieutenant-Colonel E. V. Sumner was ordered to

TROOP PICKET LINE, PINE RIDGE CAMPAIGN.

take this band of Indians to Fort Meade, but after pretending to acquiesce in the arrangement they decamped during the night. About 10 a. m., December 24th, a courier arrived from the Eighth Cavalry camp with a message from Colonel Sumner, saying Big Foot was moving south on the Deep Fork trail and would probably pass the head of Bull Creek in the Bad Lands. General Carr had been sending his troop commanders in all directions scouting and familiarizing themselves with the trails and it so happened that F troop had returned from the Bull Creek pass the night previous, up to which time there were no signs of Indians in that country.

General Carr, however, ordered "boots and saddles" sounded, and in half an hour was forcing a crossing of the Cheyenne through floating ice with four troops of cavalry and two Hotchkiss guns. Nearly all the officers and men hurried off without rations or blankets. The column moved rapidly, examining all the trails and reached the head of Sage Creek before dark, when pickets were sent to watch the pass toward which Big Foot was supposed to be working his way. Two more troops which were absent from camp when the column started joined during the night with several guides, one of whom was sent to warn Major Adam who had a squadron on White river patrolling to prevent parties of Indians from passing out into the Bad Lands.

The night, Christmas Eve, was very cold and the alkaline pools in the vicinity were frozen solid. Those who had brought any food divided with the others as far as possible, but Christmas morning dawned upon a lot of half-frozen, uncomfortable men who had spent a cheerless night, alternately heaping wood on the fires and then trying to sleep on saddle blankets.

Christmas morning, a detachment was sent up on "The Pinnacle," a high point of wall in the Bad Lands, from which the country could be seen for many miles. The command examined the valley of Bull Creek and made certain that Big Foot's band had not passed on that side of the range. The regiment returned to its camp on the Cheyenne, arriving after dark and having marched more than seventy miles, practically without food for men or horses. There was no complaint, however, for every one thought it would be General Carr's luck to overhaul these Indians, and when the officers and men stood shivering through the night, many were heard to say good-naturedly that it served them right for they ought to have known enough to put some crackers and bacon in their saddle-pockets when such an alarm for service was sounded.

On the night of December 28th, information was received that Major Whitside had captured Big Foot's band, and before morning orders came to

GENERAL CARR RECEIVING REPORT FROM A SCOUT, PINE RIDGE CAMPAIGN.

leave two troops to continue scouting the Bad Lands and for the rest of the command to move over the divide to the mouth of Wounded Knee Creek. F and I troops, under Major Tupper, were detached to scout to the north of the big village to determine if any Indians were passing out.

During the 29th, word was flashed over the heliograph line, which had been established by Lieutenant E. E. Dravo, and who had previously had charge of similar work in the Department of Arizona, to the effect that Big Foot's band had fought the Seventh Cavalry with all the dire results now so well known. The detached troops were immediately ordered to concentrate at Wounded Knee Creek, which was done by forced marches.

On the afternoon of January 1st, the pickets reported that they could hear firing several miles away on White River. Troop K, of the Third Squadron had not yet joined, and suspecting that the Indians had attacked it, "boots and saddles" was sounded and Major Tupper with his two remaining troops, F and I, proceeded at a gallop through the snow, guided only by the sound of the firing. Arriving on the bluffs overlooking White River, Troop K, under Captain Kerr, was seen with the wagon train corraled, and the attacking Indians in full view. Although the horses were blown with their run of four or five miles in the snow, the column pushed rapidly across the half-frozen river and formed line of skirmishers between K troop and the Indians, who, notwithstanding their taunting cries of "come on," gave away all along their line, and retreated in the direction of the main village as soon as the line advanced on them.

One party of three Indians, which had crawled up close to K troop, was cut off, but by abandoning their ponies they managed to creep away in a gulch between the lines and escaped into the bluffs. They were greeted with many shots as they emerged from the river bottom, one being already badly wounded and supported by his comrades. They were subsequently found and killed by Indian scouts.

The other troops directed to take part in this affair arrived, under General Carr, so promptly on the flank of the Indians that their escape would have been a very difficult matter if they had made a stand for a few minutes. The result of this attack was particularly gratifying because the Indians were seeking revenge for their losses at the hands of the Seventh Cavalry, and found the Sixth so fully prepared to give it to them, that they returned to the hostile village and acknowledged defeat and a loss of nine warriors.

The regiment continued to guard the Bad Lands flank of the Pine Ridge reservation, being out every day in very cold weather. The valleys of Wounded

Knee, and other neighboring streams, were part of the Pine Ridge reservation and contained many Indian ranches. A number of hay-stacks were located within a few miles of camp, and there being no grazing, the hay was seized for the horses and subsequently paid for as fast as the owners could be determined. Many of the Sioux ranches had been looted by Cheyennes before the troops arrived.

On January 14th, orders were received to close in and the regiment went into camp on Wolf Creek, near the beef corral, in sight of the agency. The Indians finally made up their minds to a complete surrender, and after they moved in from their fortified stronghold, the regiments which had concentrated at the agency, were encamped in a single line several miles long.

On January 24th they were assembled for a grand review by General Miles. The cavalry brigade, consisting of the Sixth, Seventh and Ninth, and a separate squadron composed of troops of several regiments, was commanded by General Carr. The ground was already covered with snow, and the review took place in a light snow-storm. No such body of troops had been brought together since the Civil War, and there can be little doubt that the sight of these well-equipped and seasoned soldiers, with truly every button and cartridge in place, made a lasting impression on the recent hostiles, for they have never given any trouble since.

The other cavalry regiments struck their tents and left the Sixth camped for several weeks on the cold, bleak prairie in deep snow, awaiting arrangements for disposing of some antagonistic elements amongst the Indians on the reservation.

The bitterness between the Cheyennes and Sioux caused the former to be moved to the Tongue River country. The remnant of Big Foot's band, which had been almost annihilated by the Seventh Cavalry, was sent to the Agency on the Missouri River, escorted by Lieutenant H. G. Gallagher and a detachment from the Sixth Cavalry. The weather was unusually severe, and the Indians—many of them women and small children—suffered intensely. Some of the soldiers actually removed their overcoats and wrapped the freezing children up in them to save their lives. It was only by superhuman exertions on the part of the detachment that this broken-hearted remnant of a once mighty band was safely delivered to their kindred.

The headquarters and Troops A, F, G, E and K were now assigned to station at Fort Niobrara, Nebraska, on the southern boundary of the Rosebud Indian reservation, where the Brule band of Sioux had been located some years before, while under that justly celebrated chief, Spotted Tail. Troops C, H and D were assigned to Fort McKinney, Wyoming, and Troop I to duty in the Yellowstone Park. Later on Troop B was relieved from duty in the east, at Washington, D. C., and ordered to Fort Washakie, Wyoming. The four stations occupied were as much out of touch with one another as if they had been on opposite sides of the continent.

The troops assigned to Fort McKinney encountered a succession of violent storms, and the suffering was intense, notwithstanding the fact that the command had been undergoing acclimatization in a winter campaign for many weeks. The troop assigned to the Yellowstone Park simply lived in mountains of snow until late the following summer. The column which marched to Fort Niobrara encountered a severe blizzard on the open prairie which would have inevitably left a trail of death but for the winter equipment which had been provided for men and horses.

These blizzards are simply indescribable, and only those who have experienced them can understand how many years of misery it is possible to concentrate in a few days. After the icy wind and snowstorm had died away, there was nothing left but to take turns in plunging through the enormous drifts, which filled every gulch. Under the intelligent care which had been bestowed upon them, nearly all the horses had come through the campaign in fine condition and were fit for any ordinary undertaking. Breaking trail in the deep snow, however, proved a hard task, and it was necessary to let the leaders fall back after a few yards, and bring up fresh horses to plunge into the drifts.

When the bridge was reached, over which the road passes before entering the post on the plateau above, a soldier was found frozen to death. He had been out with the mail, and, returning in the storm, had missed the bridge by a few yards; disheartened, he had evidently gotten on his hands and knees to crawl and was found in that position, dead.

Arriving in the post, the buildings could scarcely be discerned, for they were blockaded with snowdrifts up to the roofs. It was several hours before the drifts were cleared away so that the stable doors could be opened. To troops coming from many years of service in Arizona and New Mexico, this was anything but inviting. Similar experiences were encountered by the other columns.

The service in Yellowstone Park proved a unique experience for the guard there, which was ultimately composed of D and I troops. During the summer season each year, when the Park was filled with tourists, the utmost vigilance was required to prevent careless or malicious destruction, especially from camp-fires. The game was seldom interfered with by respectable people, but there is something in the human kind that makes men look with moderation upon law-breakers who shoot out of season or on game preserves.

Skin-hunters poached within the Park limits during the winter when the animals were frequently rendered comparatively helpless by the great depth of snow. To guard against their nefarious operations, it was necessary to have small detachments located in various isolated cabins, often for periods of several months' duration without relief. Horses were useless during the winter, and in order to perform the constant patrol duty, it was necessary for the soldiers to go about on snow shoes or Norwegian skis. Many of them became expert in the use of the skis, and this made it possible to ferret out an occasional villain who, in a few weeks, would destroy more game than could be replaced in years. Owing to the curious freaks of nature in the Park, it often happened that the ski patrols would have to remove their foot coverings and wade in midwinter through warm streams which flow from the hot-springs. While the service was active and interesting in summer, the long periods of semi-hibernation proved monotonous to those who were compelled to remain through the winter season.

The troop at Fort Washakie, on the Shoshone reservation, was constantly called upon to protect the Indians from encroachments on the part of the cattle men of the surrounding country. The Fort McKinney squadron, on the contrary, was called out to keep the cattle men from killing one another. The trouble was known as the "Rustler War," and was brought about by large cattle-owners organizing an armed party to penetrate the Big Horn and Powder River country, for the purpose of killing a considerable number of cattle-thieves who were living off the large herds. The importation into the state, of Texans and others to take part in this raid, aroused all the small cattle-owners and many joined with the Rustlers and attacked the raiders.

The Sixth Cavalry squadron was hurried to the scene of battle, rescued the raiders and escorted them to Fort McKinney. The Rustlers were indignant at the interference and endeavored to burn down the buildings where the prisoners were confined under guard. The post was in serious danger of being entirely destroyed, when it was determined to blow up a portion to save the remainder. Lieutenant Gatewood, and one or two others who volunteered for the work, entered one of the burning structures to place cans of powder to insure quick destruction. Some burning rafters parted, fell and prematurely exploded a can of powder. Lieutenant Gatewood was blown violently against the side of the building and so badly crippled that he was compelled to retire from active duty while yet a young lieutenant and with a rare record of successful Indian service.

The raiders were subsequently sent under guard to Fort Russell, near Cheyenne, Wyoming, and turned over to the civil authorities. During the spring it became necessary to order the regiment out to prevent further trouble in Wyoming, and the troops from Nebraska established Camp Elkins on La Prêle Creek, near old Fort Fetterman. The troops were sent in turn through the neighboring country, but there was no call for interference beyond warning all parties that no private "round ups" would be allowed. The general round up then followed along the Platte river from day to day, involving about 150,000 head of cattle.

Troop L, which consisted of full-blooded Brule Sioux Indians of Spotted Tail's old band, accompanied the regiment on this service and performed full duty the same as other troops. This troop was the first regularly organized and enlisted body of Indian soldiers brought into service under the experiment which, after a fair trial, was pronounced unsuccessful. Prior to that time, Indians had been constantly utilized as enlisted scouts, but they were not required to wear uniforms or cut off their hair.

These Indians were enlisted with considerable care and trained by officers of the regiment as a cavalry troop until they were able to drill with the other troops in both squadron and regimental drills. But as time passed, the novelty of the life wore off, and it became apparent that the Indian, as a regular soldier, was not equal to the white man, and that he could be utilized to much greater advantage under the old system as a scout. The troop was allowed to become a "skeleton" again by the discharge of the Indians who returned to their old life on the reservation.

During the autumn of 1892 the troops were all returned to their posts and two of them, F and G, were selected to represent the regiment at the dedication of the World's Fair Building at Chicago. The two troops were filled to the maximum of men and horses, one with iron grays and the other blood bays, all well sized, and, together with the troops from other regiments, made a creditable representation of the regular cavalry. The gray troop had the honor of heading the Grand Review and of leading the column of regular and State troops to and around the grounds to the Manufacturers' Building, where the dedicatory services were held in the presence of the largest audience ever assembled under cover in any country. Upon conclusion of the ceremonies, the troops returned to their station in Nebraska and went into quarters for the winter.

The regiment continued at the stations occupied, performing ordinary garrison duty until September, 1894, except Troop F, which was ordered in April, 1893, to the Infantry and Cavalry School at Fort Leavenworth, the garrison of which was then composed of organizations selected from different regiments, aggregating a squadron of cavalry and a regiment of infantry.

During the summer of 1894 a part of the regiment was sent to Chicago during the prevalence of the great railroad strikes, and subsequently encamped at Fort Sheridan, waiting for the turbulent element to adjust itself to normal conditions. The Coxey Army invaded the Missouri River valley in such a way as to be regarded as a menace to the public, and many were arrested and put in camp on the Fort Leavenworth reservation. They were brought before the United States Court and, to their amazement, were convicted and sentenced to imprisonment. When the fact was announced, they began to escape from the deputy marshals and would not move to the place of confinement designated. On the call of the marshal for assistance, F troop of the Sixth, was sent rapidly along the river bank cutting off escape, and surrounding the so-called army. The prisoners were then marched to the court-house and turned over to the authorities.

During the autumn of 1894 the regiment, except the two troops in Yellowstone Park, was ordered to change station, one squadron with the head-quarters being assigned to Fort Myer, Virginia, opposite Washington, and three additional troops to Fort Leavenworth, Kansas, completing, with the troop already there, another squadron.

These squadrons, for the first time in their history, found themselves provided with a fine riding hall each for winter instruction. The troops showed their appreciation of the opportunities afforded, after their many years of frontier service at undesirable stations, by going to work systematically to perfect the organizations in all details pertaining to them.

It was fitting that this regiment, which had begun the new order of horse training and cavalry instruction ten years before, should now be given an opportunity to show its degree of excellence. There were a few troops scattered through various regiments which probably equaled those of the Sixth, but it can be fairly stated, without disparagement of comrades, that there never existed in the American cavalry, regular or volunteer, two squadrons more thoroughly and uniformly instructed in all drills, from the individual training of the trooper and horse up to and including all the duties of the squadron in garrison and field, than were those of the Sixth between 1894 and 1898, when they took the field for the war with Spain.

It was a rare and unknown experience for this regiment to be so long in garrison, but now, like others, it found practice marches necessary to teach the younger officers and men the details of camp life and the practical duties of the march. Continually did they devote themselves to outpost, reconnoissance and similar duties, and to all details of offensive and defensive warfare, so far as the size of the organizations would admit. The list of daily duties for the guidance of organizations at any of the large posts of the regular army during this period looks appalling, but it is admitted by all thoughtful men that this training made the men individually athletes, and the army as a whole the fittest body of men that ever entered a campaign.

For some years officers had been required to devote much of their time to the Lyceum, and many of the essays prepared were most creditable alike to the individuals and to the whole army. The study and discussion of campaigns, which hold important places on the pages of history, by reason of their momentous effect on the fate of nations, could only result beneficially. Of fully as much, if not greater value, however, was the planning of field exercises, followed by their practical execution by the various garrisons, and terminating with decisions of selected umpires.

Few people understood the work being so quietly carried on by the army, although the high standard of instruction was occasionally illustrated by selected organizations detailed at horse-shows, fairs, or other public exhibitions. The following official programme for seven months' instruction at one of the posts garrisoned by the regiment, will give some idea of the labor involved in preparing a command for modern war:

Fort Leavenworth, Kansas, April 2d, 1896.

Circular 1.

Programme of drills and exercises for the period from April 1st to October 31st.

Drill for Infantry: Schools of the soldier, of the company, of the battalion; evolutions of the regiment; extended order for the squad, platoon, company, battalion and regiment.

Drill for Cavalry: Schools of the soldier, trooper, troop and squadron; extended order for the squad, troop and squadron.

Calisthenics, running, jumping, escalade of walls.
First aid to the injured.
Litter-drill.
Signaling.
Instruction of field musicians.
Estimating distances.
Target practice.
Castrametation.

Non-commissioned officers' patrols, reports and rough sketching.
Officers' patrols, reports and itineraries.
Reconnoissance.
Advance and rear guards.
Outposts, illustrating the several systems.
Practical problems in minor tactics by each arm separately.
Practical problems in minor tactics with the arms combined.
Practical problems with opposing forces.
Hasty entrenchments.
Practice marches.
Marches of concentration.

Company and troop commanders will follow the course of instruction as nearly as possible in the succession mentioned as far as it pertains to their separate organizations, their records to show the completion of each portion, also its resumption at subsequent periods when they deem this necessary to perfect the course.

Field officers are requested to keep similar record as pertaining to squadron, battalion and regiment. It is desired that they shall give every latitude to company and troop commanders as to apportionment of time consistent with what is necessary for squadron, battalion and regiment both in drill regulations and in minor tactics and kindred subjects.

MEMORANDUM FOR PARADES.

Mondays . . . . . 1st Battalion, 20th Infantry.
Wednesdays . . . . 2nd Battalion, 20th Infantry.
Thursdays . . . . . Cavalry Squadron.
Fridays . . . . . . Regimental, 20th Infantry.

By order of Colonel HAWKINS:

BENJ. ALVORD,
1st Lieutenant and Adjutant.

At least one day of each week was devoted to practical field work, usually the solution of a previously arranged problem. The following is a fair sample of this character of instruction and is one of many exercises arranged for and participated in by the regiment during recent years:

Field Exercise.

A force (Blue) is stationed at Weston.

A force (Brown) is posted five miles south of Leavenworth near the river.

The commander at Weston has ascertained by reconnoissance that none of the enemy is north of Leavenworth. He sends a train of 200 six-mule wagons to forage in Salt Creek valley under escort of 4 companies of infantry and 2 troops of cavalry. He also sends additional force to threaten Burlington bridge opposite Leavenworth.

The commander of the escort, knowing that the enemy is all south of Leavenworth, detaches only one platoon of cavalry to accompany the train to Salt Creek. With the remainder of his force he determines to take position for securing line of retreat across the Fort Leavenworth bridge.

The commander of Brown force learns from a farmer that a large train is foraging in Salt Creek valley. He sends 4 companies of infantry and 2 troops of cavalry to capture it. He also sends additional force to protect Burlington bridge.

To limit the field, the country west of Merritt Lake will be regarded as impassable.

Rules for field exercises heretofore published will be observed.

Written report of operations to be made within two days by the commander of the Blue and the commander of the Brown force engaged.

Such exercises could not fail to inure to the benefit of officers and men, not only by training them in the marked difference between armory and parade-ground drills in close order and the actual use of troops on varied ground, but also by accustoming them to marches and open-air work with full field equipment. So long as the west was all frontier, enterprising troops had no lack of exercise, for when not scouting after Indians there was much opportunity for hunting or fishing, both of which were officially encouraged.

The following list of Indian fights in which the regiment participated, taken from the official records of the War Department, shows that those were busy days on the old frontier which has now so completely passed away:

Date.	Place.	Troops Engaged.
July 21st, 1867	Buffalo Springs, Texas	Detachs. A, E.
August 30th, 1867	Near Fort Belknap, Texas	F.
October 17th, 1867	Deep Creek, Texas	Detachs. F, I, K, L.
March 6th, 1868	Paint Creek, Texas	F, I, K.
May 30th, 1870	Holliday Creek, Texas	Detachs. C, D.
July 12th, 1870	Near North Fork of Little Wichita River, Texas	Detachs. A,C,D,H,K,L.
October 5th, 1870	Near Little Wichita River, Texas	Detach. M.
October 6th, 1870	Near Little Wichita River, Texas	Detach. G.
November 14th, 1870	Scout from Fort Richardson, Texas.	Detach. I.
May 22d, 1872	Between Forts Dodge, Kansas, and Supply, Ind. Ter.	Detach. E.
April 11th, 1874	Bull Bear Creek, Ind. Ter.	Detach. G.
June 19th, 1874	Buffalo Creek, Ind. Ter.	Detach. K.
June 21st, 1874	Buffalo Creek, Ind. Ter.	Detach. G.
June 24th, 1874	Bear Creek Redoubt, Kansas	Detach. G.
August 19th, 1874	Adobe Walls, Texas	Detach.
August 20th, 1874	Chicken Creek, Texas	Detach.
August 30th, 1874	Mulberry Creek, Texas	A, D, F, G, H, I, L, M.
September 9th, 1874	Dry Fork of Wichita River, Texas.	Detachs. H, I.
September 9th, 1874	Sweetwater Creek, Texas	Detach. I.
September 9th to 12th, 1874.	Near Canadian River, Texas	Detach. I.

Date.	Place.	Troops Engaged.
September 11th to 12th, 1874	Near Wichita River, Texas	Detach. H.
September 11th to 12th, 1874	McLellan Creek, Texas	Detachs. I, M.
October 17th, 1874	Near Washita River, Ind. Ter.	I.
Oct. 21st to Nov. 8th, 1874	Expedition from Fort Sill, Ind. Ter.	D.
November 8th, 1874	Near McLellan Creek, Texas	Detach. D.
November 10th, 1874	Near Fort Dodge, Kansas	Detach. B.
December 2d, 1874	Gageby Creek, Texas	Detach. I.
April 6th, 1875	Near Cheyenne Agency, Ind. Ter.	M.
April 23d, 1875	North Fork, Sappa Creek, Kansas	Detach. H.
January 9th, 1876	Camp Apache, Arizona	A and D.
April 10th, 1876	San José Mountains, Arizona	Detach. H.
August 15th, 1876	Red Rock Country, Arizona	Detach. E.
October 4th, 1876	Tonto Basin, Arizona	Detach. E.
Jan. 9th to Feb. 5th, 1877	Scout in Tonto Basin, Arizona	Detach. E.
January 9th, 1877	Leidendorf Mountains, New Mexico	Detachs. H, L.
May 29th, 1877	Near Camp Bowie, Arizona	H, L.
August 29th, 1877	Near Black Rock, Arizona	Detach. F.
September 8th to 10th, 1877	Near San Francisco River, and Mogollon Mountains, New Mexico	Detachs. B, M.
December 13th, 1877	Ralston Flat, New Mexico	Detachs. C, G, H, L.
December 18th, 1877	Las Animas Mountains, New Mex.	Detachs. C, G, H, L.
January 7th, 1878	Near Tonto Creek, Arizona	Detach. A.
April 5th, 1878	Mogollon Mountains, Arizona	Detach. A.
May 20th, 1878	Smith's Mills, Arizona	Detach. I.
Sept. 29th to Oct. 1st, 1879	Cuchillo Negro River, New Mexico	Detach. A.
October 27th. 1879	San Guzman Mountains, Mexico	Detach. A.
April 7th, 1880	San Andreas Mountains, New Mex.	Detachs. D, E.
April 9th, 1880	San Andreas Springs, New Mexico	L.
May 7th, 1880	Ash Creek Valley, Arizona	Detach. E.
August 30th, 1881	Cibicu Creek, Arizona	D, E.
August 31st, 1881	Near Fort Apache, Arizona	Detach. D.
September 1st, 1881	Fort Apache, Arizona	D, E.
September 30th, 1881	San Carlos, Arizona	A, B, C, E.
October 2d, 1881	Cedar Springs, Arizona	A, F.
October 4th, 1881	South Pass of Dragoon Mountains, Arizona	A, F.
April 20th, 1882	Near Fort Thomas, Arizona	B.
April 28th, 1882	Hatchet Mountains, New Mexico	G, M.
June 1st, 1882	Near Cloverdale, New Mexico	A.
July 17th, 1882	Big Dry Wash, Arizona	E, I, K.
July 15th, 1884	Worthington Cañon, Arizona	B, F.
November 8th, 1885	Florida Mountains, New Mexico	Detach. A.
January 1st, 1891	Mouth of Little Grass Creek, South Dakota	F, I, K.

Those who have campaigned against Indians know that for every fight there were numberless scouts without result, other than to prevent raiding bands from remaining in the vicinity of settlements. In fact, much scouting and marching was done simply to let Indians and settlers know that troops were on the alert, and familiarizing themselves with the country.

With the cessation of Indian hostilities, which had really ceased to be a daily factor in frontier life after the Pine Ridge campaign, ending in 1891, many isolated stations were abandoned and regiments were concentrated as much as possible with a view to enabling all to perfect themselves in the new order of things. Target practice had, for a few years, been forced to the front to the exclusion of other instruction, but good judgment prevailed at last and it became an integral part of the whole, of recognized value, but not the only criterion of efficiency.

It was hard for the army to realize that the days of Indian campaigning had really ended. Year after year various regiments had been called to the field, sometimes under tropical suns, and again in the land of the blizzard, where the icy winds made life miserable alike to pursuer and pursued. With each recurring surrender the Indians had been gently restored to the tender mercies of the agent and his harpies, only to find their grievances multiplied. But as years wore on, and the settlers with their wire fences closed in slowly, but surely, around the reservations, the light broke upon the Indians that the days of the wild, free life of the Golden West had gone glimmering in the dead past. The march of civilization had swept away the old life and left the remnants of once proud tribes stranded as driftwood along the shores of progress.

Encountering only the worst elements, too often the mere outcasts of society, the poor warriors, shorn of the power wielded by their ancestors, turned restlessly for some light on their future to those with whom they had battled, and at whose hands they had often suffered defeat. Army officers were again installed as Indian agents and gradually laid the foundations of lasting peace by showing the Indians the utter futility of contending against inevitable fate.

CHAPTER XII.

SANTIAGO.

REGULARS TO THE FRONT—CHICKAMAUGA PARK—EXPERIENCE IN CAMP—ON TO TAMPA—JOIN FIFTH CORPS—TROOP H DETACHED—PROVOST GUARD—EMBARKS FOR PORTO RICO—AGROUND OFF PONCE—DISEMBARK—ABOUT TO ENGAGE ENEMY—NOTICE OF PEACE—RETURN HOME—CAVALRY DIVISION EMBARKS AT TAMPA—HORSES LEFT BEHIND—ARRIVAL OFF SANTIAGO—DISEMBARKATION—MARCH TO SEVILLA—EL POSO—JULY 1ST—ORDERED AS ADVANCE OF DIVISION—MOVES ON SAN JUAN HILL—ENEMY OPENS FIRE—THE ADVANCE OF SECOND SQUADRON—FIRST SQUADRON—BALLOON—COMPLETION OF DEPLOYMENT—DIVISION MOVES TO ASSAULT—ATTACK DIFFERENT PARTS LINE—MINGLING OF REGIMENTS—SUCCESS OF ATTACK—ENTRENCHING—SUPPORT BATTERIES JULY 2D—SIEGE—SURRENDER—MOUNTAIN-CAMP—SICKNESS—EMBARK FOR MONTAUK POINT—LOSSES—INTEMPERATE CRITICISM—RESULTS—BACK TO FRONTIER—THE END.

GRANT proclaimed but the reflex action of the long continued war strain when, at Appomattox thirty-five years ago, he said, "Let us have peace." The nation had learned the bitter cost of war in empty hearthstones and a burden of debt, and it seemed as if nothing but the imperiled liberties of the people could ever again drag the country to war. The tribulations of the neighboring Isle of Cuba and of the republics of Central and South America, sometimes produced war clouds of darkest hue, but it remained for an infamous wrong to arouse the nation's anger.

As the sound of the guns which bombarded Fort Sumter in 1861 echoed in every hamlet of the North, so the explosion which sunk the "Maine" in Havana harbor on that fateful night in February, shook the fabric of Spain's whole colonial system and sent a thrill of horror to every fireside of the civilized world. Diplomacy could delay, but was powerless to stem the tide of public sentiment, and when the Administration yielded to popular demand, there was no doubting that a united nation stood shoulder to shoulder to revenge the "Maine" and incidentally to free Cuba from a grinding and merciless tyranny.

The nation was not prepared for war, but right manfully did every shoulder go to the wheel, and while the machinery of the Government was set in motion to put volunteers in the field, the gallant little band of regulars was hurried from all quarters of the continent.

Camps were established at various southern points, most of the cavalry going to Chickamauga Park, near Chattanooga, where the troops of the Sixth were concentrated. The magnificent character of the regular army assembled in this great camp impressed itself upon all who were capable of judging of its capacity for war, and history will record how manfully it sustained its highest traditions in the campaign which followed.

It was eminently appropriate that the regulars should have been assembled at Chickamauga, for in all that magnificent army which struggled on this field thirty-five years ago, none bore themselves with more honor or suffered greater losses than the regulars, and it was a fitting spot from whence to draw inspiration for deeds of knightly valor in the coming conflict.

The squadrons were put en route to Chickamauga during April. The regiment established its camp there on the 21st, and participated in the drills and other exercises inaugurated for the further instruction of the troops, included in which were five regiments of regular cavalry.

The experience of the army of regulars, while located on this magnificent camp site, was far different from that of the two corps of volunteers which followed them, but this is another story which need not be detailed here. Suffice it to say that, if the nation takes its lessons to heart and applies the simple remedy of training a sufficient number of officers in time of peace to supply experienced commanders and staff to the volunteer regiments when called into service, there will be no future camp scandals. Both regulars and volunteers have since occupied the pest holes of Cuba with less loss than the volunteers suffered in healthy American camps.

On May 8th nine troops of the regiment moved to Tampa, Florida, becoming a part of the Cavalry Division of the Fifth Corps, composed almost wholly of regulars selected to bear the brunt of early battle, while the volunteers were being prepared for war.

Troop H was detached as provost guard at the great volunteer camp then being established within the limits of Chickamauga Park, and its movements will be described before proceeding further with the regiment. The troop served as escort and provost guard at General Brooke's headquarters, and accompanied the expedition to Porto Rico, sailing from Newport News on the transport "Massachusetts," July 28th, 1898. The transport arrived at Ponce, Porto Rico, August 2d, and received instructions to proceed to Guayama, where General Brooke's headquarters then were. The large vessel passed safely out of the harbor, but went hard aground immediately after. This necessitated unloading with lighters, a slow and tedious operation.

On August 8th, H troop and the First City Troop, of Philadelphia, started from Ponce to Guayama, escorting a large train and about one thousand mules en route to General Brooke's command. The two troops and train arrived at Guayama August 10th.

On August 13th, the troop broke camp and moved out to participate in the engagement about to take place at Guamani Heights, but news of the signing of the peace protocol being received, active operations ceased and the troop went into camp at Guayama, remaining until September, when it escorted General Brooke across the island to Rio Piedras, a suburb of San Juan. The troop remained in camp there until late in October.

On October 5th, the troop participated in the ceremony of raising the American flag at Carolina, on the northern coast, and about two weeks later was present at a similar ceremony in San Juan, being the first American troop to enter the island capital.

The troop was quartered in "L'escuela del Pios," a school building in San Turce, a suburb of San Juan, and remained until November 24th, when it sailed on the transport "Michigan," for Savannah, Georgia. Upon arrival at its destination the troop disembarked November 30th, and proceeding by rail to Huntsville, Alabama, rejoined the regiment December 2d, after an absence of seven months.

After arrival of the regiment at Tampa, Troops L and M, which had been skeletonized in 1890, were reorganized, the remaining troops were filled up to 100 men each, and everything possible was done to get the mass of new material assimilated before the hour of battle. It is neither expedient nor profitable to enter into the harassing obstacles encountered, for every real cavalryman knows how impossible it is to make an educated trooper out of a raw recruit in a few days.

The Fifth Army Corps was organized under Major-General Shafter, in anticipation of foreign service, but transports for an army cannot be prepared—mobilized, as it were—at a moment's warning to meet such unusual demands, even when funds are available to a lavish degree. In the course of a few weeks, however, a fleet of more than thirty transports was assembled in Tampa bay.

The wildest dreamer of the hour was not gifted with prescience enough to foretell that this hastily equipped expedition was soon to cause the whole fabric of Spain's power to crumble to dust, and that a brief campaign on a foreign shore was to convince the civilized world that the word "soldier" was typified in its highest sense in the American regular.

All this preparation at Tampa betokened early active service and gave Spain much uneasiness concerning the probable destination of the expedition. Various plans were on foot for landing the regulars on the coast of Cuba, notwithstanding the

NIGHT ALARM, TAMPA, 1898.

sickly season was at hand, but before anything definite had been determined upon the following brief cable message from Admiral Sampson, off Santiago, put further discussion at rest:

"If 10,000 men were here, city and fleet would be ours within forty-eight hours. Every consideration demands immediate army movement."

The President gave instructions for the immediate sailing of the expedition, and in communicating the orders the Adjutant-General added his favorite phrase, "Time is the essence of the situation."

The regiments composing the cavalry division received orders about "tattoo" and, notwithstanding all the arrangements made necessary through the abandonment of the horses, the regiment with its baggage was entrained during the night and arrived at Port Tampa, nine miles away, at daylight the following morning, June 8th.

There was no provision made for cavalry horses in the final plans, so each regiment was compelled to leave behind a squadron to care for the animals. The headquarters, band, and Troops A, B, C, D, E, F, G and K, averaging fifty-four dismounted men each, all selected soldiers, Lieutenant-Colonel Henry Carroll commanding, were assigned to the transport "Rio Grande." The Colonel, S. S. Sumner, had been promoted to Brigadier-General of Volunteers and assigned to command the brigade in which the Sixth was then serving.

The fleet did not sail for a week owing to a false rumor, sent in by a naval vessel, concerning the near presence of a Spanish fleet. This mythical fleet having been disposed of, the army saile on June 14th, not having been improved by the enforced confinement on board the vessels at a southern port in midsummer.

After an uneventful voyage through the Bahama Channel, the transports, convoyed by the navy, arrived off Santiago where Admiral Sampson, with his magnificent fleet, was blockading Admiral Cervera's squadron within the narrow harbor.

There were no wharves at which to disembark the troops, so the navy supplied their small boats and landed the army through the surf on the open coast as rapidly as could be done under such conditions. A moderate storm would have scattered the fleet of transports and prevented the landing.

The regiment disembarked at Daiquiri June 23d, and went into bivouac about a mile from the wharf, without baggage other than what each officer and man carried on his person. Two days later Troops F and G escorted Grimes' and Parkhurst's batteries to Siboney. Next day the two troops rejoined the regiment, when all moved forward to the Sevilla sugar house. The action at La Guasima had, in the meantime, been fought and the Spanish outposts driven in, on June 24th, by General Young's brigade, of the cavalry division.

DISMOUNTED CAVALRYMAN, SANTIAGO CAMPAIGN.

On June 30th, the regiment marched at night with the cavalry division to El Poso, and camped in the road near the Cuban contingent. About 6 a. m. the Cubans moved to the front along the road, but had proceeded only a few hundred yards when they halted, blocking the way for the cavalry following in rear. The Ninth Cavalry was directed to take the head of the column and pushed forward through the crowd of Cubans, who made way for them to pass. The leading troop, H, formed as advance guard and moved forward to the Aguadores Ford, about one mile distant. The vanguard platoon crossed over and had proceeded two or three hundred yards when about half a dozen shots were fired by the enemy; the advance halted and was promptly reenforced.

About 7 a. m., Grimes' battery, which had taken position on El Poso Hill, opened on the Spanish entrenchments along the San Juan ridge, and the Spanish guns replied immediately, the fire passing over the troops. The Cubans disappeared in the chaparral at the first casualty in their ranks.

While the Ninth Cavalry deployed to the right, the first squadron of the Sixth, A, D, E and G troops, moved across the Aguadores Creek and endeavored to form to the left of the Santiago road, but finding the underbrush impassable, returned to and moved forward on the road, the second squadron

19

having been directed to support the first. The men were stripped of their blanket rolls and haversacks, which were piled beside the road, under guard.

Captain Howze, having reported Spanish outposts directly in front, Colonel Carroll, commanding the Brigade—General Sumner was in command of the cavalry division at this time—ordered Captain J. B. Kerr forward with the second squadron, consisting of B, C, F and K troops. This squadron then formed the advance of the cavalry division, and after crossing the stream, deployed in two lines, B and K troops in the first, and C and F in the second. Advancing, the squadron drove in the sentinels and pickets, who retreated in the direction of San Juan Hill and the main blockhouse. Wire fences and entanglements were encountered as soon as the stream was crossed, but were cut by troopers who had been supplied with nippers for such an emergency.

The squadron advanced by short rushes, with long intervals, to enable the men to get through the difficult brush and grass and reform the line, which was more or less broken each time by the obstacles. The squadron advanced in this way in front of the cavalry division until a point about 400 yards from, and somewhat under, San Juan Hill, was reached. The position now occupied was partially sheltered by the nature of the ground as well as by the steep slope of the hill itself. Only the heads of the enemy could be seen and sometimes their fire continued when not even their heads were visible. This was accomplished by the Spaniards delivering their fire without any attempt at aiming. They laid their Mauser rifles on the parapet and directing the muzzles downward, pulled the triggers without exposing themselves.

Whilst the second squadron was working up to this stage of battle, the first squadron, under Captain Stanton—the regiment was under command of Major Lebo after Colonel Carroll assumed command of the brigade—moved forward and formed on the left. A troop was the extreme left of the cavalry division connecting with General Hawkins' brigade of infantry.

After the First Brigade had begun its deployment, the Second arrived and started to execute an order to move toward the El Caney road to connect with the left of General Lawton's division, to which had been assigned the task of first reducing the Spanish position at El Caney and then connecting with the right of the cavalry division in the main attack. El Caney proved more formidable than had been anticipated, and the junction was found impracticable, owing to the non-arrival of Lawton's left.

The troops had met with considerable delay in the narrow road and after about an hour they were seriously interfered with by the appearance of the chief engineer with a captive balloon, which was dragged along the road and anchored near the crossing, cutting the cavalry division into two parts. The balloon attracted an incessant shrapnel and small arm fire which was concentrated on the road and crossing, and caused many casualties without any compensation so far as could be discovered by those under fire.

When the deployment of the First Brigade was completed, the Sixth was in advance, the Ninth on its right and slightly in rear, and the Third immediately in rear of the Sixth. When the Second Brigade emerged from the crossing, the First Volunteer Cavalry led off to the right, along the bank of the stream, in the futile effort to connect with Lawton's left; the regiment was soon halted and held in reserve at a sunken road. The First Cavalry (regulars) formed in rear of the First Brigade with the Tenth on its right rear. This placed the First Volunteer Cavalry on the right of the Second Brigade.

The men laid down and waited further deployment of the army. While lying down, a dynamite gun was run up between E and G troops of the Sixth and fired two shells, when the gun became disabled and retired. These two shots, however, brought a storm of shrapnel and small arm missiles from the enemy's lines, which killed and wounded a number of men.

The whole division was now constantly under observation and fire and was losing a great many men without being able to retaliate on the entrenched enemy. It had become committed to immediate battle or the necessity of retiring with loss to some other position, an alternative not considered for a moment. At about noon, Lieutenant Miley gave General Shafter's order for the attack. The period of waiting under fire had been most trying and would have been impossible except with an army of regulars accompanied by troop leaders and subordinate officers in whose courage, training and professional ability the men in the ranks had absolute confidence and faith born of experience.

When the advance began, the second squadron of the Sixth was in the extreme front to the right of the Santiago road, and opposite the Kettle Hill. All its reserves had been put in the firing line. The first squadron was on the left, covering the Santiago road. The regiment waded the San Juan river about waist deep, and moved to the assault of both Kettle Hill and Fort San Juan. Almost immediately the troops assaulting Kettle Hill were assailed with a heavy fire from Fort San Juan on the left. Some of the troops assaulting Kettle Hill were wheeled slightly to the left and opened fire in reply, but Parker's Gatling guns were soon brought into action and silenced this enfilade fire from the fort.

The ground over which the regiment moved forward to the assault was bottom land covered with high grass. There was a pond in this bottom which proved to be obstacle enough to split the regiment. The troops which passed on the side next to General Hawkins' Infantry Brigade, moved forward past a portion of the Sixth Infantry. D and part of A troop, of the first squadron, took part in the assault on the San Juan blockhouse, and joining a few of General Hawkins' infantrymen at the foot of the slope, charged up the hill and gained the crest. Captain Blocksom, commanding D troop, was wounded before reaching the foot of the hill, but Lieutenant Short gallantly carried this part of the line forward and reached the crest amongst the first, there being only a few scattered infantrymen in sight. Lieutenant Short was wounded soon after reaching the hilltop. His conduct attracted the attention of those who first arrived at the Spanish position, one of whom made the following report:

The Adjutant General, U. S. Army,
Washington, D. C.

SIR:—I have the honor to recommend that a medal of honor be awarded to Lieutenant Walter C. Short, 6th Cavalry, for his conspicuous gallantry in leading a detachment of men of his regiment, in advance of the line of battle, to the summit of San Juan Hill, where he was among the first to arrive at the blockhouse, known as "Fort San Juan"; this on the first day of July, 1898, near Santiago de Cuba.

I was an eye-witness of Lieutenant Short's gallantry in this successful assault, and I do not hesitate to say that its happy result was as much due to Lieutenant Short's example and bravery as to that of any single line officer engaged.

As his advance took him away from the main body of his regiment, I do not know that any of his proper commanding officers witnessed his conduct. For this reason, I make this recommendation, believing that such gallantry should be duly rewarded.

General Hawkins may also remember seeing Lieutenant Short at the blockhouse, if further corroborative evidence is needed.

Very respectfully,
L. W. V. KENNON,
Captain, 6th Infantry."

Troops E and G of this squadron were deflected to the right and assaulted the San Juan house. They joined there a mixed body of troops under Major Wessels, Third Cavalry, and opened fire across the valley on the Fort San Juan ridge. After firing for some time, this part of the line advanced, crossed the second valley and carried the hill on which was located the officers' mess-house, about a quarter of a mile north of Fort San Juan. Private Tilden Hughes, Troop G, was the first soldier of the regiment to reach this strongly intrenched position and he captured a Spanish prisoner.

Soon after reaching the mess-house, Major Wessels was wounded. Captain Howze, Assistant Adjutant General, then conveyed an order to the senior officer, Captain F. West, Sixth Cavalry, to take the mixed command forward and capture the next hill to the right front, which commanded the position of the enemy as well as the line now being occupied by the cavalry division. This hill was captured and was the most advanced position taken towards Santiago, near the center of the line. Captain West detached Captain McBlain, Ninth Cavalry, to capture another commanding hill to the right, which was done with some loss. These positions constituted the most advanced part of the line occupied by the trenches of the cavalry during the siege.

While the second squadron was lying across the Santiago road closely investing the San Juan Hill and blockhouse, much of the artillery and small-arm fire, aimed at the advancing troops, passed high over the line. Heavy volleys were frequently directed at the line itself one of which killed several men and wounded a number. The squadron commander, Captain J. B. Kerr, was wounded at this time but remained on duty until the final assault of the heights.

About this time it was discovered that the right of the Sixth and the left of the Ninth had become separated in moving through the brush. The First Cavalry (regulars), which belonged to the second brigade, moved up from the rear and its commanding officer, having been informed of the situation, promptly filled the gap with Captain Tutherly's squadron of his regiment.

When this part of the line moved to the assault, the second squadron of the Sixth reached a point on the hillside about sixty yards from the crest, where it was compelled to halt for about half an hour to enable the other troops to come up. It was so close to the Spanish entrenchments as to be protected from their fire and the enemy did not venture a sortie. When the lines were somewhat closed, the final rush for the crest took place and the Spaniards broke from their entrenchments and fled to the rear, their retreat being accelerated by a deadly fire from the American lines, which also caused the reserves to retreat in haste, notwithstanding the strenuous efforts of several mounted Spanish officers, who vainly endeavored to stem the tide of defeat. The accurate fire of the Americans quickly unhorsed most of these officers.

When the effort to connect with Lawton's left was abandoned, the second brigade was in rear of the first, and consequently was directed to support the line in front. The entire cavalry division numbered less than 2500 dismounted men. The lines were very thin—mere skirmish lines—so that when the second brigade moved forward in support, portions of the two regular regiments and the First Volunteer Cavalry (Rough Riders) became mingled with the regiments in front and in the final rush the whole division participated in the onslaught on the Spanish lines.

At the close of this most successful day, during which the whole cavalry division—regulars and volunteers—had given a brilliant example of well-directed courage, the Spaniards had been driven completely from their strong position on the crests of the ridges surrounding Santiago. The regiments had become much broken up by the difficult movement through the brush and tall grass, but true to their traditions, they had all gone forward to strike the enemy at the nearest point. This caused a mixing up of organizations which it was not practicable to rectify until towards evening, when the battle was over. The Sixth was assembled on the San Juan Hill, with the left resting near Fort San Juan and the right near the Santiago road. During the night rifle-pits were dug to resist any attack by the enemy from their inner line, to which they had been forced back.

Before daylight next morning,—July 2d—three batteries of artillery were brought up on the line occupied by the regiment which then acted as a support, the men lying between the guns. As soon as there was light enough, the batteries opened and drew from the Spaniards such a concentration of fire that, after a few rounds, the guns were withdrawn from the line. The enemy, however, continued firing throughout the day, the regiment occupying the trenches dug at the close of the fight the preceding night.

About 10 p. m., July 2d, a heavy fire began and was taken up by both lines for about an hour, but no assault was made on the cavalry division. The action was resumed on the morning of July 3d and continued until noon, when a truce was pronounced which lasted until 5 p. m., July 10th. Cannonading was then resumed and lasted until noon next day, July 11th, after which no more firing took place during the siege.

On July 14th an armistice was arranged, followed by formal surrender on the 17th, when the regimental band had the honor of being selected to salute the flag as it was run up on the Palace, in the city of Santiago de Cuba, to replace the Spanish ensign which was soon to fall from every staff in the island possessions of Spain.

The day following the formal surrender the regiment marched with the cavalry division to the foot of the mountains, northwest of El Caney, and established a camp, such as was possible in the absence of all the usual baggage which had been left on the transports and was not received for more than a month, when the transports were unloaded in the harbor of Santiago. While in this camp the regiment generally was stricken with malarial and other fevers.

It had been the intention to send the cavalry and part of the infantry on the transports to participate in the Porto Rico campaign. The exposure to rain and sun without shelter during the summer season on the unhealthy coast of Cuba had so affected the troops that, when yellow fever broke out, the plan for utilizing them in Porto Rico was abandoned, and orders were given to transport all but the sick to Montauk Point, Long Island, where a large camp was established.

The Sixth was the first regiment to embark, boarding the transport "Gate City," August 7th, and sailing out of Santiago harbor next day. The regiment landed on Long Island August 13th. After spending three days in the detention camp, it was released and joined the squadron which had been left at Tampa, and later moved to Montauk Point, with the horses, to await the return of the dismounted squadrons from Santiago.

The regiment took into battle at San Juan sixteen officers and four hundred and twenty-seven men. Four officers, Lieutenant-Colonel Carroll, Captains Kerr and Blocksom and Lieutenant Short were wounded. Four men were killed and fifty wounded. Twenty-five per cent of the officers and a trifle more than twelve per cent of the men engaged being struck by Spanish bullets, is a fair indication that the regiment participated with honor.

The discipline and instruction of the regular army has always and steadfastly had for its object the preparation for battle. The nature of the fight, from the moment the Spaniards opened fire on the column in the road up to the final assault and capture of the entrenched lines of the enemy, had rendered impossible the carrying-out of all the details for battle, so carefully instilled in the minds of officers and men of the army during the past ten years, but if ever an army deserved credit for moving without reserves to the sound of the enemy's guns unwavering, resistlessly, fearlessly and successfully, it was this regular army at Santiago on that memorable July 1st, 1898.

There have been many minor criticisms of this brief campaign, and many writers, usually without military experience, have endeavored to show how everything should have been done. Volumes have been written on the meagre railroad facilities at Tampa, of the hurried and improper loading of transports, of the disembarkation and misbehavior of transport captains, etc., etc. All these complaints dwindle into insignificant trifles when weighed with the results.

Every officer and man in the regular army was anxious to go on this expedition at all hazards, knowing that aside from the climate there was little hardship to be feared which would exceed that of former years on the frontier, or that endured throughout the Civil War.

The planning and execution of such an expedition was a new and untried experience. The results obtained will remain upon the pages of history as a marvelous achievement, and the officers and men of each and every regiment which had the honor to participate, may well feel proud that through their gallantry the name of "Santiago" will remain emblazoned on their standards, and be noted in the archives so long as the Republic exists, for should the moment ever arrive when patriotism, loyalty and courage to defend its flag are no longer regarded as the highest attributes of American citizenship, that hour will mark the decline and fall of the Republic.

It seems fitting that the history of the regiment should close here with the brief story of its participation in the war with Spain. Soon after its arrival at Montauk Point, the regiment went with the cavalry division to Huntsville, Alabama, and later was scattered over the plains and mountains of the far west, even to California; back again to its duties of standing guard over the interests of the people, which have never been more safe than when in the keeping of the regulars, who have marked their guardianship on hundreds of battlefields, with the best blood of the nation.

It is a simple story, and all too brief to be dignified with the title of history. It would require volumes to fully describe the individual experiences of officers and men in the Civil War alone, and there was much of an heroic character in the daily life on the old frontier where, to the natural and manifold difficulties of the situation, there was an added element of Indian cunning and treachery to be reckoned with.

It is not probable, under the present system of promotion, that the same spirit of regimental pride and rivalry will exist as in days of yore, but let it be hoped that what the individual regiment loses, the whole service will gain in an esprit de corps comprehensive enough to include all the regiments of the best and most practical little army in the world.

AFTERMATH.

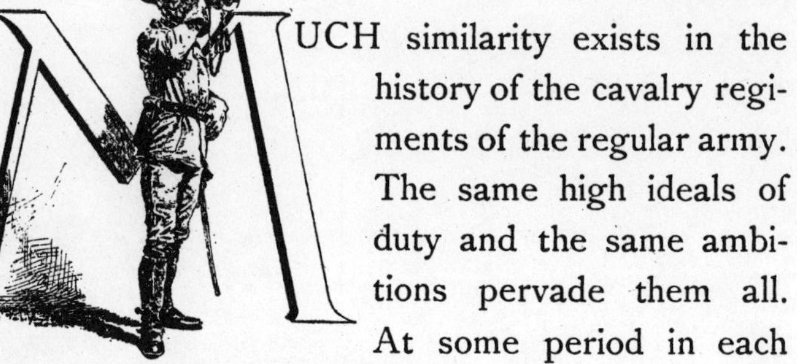

MUCH similarity exists in the history of the cavalry regiments of the regular army. The same high ideals of duty and the same ambitions pervade them all. At some period in each regimental life a forceful commander may firmly impress his individual character upon the customs of a particular organization, which, becoming traditions, may be commemorated by peculiarity of dress, features of parade, special music, and in many other significant ways.

With the exception of the Sixth, all were organized primarily for service against hostile Indians. Prior to the Civil War there was more or less rivalry in the mounted forces, the two dragoon regiments assuming that they were justly entitled to first place as compared to the more recently organized mounted rifles and cavalry regiments. The regiments vary rather in length, than in character of service, and both individually and collectively are equal to any mounted force of like size the world over.

In the hurry and rush of war many valuable lessons are lost to future generations, because those who have learned them by hard experience are apt to consider that the only school, and leave to others the acquisition of knowledge, in a similar manner.

The services of the Sixth illustrate quite thoroughly the development of the American cavalry idea. Entering the Peninsular campaign equipped as light cavalry, without carbines, it required but a brief experience for those in authority to recognize the limitations placed on cavalry, suited only to the charge, operating in a heavily wooded country with but few places sufficiently open for mounted action.

The squadron with carbines proved itself invaluable as the advance guard of the Army of the Potomac, on the march up the Peninsula, and every effort was made to similarly arm the other squadrons.

As time passed and the cavalry corps was armed with breech-loading carbines, the full value of their united action began to dawn on the enemy before it was appreciated by infantry comrades, who profited by the hard and brilliant work of the mounted force. The Confederates were for some time deceived by the intense volume of fire delivered by dismounted cavalry, and imagined themselves opposed by much larger forces because they were unaccustomed to breech-loading arms.

The frequency with which the cavalry was put into action, dismounted, often caused that arm to be referred to as mounted infantry. There is no comparison between the two organizations, and, thanks to the gallant leaders who adhered firmly to their beliefs, the Civil War developed the American cavalry into an arm capable of mounted action of which no army need be ashamed, and on the other hand left a record of dismounted fighting second to no infantry in the world. The younger generation held tenaciously to the teachings of the Civil War, and while the cavalrymen have, in the past quarter of a century, earned for themselves substantial reputation as riders on the frontier, they have never had to yield the palm of superiority in the field or on the target range to their comrades of other branches.

An arm whose traditions demand excellence in all things need never fear to meet the best cavalry of other nations in mounted combat. On the other hand the brilliant success of the dismounted cavalry division at Santiago is significant of the versatile character of the American cavalryman. Separated suddenly from their horses, put aboard ships in midsummer, disembarked in the surf of a tropical and foreign shore, placed in advance and

BATTLE MONUMENT AT WEST POINT.

carrying the same packs as their infantry comrades, they went forward promptly to the scene of battle. Without supports of any kind, the dismounted cavalry regiments moved to the assault of an entrenched position and in face of all theory and academic teaching wrested victory from their astonished opponents, and side by side with their gallant comrades of the infantry, with scant rations and shelter, entered upon the seige of a fortified town to reap the full fruits of their hard-bought victory in the open field. History does not record a more complete justification of a system than that thus rendered to the organization and training of the American Cavalry.

The progress of events in the Philippines, since the advent of one cavalry brigade in the theater of operations, gives additional proof as to the value of modern cavalry; and, in the Transvaal, the British have learned what an invaluable component of their forces the dragoons have become.

The public is always apt to exaggerate the merits of the few at the expense of the many, to whose combined efforts all success is due. In the eagerness to show honestly conceived appreciation, heroes are sometimes made of those who are not the most deserving and thus the truly great, but more modest, are defrauded of rightful honors.

Opportunity and influence must be reckoned with

by all who have ambitious dreams of military fame, and history shows a trail of broken hearts and wrongs which will never be righted, in the wake of every war. The Revolution, the Mexican War, the Civil War, and the war with Spain, have all left their scars in uneven distribution of rewards.

The officers and men who perform their allotted tasks without expectation of reward, other than that which comes from a consciousness of duty rightly done, may always be counted upon for more than a yeoman's share in the hour of battle "just for the honor of the old regiment." Their presence habitually with the colors, fitting themselves and their organizations for battle, makes success far more substantial than the theatrical display of a few human comets, who shoot across the military sky in every war and not infrequently secure the reward which rightly belongs to the many. This is fate,—even in the national wars of the present day where soldiers of fortune find no legitimate place.

But when armed men grow weary of strife and the implements of war are laid aside, the real heart of the nation goes out to the honored dead. He who gives up his life in hospital, camp or prison, from exposure and disease, is as worthy a patriot as he who dies at the cannon's mouth; but nations love most to honor those who fall in the forefront of battle, winning peace through overpowering victory.

The Battle Monument at West Point contains the names of eight officers and forty-seven men of the Sixth Cavalry, killed in action during the mighty struggle of 1861–65. The towering monolith faces the gateway of the Hudson Highlands, guarding like a giant sentinel the memory of two thousand "regulars."

The gallant men whose names are inscribed upon its tablets were the battle victims of that little army which stood at the beginning of the Civil War for all the military art the nation could command, and which for half a century had kept alive the traditions of military integrity, discipline and science, which inspired not only these men but, through them, the mighty hosts of heroic volunteers,—leaderless masses of noble men who left their peaceful avocations and offered up their lives for principle and country.

This monument to the regulars was erected by brothers to brothers, through voluntary offerings from the hard-won pay of comrades in the field within hearing of the roar of battle, and in sight of the dead, whose memory it preserves. The shaft stands for duty, professional honor and discipline, combined with the loyalty, courage and patriotism inherent in all Americans. It was not raised in an invidious or vaunting spirit, but with just pride in the great work wrought by the regulars, not only in the Civil War, but upon the remote frontiers amidst savage foes, where, as the advance guard of civilization, they protected and promoted the greatest industrial development known to history.

> "Nor shall your glory be forgot,
> While fame her record keeps,
> Or honor points the hallowed spot,
> Where valor proudly sleeps."

ROSTER.

It is not practicable to give sketches of the long and valuable service of officers and men who have distinguished themselves in the regiment. Individual volumes would be required to do justice in many instances. The regiment has the unique distinction of having furnished from among its gallant soldiers, the first officer ever promoted from the ranks who subsequently rose to the grade of brigadier-general in the regular Army. Up to the year 1900 there have been but two such promotions. Six officers and forty-four enlisted men have been rewarded with medals of honor during a period of nearly forty years, since the regiment was organized.

The accompanying list contains the names of officers who have belonged to the regiment at various periods since its organization, showing the highest rank held by them in the regiment and the highest grade attained in the service. A number of officers appear on the list who have been assigned, since the introduction of lineal promotion, and who were subsequently transferred back to their old regiments with but little service with the Sixth.

RANK IN REGIMENT.		HIGHEST RANK IN SERVICE.
COLONELS.		
David Hunter	14th May, 1861	Major-General Volunteers.
James Oakes	31st July, 1866	Brig.-Gen. Vols. (Declined.)
Eugene A. Carr	29th April, 1879	Brigadier-General, U. S. A.
George B. Sanford	22d July, 1892	Colonel, 6th Cavalry.
David S. Gordon	28th July, 1892	Colonel, 6th Cavalry.
Samuel S. Sumner	23d May, 1896	Major-General Volunteers.
LIEUTENANT-COLONELS.		
William H. Emory	14th May, 1861	Major-General Volunteers.
Samuel D. Sturgis	27th October, 1863	Brig.-Gen. Volunteers.
Charles J. Whiting	6th May, 1869	Lieut.-Col., 6th Cavalry.
Thomas H. Neill	22d Feb., 1869	Brig.-Gen. Volunteers.
William R. Price	2d April, 1879	Lieut.-Col., 6th Cavalry.
George W. Schofield	30th Dec., 1881	Lieut.-Col., 6th Cavalry.
Albert P. Morrow	17th Dec., 1882	Colonel, 3d Cavalry.
Henry Carroll	23d May, 1896	Brig.-Gen. Volunteers.
Charles S. Ilsley	29th March, 1899	Lieut.-Col., 6th Cavalry.
Theodore J. Wint	8th April, 1899	Lieut.-Col., 6th Cavalry.
MAJORS.		
Edward H. Wright	14th May, 1861	Colonel. A. A. D. C., Vols.
James H. Carleton	7th Sept., 1861	Brig.-Gen. Volunteers.
Lawrence A. Williams	7th Sept., 1861	Major, 6th Cavalry.
Robert M. Morris	11th March, 1863	Major, 6th Cavalry.
Samuel H. Starr	25th April, 1863	Colonel. (Retired.)
William W. Lowe	31st July, 1866	Major, 6th Cavalry.
Abraham K. Arnold	22d June, 1869	Brig.-Gen. Volunteers.
Charles E. Compton	28th July, 1866	Brig.-Gen. Volunteers.
James Biddle	21st Feb., 1873	Colonel, 9th Cavalry.
David Perry	29th April, 1879	Colonel, 9th Cavalry.
Emil Adam	11th June, 1886	Major, 6th Cavalry.
Tullius C. Tupper	19th October, 1887	Major, 6th Cavalry.
Edmond G. Fechét	20th April, 1891	Major, 6th Cavalry.
Adam Kramer	8th March, 1893	Major, 6th Cavalry.
Thomas C. Lebo	26th July, 1893	Lieut.-Col., 1st Cavalry.
Eli L. Huggins	13th Jan., 1897	Colonel, 8th Vol. Infantry.
Winfield S. Edgerly	9th July, 1898	Lieut.-Col., Insp.-Gen., Vols.
George S. Anderson	10th Nov., 1898	Colonel, 38th Vol. Infantry.
Alexander Rodgers	14th Sept., 1899	Major, 6th Cavalry.
Louis H. Rucker	13th Jan., 1897	Major, 6th Cavalry.

RANK IN REGIMENT.		HIGHEST RANK IN SERVICE.
	CAPTAINS.	
August V. Kautz	14th May, 1861	Brigadier-General, U. S. A.
Andrew W. Evans	14th May, 1861	Colonel, 1st Maryland Cav.
William S. Abert	14th May, 1861	Colonel, 3d Mass. Artillery.
David McM. Gregg	14th May, 1861	Brig.-Gen. Volunteers.
Joseph H. Taylor	14th May, 1861	Major, A. A. G.
William P. Sanders	14th May, 1861	Brig.-Gen. Volunteers.
J. Irwin Gregg	14th May, 1861	Colonel, 8th Cavalry.
John Savage	14th May, 1861	Captain, 6th Cavalry.
George C. Cram	14th May, 1861	Major, 4th Cavalry.
Charles R. Lowell	14th May, 1861	Brig.-Gen. Volunteers.
Henry B. Hays	5th August, 1861	Captain, 6th Cavalry.
James S. Brisbin	5th August, 1861	Brig.-Gen. Volunteers.
John J. Upham	9th Sept., 1861	Colonel, 8th Cavalry.
Sheldon Sturgeon	25th April, 1862	Colonel, 1st New Orleans Inf.
Ira W. Claflin	23d Dec., 1862	Captain, 6th Cavalry.
Benjamin T. Hutchins	19th Nov., 1863	Lieut.-Col., 1st N. H. Cavalry.
Hancock T. McLean	5th July, 1864.	Captain, 6th Cavalry.
Tattnall Paulding	20th October, 1864	Captain, 6th Cavalry.
John B. Johnson	3d February, 1865	Captain, 6th Cavalry.
James F. Wade	1st May, 1866	Major-General Volunteers.
Joseph C. Audenried	1st July, 1866	Captain, 6th Cavalry.
Henry Tucker	28th July, 1866	Captain, 6th Cavalry.
John W. Spangler	28th July, 1866	Captain, 6th Cavalry.
Curwen B. McLellan	28th July, 1866	Lieut.-Col., 1st Cavalry.
Joseph Kerin	28th July, 1866	Captain, 6th Cavalry.
Samuel M. Whitside	20th October, 1866	Colonel, 10th Cavalry.
Daniel Madden	10th May, 1867	Major, 7th Cavalry.
John A. Irwin	8th June, 1867	Captain, 6th Cavalry.
Adna R. Chaffee	12th October, 1867	Major-General Volunteers.
Thomas M. Tolman	18th Nov., 1867	Captain, 6th Cavalry.
Reuben N. Fenton	8th January, 1868	Captain, 6th Cavalry.
William A. Rafferty	14th May, 1868	Colonel, 5th Cavalry.
Edwin Mauck	10th Sept., 1869	Captain, 6th Cavalry.
Clarence E. Nesmith	22d May, 1872	Captain, 6th Cavalry.
Charles H. Campbell	20th Sept., 1874	Captain, 6th Cavalry.
William Harper, Jr.	27th Jan., 1875	Major, 1st New Jersey Cav.
William M. Wallace	17th May, 1876	Lieut.-Col., 2d Cavalry.
Edmund C. Hentig	15th Nov., 1876	Captain, 6th Cavalry.
William L. Foulk	3d March, 1873	Lieut.-Col., 7th Pa. Infantry.
Lemuel A. Abbott	3d June, 1880	Captain, 6th Cavalry.
Henry M. Kendall	15th Feb., 1881	Major. (Retired.)
Charles G. Gordon	30th August, 1881	Captain, 6th Cavalry.

RANK IN REGIMENT.		HIGHEST RANK IN SERVICE.
CAPTAINS.		
Gilbert E. Overton	30th Dec., 1881	Captain, 6th Cavalry.
Henry P. Perrine	15th Jan., 1884	Captain, 6th Cavalry.
John B. Kerr	3d January, 1885	Major, 10th Cavalry.
William Stanton	21st May, 1886	Major, 8th Cavalry.
Henry P. Kingsbury	5th October, 1887	Major, 3d Cavalry.
Frank West	19th Oct., 1887	Captain, 6th Cavalry.
Robert Hanna	7th July, 1888	Captain, 6th Cavalry.
William H. Carter	20th Nov., 1889	Lieut.-Col., Asst. Adj. Gen.
Louis A. Craig	24th Feb., 1891	Colonel, 32d Vol. Infantry.
William Baird	24th Feb., 1891	Captain, 6th Cavalry.
George L. Scott	1st July, 1891	Captain, 6th Cavalry.
Benjamin H. Cheever	8th March, 1893	Maj. and Insp. Gen. of Vols.
Augustus P. Blocksom	10th Nov., 1894	Captain, 6th Cavalry.
Elon F. Willcox	6th Feb., 1897.	Captain, 6th Cavalry.
George H. Sands	3d Dec., 1897	Maj. and Eng. Officer of Vols.
J. F. Reynolds Landis	31st May, 1898	Captain, 6th Cavalry.
Thomas T. Knox	23d January, 1889	Major and Inspector-General.
Albert L. Mills	24th Oct., 1898	Col. and Supt. Mil. Academy.
Henry T. Allen	10th Nov., 1898	Major, 43d Vol. Infantry.
John M. Stotsenburg	14th Dec., 1898	Colonel, 1st Nebraska Vols.
William W. Forsyth	2d March, 1899	Captain, 6th Cavalry.
Matthew F. Steele	2d March, 1899	Major, 30th Vol. Infantry.
DeRosey C. Cabell	23d April, 1899	Lieut.-Col., 2d Arkansas Inf.
Grote Hutcheson	9th June, 1899	Captain, 6th Cavalry.
Richard B. Paddock	15th July, 1899	Captain, 6th Cavalry.
George L. Byram	23d January, 1900	Major, 27th Vol. Infantry.
1ST LIEUTENANTS.		
Herbert M. Enos	14th May, 1861	Major and Quartermaster.
Sewell H. Brown	14th May, 1861	1st Lieutenant, 6th Cavalry.
Frederick Dodge	14th May, 1861	1st Lieutenant, 6th Cavalry.
Peter McGrath	24th Oct., 1861	1st Lieutenant, 6th Cavalry.
Stephen S. Balk	17th July, 1862	1st Lieutenant, 6th Cavalry.
Isaac M. Ward	20th Oct., 1862	1st Lieutenant, 6th Cavalry.
Albert Coats	23d Dec., 1862	Lt.-Col., 6th U. S. (Col.) Cav.
Christian Balder	23d Dec., 1862	1st Lieutenant, 6th Cavalry.
Andrew Stoll	19th Nov., 1863	1st Lieutenant, 6th Cavalry.
Nicholas Nolan	5th July, 1864	Major, 3d Cavalry.
Louis H. Carpenter	28th Sept., 1864	Brigadier-General, U. S. A.
Joseph H. Wood	20th Oct., 1864	Lt.-Col., 2d N. Y. Mtd. Rifles.
Thomas W. Simson	3d February, 1865	1st Lieutenant, 6th Cavalry.
Clarence E. Bennett	28th July, 1866	Lieut.-Col., 11th Infantry.

RANK IN REGIMENT.		HIGHEST RANK IN SERVICE.
	1ST LIEUTENANTS.	
Jeremiah C. Wilcox	28th July, 1866	Major, 5th Iowa Cavalry.
Gustavus Schreyer	28th July, 1866	Captain, 1st Missouri Cav.
Moses Wiley	28th July, 1866	Captain, East Tennessee Cav.
Theodore Majtheny	20th Oct., 1866	Captain, 1st Indiana Cavalry.
Henry B. Mellen	22d January, 1867	Major, 2d California Cavalry.
Harry E. Scott	8th June, 1867	1st Lieutenant, 6th Cavalry.
James F. Hill	17th Sept., 1867	1st Lieutenant, 6th Cavalry.
Isaac N. Walter	18th Nov., 1867	1st Lieutenant, 6th Cavalry.
William A. Borthwick	25th Nov., 1867	1st Lieutenant, 6th Cavalry.
Harrison Holt	18th August, 1868	1st Lieutenant, 6th Cavalry.
James H. Sands	1st Dec., 1869	Captain, Indiana Cavalry.
John W. Chickering	1st February, 1868	Captain, 88th Illinois Inf.
Hiram F. Winchester	1st January, 1871	1st Lieutenant, 6th Cavalry.
William I. Reese	12th June, 1872	1st Lieutenant, 6th Cavalry.
Sebree Smith	4th October, 1872	Captain, 3d Artillery.
Charles C. Morrison	27th Jan., 1875	Captain, Ordnance Dept.
Austin Henely	15th Nov., 1876	1st Lieutenant, 6th Cavalry.
Timothy A. Touey	3d June, 1880	1st Lieutenant, 6th Cavalry.
Edward E. Dravo	30th August, 1881	Lt.-Col., Cf. Com. Sub. Vols.
Charles B. Gatewood	3d January, 1885	1st Lieutenant, 6th Cavalry.
John N. Glass	20th March, 1885	1st Lieutenant, 6th Cavalry.
Thomas Cruse	28th Sept., 1887	Major, Quartermaster Vols.
John Y. F. Blake	5th October, 1887	1st Lieutenant, 6th Cavalry.
Frederick G. Hodgson	7th July, 1888	Lt.-Col., Quartermaster Vols.
Barrington K. West	20th Feb., 1891	Captain, Com. Subsistence.
Robert B. Watkins	24th Feb., 1891	1st Lieutenant, 6th Cavalry.
Robert J. Duff	24th Feb., 1891	Captain, 8th Cavalry.
James A. Cole	1st April, 1891	Captain, 9th Cavalry.
Hugh J. Gallagher	20th April, 1891	Major, Com. Sub. of Vols.
Gonzalez S. Bingham	1st July, 1891	Major, Chief Qrmr. Vols.
Charles W. Farber	5th April, 1892	1st Lieutenant, 8th Cavalry.
John T. Nance	15th August, 1892	1st Lieutenant, 6th Cavalry.
Edward C. Brooks	8th March, 1893	Captain, A. A. G. Volunteers.
Thomas H. Slavens	15th April, 1894	Captain, Asst. Quartermaster.
John A. Harman	10th Nov., 1894	Major, Ch'f Ord. Officer Vols.
Robert L. Howze	9th January, 1896	Lieut.-Col., 34th Vol. Inf.
John P. Ryan	20th May, 1896	1st Lieutenant, 6th Cavalry.
Charles D. Rhodes	8th Dec., 1896	Captain, A. A. G. Volunteers.
Francis C. Marshall	5th January, 1897	1st Lieutenant, 6th Cavalry.
Frank M. Caldwell	6th Feb., 1897	Lt.-Col., 4th Wisconsin Inf.
John W. Furlong	11th Dec., 1897	1st Lieutenant, 6th Cavalry.
Thomas M. Corcoran	26th Feb., 1898	1st Lieutenant, 6th Cavalry.

RANK IN REGIMENT.		HIGHEST RANK IN SERVICE.
	1ST LIEUTENANTS.	
Kirby Walker	14th Dec., 1898	1st Lieutenant, 6th Cavalry.
George C. Barnhardt	7th Nov., 1898	1st Lieutenant, 6th Cavalry.
Benjamin B. Hyer	2d March, 1899	1st Lieutenant, 6th Cavalry.
Herbert A. White	2d March, 1899	1st Lieutenant, 6th Cavalry.
August C. Nissen	2d March, 1899	1st Lieutenant, 6th Cavalry.
James S. Parker	8th April, 1899	1st Lieutenant, 6th Cavalry.
Alvord VanP. Anderson	9th June, 1899	1st Lieutenant, 6th Cavalry.
LeRoy Eltinge	15th July, 1899	1st Lieutenant, 6th Cavalry.
	2D LIEUTENANTS.	
Hugh McQuade	14th May, 1861	Captain, 38th New York Inf.
Henry McQuiston	17th July, 1862	2d Lieutenant, 6th Cavalry.
John C. Rousseau	17th July, 1862	2d Lieutenant, 6th Cavalry.
Joseph Bould	1st June, 1863	2d Lieutenant, 6th Cavalry.
Henry H. Wilson	9th April, 1866	Lt.-Col., 104th U.S. (Col.) Inf.
William P. Dixon	18th June, 1866	2d Lieutenant, 6th Cavalry.
Charles A. Rossander	5th June, 1867	1st Lieut., 3d R. I. Artillery.
David C. McIntyre	25th Sept., 1867	Captain, 1st Iowa Cavalry.
Henry Lazenby	11th Oct., 1867	2d Lieutenant, 6th Cavalry.
Harry P. Eakin	15th Oct., 1867	Captain, 3d Maryland Cav.
Frank W. Russell	15th June, 1868	2d Lieutenant, 6th Cavalry.
Sumner H. Bodfish	15th June, 1868	2d Lieutenant, 6th Cavalry.
Edward W. Brady	15th June, 1869	2d Lieutenant, 6th Cavalry.
Dexter W. Parker	15th June, 1870	2d Lieutenant, 6th Cavalry.
Vinton A. Goddard	12th June, 1871	2d Lieutenant, 6th Cavalry.
William B. Wetmore	14th June, 1872	2d Lieutenant, 6th Cavalry.
Thomas B. Nichols	14th June, 1872	2d Lieutenant, 6th Cavalry.
John A. Rucker	27th July, 1872	2d Lieutenant, 6th Cavalry.
Edward A. Benjamin	12th Dec., 1872	2d Lieutenant, 6th Cavalry.
Duane M. Greene	27th July, 1872	Captain, 6th California Inf.
J. Scott Payne	3d February, 1873	Captain, 5th Cavalry.
Wallis O. Clark	31st Dec., 1877	Captain, 12th Infantry.
Albert S. Bailey	14th June, 1878	2d Lieutenant, 6th Cavalry.
Lewis M. Koehler	14th June, 1885	Captain, 4th Cavalry.
John J. Pershing	1st July, 1886	Major, A. A. G. Volunteers.
Seward Mott	1st July, 1886	2d Lieutenant, 10th Cavalry.
George McK. Williamson	28th Sept., 1887	Captain, Asst. Quartermaster.
Francis H. Beach	5th October, 1887	1st Lieutenant, 7th Cavalry.
Alonzo Gray	19th October, 1887	1st Lieutenant, 5th Cavalry.
Lunsford Daniel	17th Dec., 1889	2d Lieutenant, 6th Cavalry.
Harold P. Howard	12th June, 1891	1st Lieutenant, 3d Cavalry.
Elmer Lindsley	12th June, 1891	1st Lieutenant, 1st Cavalry.

RANK IN REGIMENT.		HIGHEST RANK IN SERVICE.
	2D LIEUTENANTS.	
Ervin L. Phillips	1st August, 1891	1st Lieutenant, 3d Cavalry.
Walter C. Short	7th October, 1891	Major, 35th Vol. Infantry.
James H. Reeves	11th June, 1892	1st Lieutenant, 2d Cavalry.
Samuel Hof	12th June, 1894	1st Lieutenant, Ord. Dept.
Casper H. Conrad, Jr.	12th June, 1895	1st Lieutenant, 7th Cavalry.
Harry H. Stout	12th June, 1895	1st Lieutenant, Ord. Dept.
Elvin R. Heiberg	12th June, 1896	1st Lieutenant, 6th Cavalry.
Abraham G. Lott	12th June, 1896	2d Lieutenant, 8th Cavalry.
George T. Summerlin	12th June, 1896	Captain, 32d Vol. Infantry.
Frederick T. Arnold	11th June, 1897	2d Lieutenant, 4th Cavalry.
Edgar A. Sirmyer	11th June, 1897	Major, 33d Vol. Infantry.
John C. Raymond	11th June, 1897	2d Lieutenant, 6th Cavalry.
Malin Craig	26th April, 1898	2d Lieutenant, 6th Cavalry.
Wallace B. Scales	26th April, 1898	2d Lieutenant, 6th Cavalry.
Warren Dean	7th January, 1899	2d Lieutenant, 6th Cavalry.
James F. McKinley	3d February, 1899	2d Lieutenant, 6th Cavalry.
Patrick W. Guiney	15th Feb., 1899	2d Lieutenant, 6th Cavalry.
Stuart Heintzelman	15th Feb., 1899	2d Lieutenant, 6th Cavalry.
Fred. E. Buchan	1st June, 1899	2d Lieutenant, 6th Cavalry.
William L. Karnes	1st Dec., 1899	2d Lieutenant, 6th Cavalry.
Joseph A. Baer	13th June, 1900	2d Lieutenant, 6th Cavalry.
Willis V. Morris	13th June, 1900	2d Lieutenant, 6th Cavalry.
Walter S. Grant	13th June, 1900	2d Lieutenant, 6th Cavalry.

INDEX